THE BEETHOVEN
QUARTET COMPANION

The four quartet instruments presented to Beethoven by Prince Karl Lichnowsky in 1800. In the mid-nineteenth century the violins were said to be by
Giuseppe Guarneri (1718) and Niccolò Amati (1667), the viola by Vincenzo
Ruger (1690), and the cello by Andrea Guarneri (1712). More recent research
suggests that these attributions were overly generous. (Reproduced by permission of the Beethoven-Archiv, Bonn.)

THE BEETHOVEN QUARTET COMPANION

EDITED BY

ROBERT WINTER AND ROBERT MARTIN

UNIVERSITY OF CALIFORNIA PRESS
BERKELEY   LOS ANGELES   LONDON

The publisher gratefully acknowledges the generous contribution provided by the Roth Family Foundation toward the publication of this book.

University of California Press
Berkeley and Los Angeles, California

University of California Press, Ltd.
London, England

Library of Congress Cataloging-in-Publication Data

The Beethoven quartet companion / edited by Robert Winter and
    Robert Martin.
        p.   cm.
    Includes bibliographical references and index.
    ISBN 0-520-08211-7 (cloth: alk. paper)
    ISBN 0-520-20420-4 (pbk.: alk. paper)
        1. Beethoven, Ludwig van, 1770–1827. Quartets, strings.
    2. String quartets—Analysis, appreciation. I. Winter, Robert,
    1945–   . II. Martin, Robert L., 1940–   .
    MT145.B425B4   1994   92–40668
    785'.7194'092—dc20   CIP
                                                                MN

Printed in the United States of America
9 8 7 6 5 4 3 2 1

Michael Steinberg's "Notes on the Quartets" are based on his program notes for the San Francisco Symphony, © 1980. A few sentences of the original version survive, and their use here is gratefully acknowledged.

The paper used in this publication meets the minimum requirements of the American National Standard for Information Sciences—Permanence of Paper for Printed Library Materials, ANSI Z39.48-1984. ⊖

To the memory of our friend and UCLA colleague Montgomery Furth.

Contents

Acknowledgments

Initial steps toward the publication of this volume began with a 1984 proposal from the Sequoia String Quartet Foundation to the National Endowment for the Humanities. The proposal was funded, and a generous grant of matching funds was committed by the University of California Press. Work stretched over a period far longer than we ever imagined. We gratefully acknowledge the help of Herbert Morris and A. Donald Anderson, presidents of the Sequoia String Quartet Foundation during the relevant period; Ara Guzelimian, who wrote the grant proposal to the NEH; and Doris Kretschmer, editor at the University of California Press, who has been our partner throughout. Finally, we thank each other.

Introduction

The seventeen Beethoven string quartets are to chamber music what the plays of Shakespeare are to drama and what the self-portraits of Rembrandt are to portraiture. Our relationship with these masterworks can benefit from a companion—a *vade mecum* ("go with me"), as such books used to be known—for the nonspecialist, offering perspective and guidance. Such a companion should enhance the experience of listening to the quartets in live performance or on recordings. It should also enrich our understanding of the context and significance of the quartets as cultural objects.

These dual purposes—enhancing the listening experience and enriching our understanding of the cultural context—are reflected in the approach we have taken to assembling this companion. To serve the first, we asked Michael Steinberg, formerly critic of the *Boston Globe* and more recently Artistic Advisor of the San Francisco Symphony and the Minnesota Orchestra, to write individual essays on each of the quartets. These essays, grouped into three chapters that make up the second part of this book, succeed admirably, we believe, in providing movement-by-movement guideposts for the listener. Steinberg has also contributed a glossary of musical terms that is helpful not only for his essay but for those of the other contributors as well.

The motivating concern connected with the second purpose of our companion was with the society and culture of Beethoven's time and, to some extent, the context in which the quartets are performed today. We asked for contributions from writers whom we trusted to be both original and accessible, without concern for comprehensiveness or consistency among essays. We favored interdisciplinary perspectives that reflect the diversity of approaches characteristic of the last twenty years. There is no particular order in which these essays should be read; we hope each reader will find something of interest to begin with and that the threads of connection will lead to the other essays.

Joseph Kerman's essay, "Beethoven Quartet Audiences: Actual, Potential, Ideal," examines in detail one aspect of the reception history of the quartets: to what changing audiences did Beethoven address these works? This apparently simple question opens complex and fascinating issues. For example, Kerman develops a connection between the art-historical notion of "absorption," developed by Michael Fried in connection with certain eighteenth-century painters ("the supreme fiction of the beholder's nonexistence"), and the fact that in certain of Beethoven's late quartets "the sense of audience superfluity is almost palpable."

Robert Winter's essay, "Performing the Beethoven Quartets in Their First Century," brings together information on how and under what circumstances the quartets were performed before the era of sound recordings. We learn of the extent of French influence on those who first performed the quartets and of their mix of partly modern, partly old-fashioned instruments. Through the eyes of three popular nineteenth-century German and American music periodicals, Winter examines the often surprising manner in which the nineteenth century viewed and consumed the quartets. For example, until well after mid-century, string quartet ensembles consisted most frequently of either family groupings or of the principal players from permanent orchestras who came together for a handful of concerts each year.

Maynard Solomon opens his essay by pointing out that nineteenth-century musicians and critics viewed Beethoven as the originator of the romantic movement in music; indeed he was lifted to mystical status as a romantic paradigm. Beginning with the work of the German scholar Arnold Schmitz in the 1920s and culminating in the influential work of Charles Rosen in the 1970s and 1980s, the pendulum swung in the opposite direction, transforming Beethoven into the archetypal classicist. The question, Solomon argues, is not simply how Beethoven should be viewed by historians of culture but how his music is to be heard: the issue "has an important bearing on whether we perceive and perform works such as the quartets primarily as outgrowths of eighteenth-century traditions and performance practices or as auguries of fresh traditions in the process of formation."

Leon Botstein—social historian, conductor, and college president—

has contributed a wide-ranging essay that places the quartets in the context of Viennese society, philosophy, theater, and literature. Connections to other essays in this volume emerge at every turn; there is discussion of the context of the earliest performances (Winter), of the special relationship of audience to chamber music performance (Kerman), of the reception of the quartets and views as to their "place" within the musical scene (Solomon); there is even discussion, in connection with the twentieth-century Austrian philosopher Ludwig Wittgenstein, of expression and meaning in the quartets that intersects with Robert Martin's discussion of performance and interpretation.

Drawing on his experience as cellist of the Sequoia String Quartet, Robert Martin looks at the quartets from the perspective of the performer, asking what sorts of interpretive decisions are made and on what basis. Martin takes advantage of the circumstance that in chamber music, rather more than in solo or orchestral playing, players are led to verbalize their reasons for musical decisions in order to persuade their colleagues. Martin asks about the relationship between performers, composer, and score; he examines a literalist, a "buried treasure," and a textual interpretation of this relationship before settling on what he calls a collaborative view.

As a young man Beethoven inherited the highly developed quartet models of Haydn and Mozart. They had devoted many of their finest efforts to string quartet writing, for reasons that went to the heart of the Viennese style. Viennese musicians viewed the members of the violin family as the most subtle of the crafted instruments, capable of challenging the human voice in their powers of expression. String trios were considered less than ideal because only by using multiple stops or through acoustical deception could they replicate four-part chords—the most complex in the Viennese musical vocabulary. The string quintet, mastered especially and unforgettably by Mozart, tilted the intimate balance of voices toward orchestral textures. The string quartet was seen as perfect both expressively and texturally, intimate yet complete. The four performers exemplified the Viennese ideal of civilized discourse, in which one could follow the separate voices with relative ease—more so, for example, than in a string quintet.

To be sure, Beethoven experimented first in Vienna with string trios, a genre in which he was less likely to be compared to Haydn and Mozart. Within a few years he was drawn into a full set of six quartets

(Op. 18) that displayed both their debt to Haydn and Mozart and their originality. However we deal with the issue of Beethoven's "style periods" (addressed in this volume by both Joseph Kerman and Maynard Solomon), the seventeen quartets are in many ways a surer guide to the debate than the sonatas (often used by Beethoven as a proving ground) or the symphonies (whose public character imposed more stylistic limits than chamber music).

String quartet writing was deeply important to Beethoven throughout his career, as we know from many letters, documents, contemporary reviews, eyewitness accounts, and, of course, the music itself. But his return to the medium in the very last years and months of his life testifies movingly to the centrality of the string quartet in his musical and personal identity. Having completed the two largest public works of his career—the Ninth Symphony and the *Missa solemnis*—and having received from the May 1824 premieres critical adulation of the kind that had slackened during the previous decade, Beethoven might have been expected to continue in the public spotlight. He had an almost standing invitation to go to England. There were numerous opera projects to be considered. And we know that in 1822, 1824, and 1825 he made tentative sketches for a "tenth" symphony.

But Beethoven came home to quartet writing, though it offered little potential for income and even less for public acclaim; only the first three of the five late quartets were commissioned, and the money from that commission never materialized. We get some sense of the scope of his preoccupation from the fact that, in 1826, Beethoven needed more than 650 pages of sketches to fashion the C-sharp minor Quartet, Op. 131— more than four times as many as he needed to write out the finished score in its entirety. Indeed, as Joseph Kerman suggests, Beethoven seems to have created these last quartets "without any listener in mind but himself."

Robert Winter & Robert Martin
Los Angeles
July 1992

Perspectives

Playing to the twentieth-century concert audience: the Lark String Quartet in a 1993 performance in Weill Recital Hall, the 268-seat chamber music and recital space in Carnegie Hall. (Photo © 1993 Steve J. Sherman.)

Beethoven Quartet Audiences:
Actual, Potential, Ideal

JOSEPH KERMAN

Most of us have known about Beethoven's "three periods" for about as long as we have known *Für Elise* and the Minuet in G. Deep disparities in style and feeling exist across the extent of Beethoven's works, disparities that seem to need explanation, and we cannot read much about Beethoven without learning what critics, biographers, and historians have come up with to answer this need. A main explanatory construct that has served them is the idea of the three style periods, matched to the life-phases of youth, maturity, and age. We cannot read much about Beethoven's string quartets, in particular, without soon meeting up with this idea in a notably tidy version.

Thus Beethoven's earliest essays in the genre, the set of six Quartets Op. 18, can be seen (or can be said) to strain restlessly but not very effectively against the classic norms established by Mozart and Haydn. Composed between 1798 and 1800, their very dates straddle the eighteenth and nineteenth centuries as though to symbolize Beethoven's so-called "formative" first period. His next quartets, the three dedicated to Count Razumovsky, were composed only five years later. Yet they seem to inhabit a different world, the world of the *Eroica* Symphony and *Leonore,* compositions that most famously define the second period. Archetypically "third period" is the celebrated group of five late quartets, including the *Grosse Fuge*—the great compositional project that occupied Beethoven for two years just prior to his death in 1827. Two works hover somewhat less tidily between the last two periods: the "Harp" Quartet in E Flat, Op. 74, and especially the F-minor work that Beethoven called *Quartetto serioso*, Op. 95.

In his recent collection *Beethoven Essays,* Beethoven's biographer Maynard Solomon subjects the doctrine of the three periods to close and skeptical scrutiny.[1] A threefold categorization of an artist's life-work was a cliché among nineteenth-century artistic biographers, who applied it just as readily to Michelangelo and Raphael as to Beethoven; and many works by Beethoven resist such triadic categorization—the F-minor quartet is not the only one. Yet the basic framework of the three style periods survives skepticism, Solomon concludes. For in fact many historical factors apart from musical style converge to reinforce it. Among these factors are the significant changes in Beethoven's inner life, in his fundamental modes of patronage, and indeed in the Viennese zeitgeist at large.

To these can be added, for the purposes of this chapter, developments in the history of the string quartet. The kind of history I have in mind is a sort of reception history, loosely defined: an account of the different audiences to which string quartets were principally directed over the course of Beethoven's activity.

The first audience, which I call the collegial audience, can be introduced appropriately by Karl Amenda, a name remembered today solely but fondly by aficionados of the Beethoven string quartets.

An enthusiastic violinist about Beethoven's age, Amenda became a close friend and confidant of the young composer during the few years he spent in Vienna as a fashionable music teacher. He left for good in 1799. In a letter written two years later, Beethoven mentioned a string quartet that he had given to Amenda and asked him not to circulate it. "I have made some drastic alterations. For only now have I learnt how to write quartets; and this you will notice, I fancy, when you receive them."[2]

The composition in Amenda's copy has, providentially, survived. The set of players' parts, in the hand of a professional copyist, bears Beethoven's affectionate inscription to his friend. The music is appre-

---

1. Maynard Solomon, *Beethoven Essays* (Cambridge, Mass., 1988), 116–25.
2. Ludwig van Beethoven to Karl Amenda, in Emily Anderson, ed., *The Letters of Beethoven,* 3 vols. (London, 1961), letter 53.

ciably different from the piece that Beethoven had by now (1801) published—and had evidently sent to Amenda—and that we know as the Quartet in F Major, Op. 18 no. 1. Comparing Amenda's early copy with the published score, the musicologist Janet Levy has been able to trace an illuminating account of Beethoven's self-criticism and self-improvement.[3] There has even been a recording made of the "Amenda version" of Op. 18 no. 1, by the Pro Arte Quartet (Laurel 116, 1987).

It is not necessary, however, to follow the details of the comparison between the two versions in order to grasp their symbolic importance. The very existence of this music in two forms tells us something about the ambience of the string quartet at that period. It tells us that pieces circulated in what might be called "trial versions," works in progress that would evidently be touched up or recast after being played and discussed by friends and patrons. The "finalization" represented by publication could be left for later. Nothing similar is known with Beethoven's music in other genres, such as sonata or song (it would be inconceivable, of course, with symphony or opera). Nor was this the only Beethoven quartet that circulated in a trial version. Another musicologist, Sieghard Brandenburg, has argued that Op. 18 no. 2 and probably others must also have existed in earlier forms, forms that can be reconstructed to some extent from the composer's sketches.[4]

The players themselves, then, formed the hard core of the string quartet's audience in Beethoven's early years. The ambience in which the genre flourished was essentially collegial, its milieu in the best sense of the word amateur. Quartets were played and discussed in salons of the aristocracy and the upper middle class. Vienna, music's capital city in the late eighteenth century—Amendas as well as Beethovens flocked there—was a veritable hotbed of the string quartet.

By "amateur" we do not mean, of course, anyone who had had a few years of lessons on the violin. The picture given in Peter Shaffer's *Amadeus* of Emperor Joseph II as a keyboard klutz is, as so often, just the wrong picture. These were devoted amateurs of considerable cultivation who played chamber music with the same passion with which we until recently played bridge. In Berlin, King Friedrich Wilhelm II of Prussia was a cellist; in Vienna, Prince Lobkowitz and Count Razumovsky were

3. Janet M. Levy, *Beethoven's Compositional Choices: The Two Versions of Op. 18, No. 1, First Movement* (Philadelphia, 1982).

4. Sieghard Brandenburg, "The First Version of Beethoven's G-Major String Quartet, Op. 18 No. 2," *Music & Letters* 58 (1977): 127–52.

violinists, Prince Moritz Lichnowsky another cellist. His violinist brother Karl, Beethoven's special patron, held quartet parties weekly. Amateur quartet playing on another level is memorialized in a stellar Viennese pick-up group that met at least occasionally in the 1780s, consisting of Haydn, Mozart, and two other leading composers of the time, Dittersdorf and Vanhal.

In the 1790s Beethoven attended quartet parties that took place twice a week at the home of an older composer named Emanuel Aloys Förster. Though Beethoven had played viola in the Bonn court orchestra, he seems to have been too rusty now to sit down with professionals like his friends Amenda and Schuppanzigh (of whom more presently). When Prince Karl Lichnowsky gave Beethoven a gift of four quartet instruments in 1800, he did not expect Beethoven to play them. The gesture was less practical than symbolic: once again, a token of musical collegiality. It was exactly for such a gesture that the string quartet provided so seemly a channel (and, in this case, so princely a one: the violins were by Amati and Giuseppe Guarneri, the cello by Andrea Guarneri).[5]

Corresponding to the collegial, amateur ambience of the early string quartet was its aesthetic ideal as the art of musical conversation. By the time the genre emerged—not, one might add parenthetically, without a good deal of anxious legislation from musicologists—this ideal was already clearly established. The eighteenth century itself delighted in comparing the players of a quartet to conversationalists. Thus the first published quartets by Joseph Haydn, in 1764, were already described as *quattuors dialogues* (if somewhat prematurely, according to Paul Griffiths, in his recent history of the string quartet).[6] Haydn perfected this art of conversation in the famous set of six Quartets, Op. 33, of 1781. Sometimes called the "Scherzi," this set was the principal model for Mozart in the even more famous six quartets that he dedicated to Haydn. The imprint of Haydn's Op. 33 can still be traced in Beethoven's Op. 18.

As Griffiths emphasizes, string quartet "conversation" is not to be equated with traditional counterpoint. "Fugue, in its ordained responses, its direct imitation and its lack of characterization in the voices, is the

5. But see n. 4 in Winter's chapter, p. 33.
6. Griffiths has not been able to satisfy himself that a passage that counts as truly "conversational" exists in a Haydn opus before 1769; Paul Griffiths, *The String Quartet* (New York, 1983), 22.

very antithesis of dialogue." Even other baroque contrapuntal textures—textures that are less formal than fugue—are more comfortably compared to debates, logical arguments, or question-and-answer sessions rather than to the elegant, witty conversations so prized by the Enlightenment. The classical obbligato style developed by Haydn is a kind of counterpoint, to be sure, but it is counterpoint of a new kind: informal, lightly etched, individualized, mercurial, and above all infinitely interactive.

In "abstract" musical terms, furthermore, if one may employ such an expression, the conversational style of the string quartet allowed composers to develop subtleties of technique that could not easily be achieved in genres such as the sonata or the symphony. This was especially true in the area of textural detail. For the pianoforte lacked the capability and the sensitivity of the four instruments of the quartet, while the orchestra lacked their flexibility and intimacy.

Förster's quartet sessions must surely have featured all Haydn's newest works in the genre. Though Beethoven's student days with Haydn, never too cordial, were now over, he was of course paying the greatest attention to Haydn's seemingly endless flow of new music in all genres: symphonies, quartets, Masses, oratorios. (Later, when the master congratulated the student on his ballet *Prometheus,* the subtext to Beethoven's quip that it was "no *Creation*" was not lost on the older composer.) As compared to orchestral and choral music, quartets were easier to hear, easier to get a hold of, easier to study. In the five-year period from 1795 to 1799, Haydn published annually—missing, astonishingly, just one year—Op. 71 (three numbers), Op. 74 (three, including "The Horseman," in G minor), Op. 76 (six, including the "Emperor," the "Sunrise," and the "Quinten"), and Op. 77 (two).

As far as immediate musical influence is concerned, however, Beethoven was less open to Haydn than to Mozart. That is not so strange in human terms, considering the human we are discussing. For it seems clear that, to Beethoven, Haydn was an annoyingly concrete father figure whereas Mozart, whom his real father had tried to make him emulate, and whom he had met briefly as a boy, was a dead legend. And Mozart, by publishing his first Viennese string quartets with a conspicuous dedication to Haydn, had publicly proclaimed a debt that Beethoven seems to have preferred to incur at second hand. There survive two copies of Mozart quartets made by Beethoven at the time of his Op. 18 project. They are the G major and the A major, K. 376 and K. 464;

EXAMPLE 1

a. Op. 18 no. 5, fourth movement, mm. 217–23

b. Piano Sonata in C Minor, Op. 13, third movement, mm. 99–102

copying was one way that Beethoven "learned how to write string quartets," as he put it in the letter to Amenda. Indeed Mozart's Quartet in A Major, K. 464, furnished the compositional model for Beethoven's own A-major Quartet, Op. 18 no. 5. It was an extraordinarily close model, as such things go.

Only one thing about the modeling process need be mentioned here. Thanks to Mozart, Beethoven appears now to have mastered more fully than ever before the art of musical conversation that is at the heart of the classical quartet aesthetic. Listen, for example, to the passage from the finale shown in Example 1a; Beethoven had not written many earlier passages with quite the relaxed, conversational give and take of this one. Beethoven's airy dialogue manipulates three distinct musical ideas, if we count the quiet ricocheting syncopations (which emerge as a new development, in diminution, from the phrase antecedent to the one illustrated). To place this passage against a similar passage from the *Pathétique*

Sonata, written a year or two earlier, is to illustrate the richness of texture available to the string quartet, as compared to the piano (Ex. 1b).

But if Beethoven may have fine-tuned his art of musical conversation under the inspiration of Mozart, he was also impressed by a very different aspect of Mozart's work. It was an aspect that was to have special resonance in Beethoven's later activity as a quartet composer.

Among the Mozart quartets there are a few movements that from early times acquired the reputation as arcana. One is the chromatic and dissonant slow introduction in the last number of the set dedicated to Haydn, the Quartet in C Major, K. 465. This music was still regarded as opaque (and ugly) by major critics such as François-Joseph Fétis in the nineteenth century and Ernest Newman in the twentieth. Beethoven, on the other hand, was fascinated by it. He imitated Mozart's slow introduction in two introductory movements of his own, located within the last numbers of his Op. 18 and Op. 59 sets. (These two movements are specially marked by titles—one of them surprisingly evocative: *La Malinconia* in the Quartet in B Flat, Op. 18 no. 6—and "Introduzione" in the Quartet in C, Op. 59 no. 3.) To be sure, what he imitated in both cases was more the notion of chromatic mystery than any specific musical details; *La Malinconia,* in particular, develops a highly Beethovenian concept in its utter self-absorption. At other points in the C-major "Razumovsky" quartet, however, Beethoven acknowledged his inspiration by citing other fragments of Mozart's K. 465 almost verbatim.

Beethoven's interest in Mozart's Quartet in A Major, K. 464, has already been mentioned. Coming upon the score some years later, Beethoven remarked to his student Carl Czerny that with it Mozart was telling the world, "Look what I could do if you were ready for it!" The presumption here is that the world was *not* ready. Then as now, this particular work was regarded as somewhat esoteric, mainly on account of its dense and disturbed—and, again, highly chromatic—first movement. In 1800 Beethoven's modeling of his own A-major quartet upon Mozart's extended only to the later movements; his first movement is much lighter than Mozart's opening *Allegro* and borrows nothing from it.[7] Twenty-five years later, however, Beethoven cited this very *Allegro* in his A-minor Quartet, Op. 132: a gesture that we may be inclined to

7. Jeremy Yudkin to the contrary notwithstanding: see his "Beethoven's 'Mozart' Quartet," *Journal of the American Musicological Society* 45 (1992): 30–74.

see as an acknowledgment of unfinished business. Beethoven had done less than full justice to K. 464 in 1800, we may feel—less, in any case, than in his transaction with K. 465 in the C-major Razumovsky quartet.

Did Beethoven recognize, during the two years when he was composing Op. 18, that he was in a way reliving Mozart's own experience? It is not impossible. About a year and a half after arriving in Vienna, Mozart, beginning at the age of 26, had written his six quartets in a period of just over two years, from 1782 to 1785. More than any other works, these quartets warranted his claim to share space with Haydn. (That is what Mozart's dedication is about, among other things.) Beethoven, beginning at the age of 28, six years after coming to Vienna, spent an intense period writing quartets from 1798 to 1800. They too mark a decisive step forward in the young composer's career. And as he was writing them, Haydn at last fell silent as a quartet composer.

Another parallel with Mozart could not have escaped Beethoven's notice. In 1796, Lichnowsky took him on a concert tour to Berlin to see the same cellist king to whom he had taken Mozart half a dozen years earlier. Two similar fishing expeditions—with significantly different outcomes. Mozart eventually came up with three string quartets featuring prominent cello parts for the king's own use and delectation. Beethoven wrote a pair of sonatas for the king's virtuoso cellist, Jean-Pierre Duport. And the Op. 5 Cello Sonatas of 1796 are perhaps the first Viennese virtuoso sonatas. Concerto-like, and sprouting cadenzas, they are true precursors of the formidable "Kreutzer" Sonata, dedicated to another virtuoso (and composed for still another) a few years later.

We can also regard them as heralds of a new kind of string quartet, one that will bear the ineluctable marks of concert performance. Indicative here is the career of Ignaz Schuppanzigh, the violinist who was closely associated with Beethoven—and with his quartets—throughout his life. Though in his day Schuppanzigh also made his mark as an orchestral violinist, conductor, and manager, he is remembered today as the first important musician to achieve fame primarily as a quartet player. Among the groups he led was one for Lichnowsky in 1795 and another for Count Razumovsky in 1808. His return to Vienna in 1823, after a stay in St. Petersburg, is traditionally seen as one of the stimuli that turned Beethoven to the composition of string quartets again during his last years.

From the historical point of view, the most notable of Schuppanzigh's groups was the one he formed in 1804 for the express purpose of presenting public concerts in Vienna. This was an obvious harbinger of the professional world of the string quartet as we know it. The genre today addresses principally not its own players but a concert audience; its aural field is no longer a closed circle but an open-ended cone. As the ambience of the genre changed from amateur to professional, the virtuoso violinist was invited into the quartet's conversational circle. Rode and Baillot, Vieuxtemps, Ole Bull, Joseph Helmesberger, Adolf Busch, Mischa Elman, Gidon Kremer—these and other great virtuosos took their turns as quartet leaders.

Schuppanzigh's experiment did not catch on, it appears, yet it also appears that Beethoven's Op. 59 Quartets were conceived with the Schuppanzigh concerts in mind and premiered there. And to compare Beethoven's Op. 59 with his Op. 18 is to see in the music itself a leap in style and concept that bypasses the sociological move adumbrated by Schuppanzigh's public concerts. Think of the beginning of the first "Razumovsky" and the end of the last one; there's not much conversation in evidence on either page. A better term might be determined ensemble shouting. At one time happy to converse, the string quartet has now acquired a new ambition: to project.

The feel of this music is symphonic—the characteristic feel of Beethoven's second-period music. For some years after the composition of the *Eroica* Symphony, in 1803, Beethoven was obsessed by the symphonic ideal. Piano sonatas like the "Waldstein" and the "Appassionata" are as symphonic in spirit as the "Razumovsky" quartets. One can trace actual technical parallels between the first movement of the *Eroica* Symphony and the first movement of the Quartet in F, Op. 59 no. 1, as I did in a chapter called "After the *Eroica*" in my study of the Beethoven quartets.[8] Both movements derive their harmonic plan from an obtrusive "sore" note in the opening theme, a note destined to be reinterpreted later in dramatic ways—D flat in the symphony movement, G in the quartet. Both movements grow enormously expansive in their development section, which in each case develops a fugato that leads into a shattering passage of breakdown. The codas in both movements are momentous. These technical parallels between the two movements drama-

8. Joseph Kerman, *The Beethoven Quartets* (New York, 1967), 89–116.

EXAMPLE 2.   Op. 59 no. 1, third movement, mm. 126–32

tize Beethoven's ambition in the Razumovsky series in a specially vivid way: the ambition to transform the smooth conversation of the string quartet into the heroic discourse of the symphony.

　　If the concept of Beethoven's second-period quartets is often symphonic, their technique is often virtuoso, as illustrated in Example 2. "Do you suppose I am thinking about your wretched fiddle when the spirit moves me?" Beethoven is supposed to have retorted when Schuppanzigh remonstrated about some difficulty or other. (Like so many other deeply suspect anecdotes about Beethoven, on the deepest level this one feels only too authentic.) It is hardly surprising that Op. 18 achieved popularity at once and maintained its popularity, while Op. 59 was at first given a wide berth.

　　But that was just at first. In the nineteenth century, a concert-giving string quartet that shied away from Beethoven's grander contributions to the genre would have been no more viable than an orchestra that side-stepped Beethoven's later symphonies. It is probably not too much to say that Op. 59 doomed the amateur string quartet. And in the next twenty years, Beethoven penned (among other such passages) the virtuoso first-violin cross-the-string passage in the coda of the "Harp" Quartet first movement, the greased-lightning finale in F major to the Quartet, Op. 95, and several hundred bone-crushing measures in Op. 133, the *Grosse Fuge*.

With Beethoven's last quartets, the project to which he turned at the end of his life, after the exhaustive public statements of the *Missa solemnis* and the Ninth Symphony, the quartet assumed a new aesthetic stance. Though the late scores were played in public as soon as they were composed—indeed, the composer took some trouble about this—directly afterwards they dropped ominously out of sight and sound. As Beethoven's musical imagination turned inward, the quartet turned away from its earlier audiences. At the risk of oversimplification, one can say that whereas in Beethoven's first period the essential audience for his quartets had been the quartet players, and in his second period the concert public, in the late period the audience was primarily the composer. Beethoven at the end of his life achieved the privatization of the string quartet.

Oversimplification, to be sure. This is only one-half of the story—and it is the half that was downplayed in my 1967 book. The particular kind of inwardness of Beethoven's last style period has impressed many listeners as complex, involuted, and esoteric; and this was an impression that the book questioned and tried to counter. I argued that Beethoven's late music was *not* arcane, that in it Beethoven had deliberately sought the simple, the direct, and the immediately communicable. Evidence for this can be found in the very many simple dance phrases that come up in the late quartets, also in Beethoven's repeated recourse to various kinds of vocal forms, styles, and genres. These works

are drenched in evocations of the human voice. These evocations mean to sing or to speak instantly to the heart, like the songs imagined by Beethoven's poet at the climax of *An die ferne Geliebte*:

> was mir aus der vollen Brust
> ohne Kunstgepräng' erklungen
> nur der Sehnsucht sich bewusst . . .

> what from my full breast
> has sounded artlessly,
> conscious only of its longing . . .

In [Beethoven's] last period, the illusion of art concealing art, of communication "without the adornments of Art," is among Beethoven's very particular studies. One is carried away, astonished, and ravished by the sheer songfulness of the last quartets—by recitative and aria, lied, hymn, country dance, theme and variations, lyricism in all its manifestations.[9]

As for the country-dance phrases, composed with a studied naiveté, they can look rather overwhelming when a lot of them are lined up together, as in Example 3.

Twenty-five years have changed or at least softened my view of this question. I do not think that my evidence was wrong, but I also do not think that this is the sort of question that can be settled on evidential grounds. Despite voice and song and country dance, Beethoven's late music also enlarges upon the quality of self-absorption that he had first tapped so remarkably in *La Malinconia,* from the Quartet in B Flat, Op. 18 no. 6, written in 1800. At one moment in the late quartets listeners are addressed, wooed, and confronted. At the next moment they are forgotten, left standing by as the artist wrestles alone with musical issues of his own imagining.

This novel sense of audience—of a singular audience, so different from those of the first- and second-period string quartets—seems to be an essential component of the emotional quality of numerous famous individual movements in the late works. We should say "qualities" rather than "quality," for each movement is different; intense but private and rarefied, each is in its own way abidingly strange, awe-inspiring, unsettling. At all events, this is certainly how they struck listeners of Beethoven's generation and several generations that followed in the nineteenth century. We lose something essential if, in the twentieth century, we work too hard to domesticate them. However many "public" movements may be contained in the late quartets, the "private" ones tend to stay in the ear and haunt the memory.

In Op. 127 the half-fugal scherzo is such a movement, in Op. 131 the opening fugue. Today's sanguine Beethovenian may be surprised at the lack of response this movement elicited from some very eminent musicians of the past. Richard Wagner's famous centenary book *Beethoven* of 1870 included an enthusiastic tribute to the Quartet in C-Sharp Minor, but Cosima Wagner's diary tells us how little the Master had really entered into the spirit of the fugue: "R. glanced at Beethoven's C-sharp

9. Ibid., 195.

EXAMPLE 3

a. Op. 127, first movement, mm. 7–14

b. Op. 127, fourth movement, mm. 21–28

c. Op. 130, second movement, mm. 1–8

d. Op. 130, sixth movement, mm. 113–20

(continued)

EXAMPLE 3   *(continued)*

e. Op. 130, fourth movement, mm. 1–8

Alla danza tedesca

f. Op. 131, fifth movement, mm. 69–76

g. Op. 131, fifth movement, mm. 141–48

h. Op. 132, second movement, mm. 182–85

i. Op. 135, fourth movement, mm. 61–68

Minor Quartet and pointed to the 3rd bar in the second line; he says he finds it [evidently the cross-relation] unpleasant, it does not sound well, altogether he finds the whole movement distasteful." [10] "Everything lies in the first 4 [!] notes at the beginning," Wagner remarked on another occasion, "then he busies himself with some fugal writing, which is not very interesting—even for musicians." [11]

In Op. 132, the bewildering "interior" movements are the Song of Thanksgiving and also the glassy *Allegro ma non tanto* that precedes it as the quartet's second movement. (The childlike and entrancing trio to the *Allegro ma non tanto* makes the main section itself seem even stranger, and doubly strange in the da capo.) And in Op. 130, of course, the sequence of six movements originally culminated in a staggering fugal finale. Stravinsky's characterization of the *Grosse Fuge*—"this absolutely contemporary piece of music that will be contemporary forever"—is at once gratifying as a tribute and more than a little disquieting as a twentieth-century co-option. As for the nineteenth century, a whole book has been written about the bewilderment the fugue caused at that time. [12] It remained an utter mystery to the conservative American composer Daniel Gregory Mason when he wrote his book *The Quartets of Beethoven* as late as 1947.

As is well known, in Beethoven's own time the *Grosse Fuge* caused such consternation that the composer was persuaded to replace it by a simpler, more "public" finale. He had never done such a thing before. His decision has been deplored; even his motives have been questioned. But Beethoven must have understood that the world he had pronounced unready for Mozart's Quartet in A Major, K. 464, was hardly ready for the *Grosse Fuge,* even twenty years later—even after twenty years of Beethoven.

Incidentally, many explanations have been offered for the rubrics "Muss es sein?" and "Es muss sein!" that Beethoven wrote on the finale of the last of the late quartets, the Quartet in F, Op. 135. (The most recent proposal devolves upon the importance of the pitch E flat—*Es*

10. *Cosima Wagner's Diaries,* ed. Martin Gregor-Dellin and Dietrich Mach, trans. Geoffrey Skelton, 2 vols. (New York, 1980), 2:262. References to the Beethoven quartets occur in 1:240, 302, 326, 337, 350, 744, 750, 869, 872, and 1000; and in 2:44, 262, 371–73, 376, 502, 517, 550, 573, 731, 756, 845, 850, and 949–50.

11. Ibid., 2:573.

12. Ivan Mahaim, *Beethoven: Naissance et renaissance des derniers quatuors* (Paris, 1964).

in German—in the work's tonal architecture.)[13] Perhaps Beethoven was also remembering his experience with Op. 130. This time, perhaps he meant to say, the finale will stay put: "Es muss sein!" This must be it!

To bring up Op. 135, however, is to recognize again how much in the late quartets remains "available." Neither the private nor the public aspects of this supreme body of music should be overstressed. "The unique richness of the last period derives exactly from the duality of introspection and solicitation, the inward-outward, public-private aspect of the art"—that is a declaration from my 1967 book that I still think puts the situation in about the right dialectical balance.

And to bring up Op. 135 is also to realize how the old ideals of collegiality and musical conversation had retained their attraction to the composer of the "Razumovsky" virtuoso flights and the *Grosse Fuge*. The dialogue here is literal—verbal—as has just been said; and indeed the conversational tags "Muss es sein?" and "Es muss sein!" refer to an in joke concerning an actual quartet concert by Schuppanzigh and his colleagues.[14] In the music itself, textures sprout up again that would have delighted Haydn, Förster, and Lichnowsky (see Ex. 4). With all that counts as new and extraordinary about the late quartets, other retrospectives features can also be noted in them, in addition to the genial stylistic return of Op. 135. The initial commission for the pieces came from another devoted quartet amateur in the old tradition, the cellist Prince Galitzin. They were played by that pioneer of quartet professionalism, Schuppanzigh, who had introduced the "Razumovsky" series. In an ap-

---

13. Christopher Reynolds, "The Representational Impulse in Late Beethoven, II: String Quartet in F Major, Op. 135," *Acta Musicologica* 60 (1988): 180–94.

14. A Viennese civil servant and quartet-party veteran, Ignaz Dembscher, had skipped the premiere of Op. 130, given by Schuppanzigh in March 1826, saying he would have the work played at home, "since it was easy for him to get manuscripts from Beethoven for that purpose. He applied to Beethoven for the Quartet, but the latter refused to let him have it, and Holz, as he related to Beethoven, told Dembscher in the presence of other persons that Beethoven would not let him have any more music because he had not attended Schuppanzigh's concert. Dembscher stammered in confusion and begged Holz to find some means to restore him to Beethoven's good graces. Holz said that the first step should be to send Schuppanzigh 50 florins, the price of the subscription. Dembscher laughingly asked 'Must it be?' ('Muss es sein?') When Holz related the incident to Beethoven he too laughed and instantly wrote down the following canon: 'Es muss sein! ja, ja, ja, ja, Heraus mit dem Beutel!'" (WoO 196) (Elliot Forbes, ed., *Thayer's Life of Beethoven* [Princeton, 1967], 976).

EXAMPLE 4.   Op. 135, first movement, mm. 166–73

proximate way, the entire late quartet project can be seen to recapitulate the changing sociology of the genre through Beethoven's lifetime.

There also exists a document that recalls the collegial, amateur phase of the string quartet in Beethoven's youth. It is a close analog to the early copy of the F-major Op. 18 Quartet presented to Karl Amenda when he left Vienna in 1799. In 1826 a copyist prepared manuscript string parts for the fugal first movement of the Quartet in C-Sharp Minor, Op. 131.[15] And he made this copy when the work was in an otherwise unknown early stage, a stage that differs from the final version in many details. One famous place can serve as an example—a place at which the final version has a new catch in the voice (Ex. 5).

The set of manuscript parts offers no indication that the rest of the piece was copied at this point. For whom were these parts prepared?

15. See Emil Platen, "Eine Frühfassung zum ersten Satz des Streichquartett op. 131 von Beethoven," *Beethoven-Jahrbuch* 10 (1978–81): 277–304.

EXAMPLE 5. Op. 131, first movement, mm. 68–75

a. Early version

b. Final version

Did Beethoven imagine that an actual performance of this trial version would give him an insight into nuances that he could not tell about in the abstract? He was stone deaf by this time. Was there some expectation that Schuppanzigh or his new second violinist Karl Holz—the composer's latest crony—would favor him with one or two suggestions after a rehearsal?

A small mystery remains to be cleared up here. What is clear already is that after the piece was copied (and presumably played in the Beethoven circle) in this provisional version, Beethoven returned to it, just as he had returned to Amenda's version of Op. 18 no. 1, in order to refine and touch up details. An archival document sheds an already oblique light on the older collegial period of the string quartet.

At the beginning of this essay, I suggested that the traditional association of Beethoven's three main groups of quartets with the three famous style periods was one that could be supported by information from the history of the string quartet. But to consider the history of the string quartet is to assess how Beethoven with his three periods was caught up in that history, as much as how he contributed to it. If we are to see three phases in the history of the quartet during Beethoven's lifetime—the amateur, the public, and the private—we must also see how Beethoven's relation to each was different. In the first his role was that of participant. To the second he served as a sort of prophet. The third was his own unique, private vision.

It would be better, in any case, to shift the metaphor from successive stages of an evolutionary process to different light-catching surfaces of a jewel. For each of the categories of our typology has, or had, a different ontological status; the word "audience" is being used here in different ways. Only what I have identified as the first audience of the string quartet was an actual flesh-and-blood audience. The collegial, amateur phase of the string quartet is a special moment that can be isolated in time and place. Beethoven arrived in Vienna at exactly the right time to accommodate himself to it.

On the other hand, the professionalization of the genre adumbrated in Vienna by Schuppanzigh in 1804 was not a moment but a process, a disorderly process that extended over many years. By 1804 the process had already been initiated in Paris and London, and the real sociological impact of the development lay in the future. Hence the string quartet's second audience, the public audience, was only a potential in Beethoven's lifetime. While Beethoven responded magnificently to the virtuoso implications of this potential, there is a sense in which he can be said to have done so prematurely. To see this, one only has to compare the "Razumovsky" quartets with the contemporary (and earlier) *quatuors brillants* by virtuoso composers such as Rode, Kreutzer, and Baillot.

The final privatization of the string quartet was Beethoven's special contribution, one that—except for the overriding historical impact of his works—stands outside of history. As Beethoven turned the genre inward, it revealed an esoteric facet which was not entirely unprecedented, as we have seen, but which had never been exposed so fully. Once again: we catch this intense, inward-flickering light only during certain famous and memorable movements. Other movements ask for other auditors, more traditional and tangible. While a proleptic experiment such as *La Malinconia* of 1800 anticipates some of the most self-absorbed episodes of the late quartets, these works on their part assimilate many retrospective currents from the world of Haydn and Mozart.

The first audience of the string quartet was an actual audience; the second can only be thought of in terms of potential, and the third was an ideal audience that consisted, paradoxically, of no audience at all. Here I am reminded of the art historian Michael Fried's analysis of certain eighteenth-century paintings, whose aesthetic depends, he says, upon "the supreme fiction of the beholder's nonexistence."[16] These paintings depict figures so intensely absorbed in either dramatic actions or contemplative states, says Fried, that they seem oblivious to any possible observer. Likewise with Beethoven's late quartets, the sense of audience superfluity is almost palpable. Engrossed, the composer is now writing without any listener in mind but himself. To put it this way involves some oversimplification, as has already been said; but there are times when the risk of oversimplification ought to be accepted. Beethoven's late music has often lost its audiences because it was composed so as to shut them out.

And because in his last period Beethoven often gives the impression of shutting out an audience, listeners ever since have had to get used to a situation in which they are suddenly made privy to a singular colloquy, now hushed, now strident, but always self-absorbed. The conversation of

16. Michael Fried, *Absorption and Theatricality: Painting and Beholder in the Age of Diderot* (Berkeley and Los Angeles, 1980), 103. See Joseph Kerman, "Remarks from the Chair," in *Atti del XIV Congresso della Società Internationale di Musicologia, Bologna 1987* (Bologna, 1991), 1:677–84.

the classical string quartet is obviously designed to be heard and, within a discreet circle, overheard. The discourse of the professional quartet is meant to be broadcast. Listening to certain movements in the late Beethoven quartets, one feels sure that neither of these situations holds. The music is sounding only for the composer and for one other auditor, an awestruck eavesdropper: you.

ALLGEMEINE
MUSIKALISCHE ZEITUNG.

Den 23sten July.   №. 30.   1828.

Auf Veranlassung von:

1. *Grand Quatuor — pour deux Violons, Alto et Violoncelle,* comp. — — *par Louis van Beethoven.* Oeuvr. 131. Mayence, chez les fils de B. Schott. (Preiss 4 Fl. 30 Xr.)

2. *Grand Quatuor* — — — *en partition* — — — (Pr. 2 Fl. 42 Xr.)

von Friedr. Rochlitz.

Es ist schwierig und bedenklich, jetzt über die letzten grossen Werke Beethoven's zu schreiben. Diess Schwierige und Bedenkliche liegt theils in den Umständen, theils in den Werken selbst. Wir erklären uns darüber, obgleich diess keine Recension jenes Quartettes (eher eine, des Recensenten) abgibt. Es scheint uns nämlich überhaupt der Erklärung nicht unwerth, mehren Lesern zur Erwägung, wo nicht nöthig, wenigstens nützlich, und selbst um gewisser neuester Ereignisse willen, die wir nicht weiter bezeichnen wollen, rathsam und wohlgethan.

Das Schwierige und Bedenkliche, jetzt über die letzten grossen Werke Beethovens zu schreiben, liegt, sagten wir, theils in den Umständen. B. ist entschieden der Held der musikalischen Welt in deren jetziger Periode; er ist dafür, und mit vollem Rechte, anerkannt und proclamirt von allen rechtmässigen Wählern und selbst von denen, welche selbst in die Wahl kommen könnten; er ist es sogar (nach dem, was verlautet) einstimmig, wenn nicht in allen Richtungen seiner Kunstthätigkeit, doch gewiss in der, zur Instrumentalcomposition. Für den anerkannten Helden irgend einer Zeit, und worin er's sey, entzündet sich der Enthusiasmus; durch diesen wird sogar er selbst erst vollendet, nicht nur äusserlich, in seinen Wirkungen, sondern selbst innerlich, in seinen Vorzügen. Das

soll auch so seyn. Durch jeden Helden der Zeit soll ja Etwas werden in dieser Zeit, und zwar etwas, innerhalb seiner Sphäre Grosses und Weitausgreifendes: was wird denn aber Grosses und Weitausgreifendes in der Welt überhaupt, ganz ohne Enthusiasmus? Auch etwas Neues, ganz Ungewohntes soll werden; das findet unvermeidlich Hindernisse, die nun weggeräumt, Schwierigkeiten, die besiegt seyn wollen — Hindernisse, Schwierigkeiten, nicht nur in der bisherigen Lage der Dinge im Allgemeinen, sondern auch in jedes Einzelnen eigenem Innern, in seinen bisherigen Gewöhnungen, Vorneigungen, oft auch in seinen Fassungsfähigkeiten: wie gelänge diess aber, ganz ohne Enthusiasmus? Für unsern Beethoven wird nun eben jetzt dieser Enthusiasmus noch gesteigert (allerdings zunächst durch das endliche Durchdringen seiner vortrefflichsten Werke selbst; wovon wir aber hier nicht sprechen, sondern von den Umständen) durch seinen Tod und das lebendige Gefühl für die Lücke, die dieser geschlagen hat und die auszufüllen Keiner vorhanden ist; durch den, auf diese Veranlassung von neuem und lebhafter erregten Antheil an dem grossen Leiden, das unnachlassend eine Reihe von Jahren überschwer auf ihm gelegen, unter dessen Last er dennoch sich so mächtig hervor in's Freye gearbeitet und so Treffliches, auch so Vieles, und zum Theil selbst so Heiteres hervorgebracht hat; durch den, auf dieselbe Veranlassung von neuem und lebhafter erregten Antheil an der betrübten Lage, in die er zumeist durch jenes Leiden versetzt wurde, ohne auch nur im Mitgenusse seiner eigenen Werke entschädigt und erfrischt werden zu können, u. dgl. m. Wenn nun, wer über B.s neueste Werke jetzt schriebe, neben dem, was zu preisen, was aber als fast erschöpft, in der Darstellung nicht mehr sonderlich wirken könnte, auch Manches auszusetzen, (der Held blieb ja doch, wie jeder, ein

---

Beethoven's quartets were the subject of lively analysis and discussion in periodicals such as the *Allgemeine musikalische Zeitung*. The issue of 23 July 1828 includes a particularly probing article by the critic Friedrich Rochlitz, who confesses in his opening sentence that it is "difficult and hazardous to write about Beethoven's last works."

Performing the
Beethoven Quartets
in Their First Century

ROBERT WINTER

The fame of the Beethoven quartets has rested appropriately on their musical virtues. As might be expected, the substantial literature on the quartets has focused on Beethoven's stylistic contributions to this central pillar of the chamber music repertoire. While several recent studies have dealt with sketches or with biographical and programmatic aspects of the quartets, none has inquired into how—and on what kinds of instruments—these works might have been performed before the era of sound recordings, into the performers who brought them to a growing public, or into the circumstances under which they were performed.[1]

---

1. Recent studies in English include: Kathryn Laura Bumpass, "Beethoven's Last Quartet" (Ph.D. diss., University of Illinois, 1982); Richard Kramer, "Ambiguities in *La Malinconia:* What the Sketches Say," *Beethoven Studies* 3 (1982): 29–46; Janet M. Levy, *Beethoven's Compositional Choices: The Two Versions of Op. 18, No. 1, First Movement* (Philadelphia, 1982); Alan Tyson, "The 'Razumovsky' Quartets: Some Aspects of the Sources," *Beethoven Studies,* ed. Alan Tyson (Cambridge, 1982), 107–40; Donald Tobias Greenfield, "Sketch Studies for Three Movements of Beethoven's String Quartets, Opus 18, Nos. 1 and 2" (Ph.D. diss., Princeton University, 1983); John Edward Crotty, "Design and Harmonic Organization in Beethoven's String Quartet, Op. 131" (Ph.D. diss., University of Rochester, 1986); Bruce Benedict Campbell, *Beethoven's Quartets Op. 59: An Investigation into Compositional Process* (Ann Arbor, 1987); Timothy H. Lindemann, "Strategies of Sonata Form in the First Movements of the Beethoven String Quartets" (Ph.D. diss., Indiana University, 1987); and Christopher Reynolds, "The Representational Impulse in Late Beethoven, II: String Quartet in F Major, Op. 135," *Acta Musicologica* 60 (1988): 180–94.

Since the Beethoven quartets occupy the same lofty position in the domain of chamber music as the symphonies do in orchestral music, neglect on this scale seems, at first glance, puzzling. Great energy has been expended, for example, studying the manner in which Beethoven's keyboard and orchestral works were performed during the nineteenth century. We know a great deal about the lineage of pianists that leads from Beethoven to Carl Czerny to Franz Liszt and beyond. We know almost as much about the procession of permanent orchestras founded in Leipzig, Vienna, Berlin, Boston, and elsewhere during the nineteenth century. But we know much less about the lineage that leads from the first Schuppanzigh Quartet of 1804 to the Rosé Quartet founded in 1882.

If we consider for a moment the place of chamber music within the musical galaxy, the neglect is less puzzling. Romantic pianists were viewed as conquering titans whose individual feats expressed the heroic dimension of human nature. The introduction of the solo recital around mid-century institutionalized a framework within which pianists presented themselves to the public. Pianists invited a kind of hero worship that an ensemble of four string players engaged in intimate conversation could scarcely hope to arouse.

At the other end of the spectrum, orchestras were expressions of civic and regional pride. Once founded, their future existence was a near certitude. This was true even though their personnel (including the conductor/music director) often changed frequently. While principal players might earn a degree of notoriety, the departure of one or even several principals from an individual orchestra did not undermine the continued existence of that ensemble. Standing orchestras were among the first to put together subscription series that created stable, predictable frameworks within which public music making occurred. Quartets, as we shall see, were far less permanent.

Finally, the rapid evolution in instrument design that took place throughout the nineteenth century was by and large a response to the demands of the largest public forms of music—symphony, concerto, and opera. To fill the spacious new middle-class concert halls sprouting up all over Europe, louder instruments were essential. The changes in the construction of string instruments inevitably transformed the character of chamber music from an intimate private pastime into a public concert-oriented medium scarcely distinguishable in social terms from other forms such as symphony or opera. Although we might argue that

Dvořák's quartets at the end of the century are more intimate than those, say, of Brahms, both composers were by then writing for the 400–500 seat "chamber music" halls that were usually incorporated into the newest concert complexes.

It makes sense to begin with the instruments since they might appear to be the only constant in the otherwise rapid developments that took place. There is a widespread belief that the string family changed far less in the nineteenth century than instrument families such as woodwinds and brass. The nearly blind can glance at a Mozart fortepiano weighing 70 kilograms, made entirely of wood, and with a range of sixty-one notes and distinguish it from a late romantic instrument weighing over 400 kilograms, incorporating a huge cast-iron plate, and with a range of eighty-eight notes. The differences in sound between the two instruments are equally substantial—the fortepiano's silvery, quickly decaying tone versus the modern piano's full, sustained, and less transparent tone.

Likewise, the distinctions between a valveless French horn of the late eighteenth century and a modern triple-valved horn can be both seen and heard. The earlier horn produces a purer sound in the natural overtone series but is darker and more covered in chromatic passages. The evenness of the modern horn is produced at the expense of the purity of the earlier instrument. A five-keyed flute from the late eighteenth century looks and sounds very different from a mid-century Boehm instrument. And so on.

Yet even professional musicians have difficulty distinguishing between the look of a late eighteenth-century violin and that of a late nineteenth-century one. Perhaps more can distinguish between the sounds produced by each, but almost all will agree that the differences are subtle, especially when compared to pianos, horns, or flutes. We have been led to believe that the last major transformation of the violin occurred by 1800, about the time Beethoven published his Op. 18 Quartets.[2] According to this scenario, the newer (or, more frequently, altered older) violin featured a longer neck at a sharper angle, a longer and thicker bass

2. Others set the stabilizing of the instrument—and its performance techniques—even earlier. The most influential book on the history of violin playing, David Boyden's *History of Violin Playing from Its Origins to 1761* (London, 1965), concludes with the 1761 treatise of L'Abbé le fils (reprinted in facsimile in 1976)—the last major publication on violin playing before the advent of the Tourte bow. Boyden implies that the changes in violin technique after 1761 are refinements compared to the dramatic evolutions before 1761.

bar, a thicker soundpost, and stronger strings and used a modern concave bow of the type introduced around 1785 by the French maker François Tourte.

But this picture is overly simplified. The G string (the lowest of the four strings on a violin) of the first half of the nineteenth century was not wound in the gold or silver common today but rather with gut. The gut D and A strings may not have been wound with anything until after mid-century. The E string was gut until the early twentieth century, when it finally changed to steel. These earlier dispositions produced a tone that was less powerful but more transparent and intimate than the eventual all-steel coverings. Players who have experimented with gut strings today report a more responsive and "speaking" tone, albeit one in which unexpected squeaks are a greater threat than with modern strings.

Until about 1820, violins had no chin rest, which meant that the left hand was heavily involved in supporting the instrument. The German Ludwig Spohr, who introduced the chin rest (which he called a "fiddle holder"), placed it at the center of the tailpiece. It was not until mid-century that the chin rest was routinely located on the left side of the instrument. Hence any early performers of the Beethoven quartets—certainly including all those during Beethoven's lifetime—could not shift hand positions with the freedom and abandon of modern performers, nor could they apply the degree of bow pressure possible on the modern instrument. Their range of volume was circumscribed but in some ways more subtle.

One more factor must be taken into account in the Vienna of Beethoven (and even of Brahms). Vienna was the most conservative major city in Europe when it came to instrumental innovations. The piano is again the best example. The Viennese action was first challenged around 1800 by the English grand action and a few decades later by the modern double-escapement action introduced in Paris by Sébastien Erard. Yet the Viennese maintained a near-fanatical loyalty to their simpler action until well into the twentieth century. Nor was their loyalty entirely chauvinistic. The Viennese action placed the performer in a more direct, and thereby more intimate, contact with the hammer striking the string. Players were happy to sacrifice power to intimacy, and there is little reason to suppose that the Viennese view of stringed instruments was any different. It was no accident that Leopold Mozart's *Violinschule,* originally published in 1756, was still popular in nineteenth-century reprintings in Vienna.

Although the histories of the viola and cello are even less complete than that of the violin, we have no reason to think that their development was radically different. Both in the orchestra and in chamber music, the strings were now viewed as a homogeneous family whose ability to blend was one of its greatest strengths. Yet it is very likely that the ad hoc orchestras convened for the occasional orchestral concerts known as *Akadamien* consisted of mixed groups of players, some with fully modernized instruments and Tourte bows and others who clung tenaciously to unaltered instruments with flat "transition" bows. Such a group may well have played the premiere of Beethoven's Ninth Symphony in 1824. And there is certainly every reason to suppose that the groups of chamber music lovers who convened informally to read through the newest quartets of Beethoven also consisted of altered and unaltered instruments.

Throughout the first half of the nineteenth century, piano arrangements of instrumental works became more and more frequent, signaling a gradual shift from a string-based musical culture to a keyboard-based one. Though symphonies and operas were favored, quartets were not ignored. An 1820 review of an arrangement of the C-minor Quartet, Op. 18 no. 4, for piano four hands acknowledged that "Beethoven's quartets on the piano, when not arranged very well, lose more than those of other masters such as Mozart; the reasons lie in both the content and the manner of writing."[3]

Stringed instruments nevertheless remained the steadfast choice of Vienna's musical connoisseurs until well after Beethoven's death. Although known as a keyboard virtuoso, Beethoven was more than a passable violinist/violist and certainly understood the idiomatic characteristics of the entire string family. We even have the quartet of string instruments presented, according to Alois Fuchs, to Beethoven in 1800 by Prince Lichnowsky at the urging of the violinist Ignaz Schuppanzigh.[4] Alas, they tell us little about how they might have sounded in Beethoven's lifetime. All of them have been modernized, though we cannot be sure when the alterations were carried out (old instruments continued to be

3. *Allgemeine musikalische Zeitung* (hereafter *AmZ*) 22 (1820): col. 784.
4. On permanent display at the Beethovenhaus in Bonn; see frontispiece. These instruments are said to be a Giuseppe Guarneri violin of 1718, a Niccolò Amati violin of 1667, a Vincenzo Ruger viola from 1690, and an Andrea Guarneri cello of 1712. These nineteenth-century attributions are now questioned, although no one has made a detailed study.

altered into the twentieth century). Strings, of course, were replaced frequently. Nor do we have any of the bows used by Schuppanzigh and his numerous quartet partners while Beethoven was alive. We do not even know to what extent he used these tokens of Lichnowsky's esteem. Curiously, although Beethoven's poorly restored Graf of 1825 (a loan from its maker) has been used for several recordings, no group has made a commercial recording on the quartet of string instruments.

The Viennese violinist Ignaz Schuppanzigh is almost synonymous with performances of the Beethoven quartets during the composer's lifetime.[5] Schuppanzigh was born in Vienna in 1776, the son of a professor at the Realschule (a preparatory school). Having started out as a violist, he made the switch to violin in his teens. As early as 1793, according to Franz Wegler, the 16-year-old Schuppanzigh was leading informal quartet concerts at the apartments of Prince Lichnowsky (one of Beethoven's most important aristocratic patrons) every Friday morning—a custom that lasted for several years. By the time Schuppanzigh was twenty, according to Theodor Frimmel, he already belonged to a "paid quartet of Prince Lichnowsky's."[6]

Although Lichnowsky's performers played trios and other chamber works, a string quartet provided the core group. We cannot be certain who Schuppanzigh's violin partner in such a quartet was, nor with which of several cellists he played. Frimmel drew his list of performers directly from the 1838 *Biographische Notizen über Ludwig van Beethoven* of Ferdinand Ries (a pianist/composer who studied piano with Beethoven for several years around 1800), in which the artists mentioned include the violist Franz Weiss (1778–1830) and as many as four cellists: Anton Kraft (1752–1820) and his son Nikolaus (1778–1853); the amateur cellist and friend of Beethoven, Nikolaus Zmeskall (1759–1833); and possibly Josef Linke (1783–1837). Without citing a source, Thayer-Forbes mentions as the second violin Louis Sina, a youthful French pupil of the Silesian composer Emanuel Aloys Förster (1748–1823), whose string quartets Beethoven admired.[7] The performers in what was apparently the most common configuration at Lichnowsky's—Schuppanzigh, Sina, Weiss,

---

5. The most detailed general article on Schuppanzigh in English is Donald McArdle's "Beethoven and Schuppanzigh," *The Music Review* 26 (1965): 3–14.

6. Theodor Frimmel, *Beethoven Handbuch* (Leipzig, 1926), 2:161.

7. Elliot Forbes, ed., *Thayer's Life of Beethoven* (Princeton, 1967), 156. (Hereafter, this work will be cited as Thayer-Forbes 1967.)

and Nikolaus Kraft—ranged in age from 14 to 17 years, which must have delighted the newcomer Beethoven. The notion of a fixed, permanent quartet of players, however, would have been foreign to all of the participants.

Schuppanzigh—who early on attained a corpulence that earned him the Beethovenian sobriquet of "Falstaff"—was no more able to earn a living exclusively as a player of chamber music than was any other Viennese musician. Beethoven probably studied violin with Schuppanzigh three times a week during 1794. In 1795 Schuppanzigh led the orchestra in the summer concerts offered at the Augarten (a local restaurant with a music-loving proprietor); from 1798 he assumed the management of the series.

In the winter of 1804–5, Schuppanzigh formed his own quartet for the express purpose of giving public quartet concerts—a historic first, according to the primary chronicler of Viennese concert life, Eduard Hanslick.[8] Joseph Mayseder (a brilliant pupil of Schuppanzigh's who was 15 when the concerts began) played second violin, Schreiber (a violist in the Kärntnerthortheater orchestra whose first name is not known) played viola, and the elder Kraft played cello. This was presumably the group that, early in 1807, played the first performances of the three Op. 59 Quartets commissioned by Count Andreas Razumovsky, the Russian ambassador to Vienna.[9] The concerts of 1804–5 took place initially in a private house, the Heiligenkreuzerhof, and later—as was common in a city without formal concert halls—in the hall of a popular restaurant, Zum römischen Kaiser. In neither case could the audience have numbered more than a hundred. The correspondent for the *Allgemeine musikalische Zeitung* (or *AmZ*) says nothing about the exact circumstances of the Op. 59 performances; earlier in the same paragraph he says that a performance of Beethoven orchestral works was attended by "a very select audience," and we can safely assume the same for the quartets.

While these performances were clearly not of the informal, pick-up variety that had been the lifeblood of quartet playing in Vienna for a generation, they were just as clearly not the kind of fully public chamber music concerts that became regularized in series after Beethoven's death. The description of the quartets by the same correspondent as "long and difficult" points to a growing emphasis on professional performers. From

---

8. Eduard Hanslick, *Geschichte des Konzertwesens in Wien* (Vienna, 1869), 202–3.
9. The presumed premiere is noted in the *AmZ* 9 (1807): col. 400.

the exposed cello theme at the opening of Op. 59 no. 1 to the blatantly virtuosic closing fugue of Op. 59 no. 3 (with its exposed first entrance in the usually submissive viola), the increased demands over Op. 18 are considerable. By May the *AmZ* correspondent writes that these "difficult but profound quartets please more and more; admirers hope that they will soon be engraved."[10] After three seasons at most, Schuppanzigh's noble experiment was terminated.

Difficulties were on the minds of almost all of Beethoven's contemporaries who encountered the quartets. Already in 1801 the reviewer of the first batch of Op. 18 Quartets felt obliged to warn readers that "they must be played frequently and very well, for they are very difficult to perform and in no way popular."[11] The otherwise enthusiastic 1811 reviewer of the Quartet in E-Flat Major, Op. 74, describes the opening *Allegro* as "just as difficult to perform as its wondrous intricacies are to follow." He concludes his expansive review cryptically: "That this quartet is difficult to perform scarcely needs to be mentioned."[12]

Schuppanzigh's most publicized contribution to Viennese musical life resulted from his heading a second quasi-permanent quartet. In the late summer or early autumn of 1808, Razumovsky commissioned Schuppanzigh—whom Razumovsky named *violino primo* for life—to assemble "the finest string quartet in Europe." Razumovsky was himself a competent second violinist who had pleaded in vain in 1800 with Beethoven for lessons in quartet writing (Beethoven sent him instead to Förster).

The group assembled by Schuppanzigh included Sina (who, according to some accounts, played second violin only when Razumovsky was not available), the violist Weiss, and the cellist Linke. Weiss and his family were even supplied lodgings on the grounds of the Razumovsky palace. There are no firm records of this second group performing in public, and in some respects—the increasingly public character of Beethoven's quartet music aside—it seems a throwback to the earlier practice of domestic music making. Razumovsky's dream quartet remained in existence until the disastrous fire of 31 December 1814, which completely destroyed the palace and, with it, the count's fortune.

After a year of participating in public concerts, Schuppanzigh made the bold decision in 1816 to try his fortunes in Russia. He settled for six years in St. Petersburg, where, with great success, he introduced

10. Ibid., col. 517.
11. Ibid., 3 (1801): col. 800.
12. Ibid., 13 (1811): col. 350; 352.

Beethoven's orchestral and chamber works to the Russians. Schuppanzigh returned to Vienna in 1823 in time to take part in the premieres of the Ninth Symphony (as leader of the orchestra) and several of the late quartets, including Op. 127, Op. 130, and Op. 132.

What was Schuppanzigh like as a performer? The few comments that survive paint only a general picture. Early reviews of his leadership of the Augarten concerts praised his "accuracy" and "brilliance." Reviews a few years later continued to praise his "brilliant playing" but added that "we cannot agree with the general position that he is a great conductor." A reviewer in the *AmZ* of 1800 commented that "In double stops or in higher positions he often plays out of tune, perhaps as a result of his fleshy hands."[13]

A fuller comment on his performance of chamber music was offered by a traveling musician, Friedrich Reichardt, about some chamber concerts he heard at the end of 1810:

Herr Schuppanzigh himself has an original, piquant style most appropriate to the humorous quartets of Haydn, Mozart, and Beethoven—or, perhaps more accurately, a product of the capricious manner of performance suited to these masterpieces. He plays the most difficult passages clearly, although not always quite in tune. . . . He also accents very correctly and significantly, and his *cantabile,* too, is often quite singing and affecting. He is likewise a good leader for his carefully chosen colleagues, who enter admirably into the spirit of the composer, though he disturbed me often with his accursed fashion, generally introduced here, of beating time with his foot.[14]

Even fewer comments survive about Schuppanzigh's partners. The violist Franz Weiss was born in Silesia but came to Vienna at a young age. He seems to have spent his entire life there and is mentioned even more frequently than Schuppanzigh in the lists of performers at chamber and orchestral concerts of Beethoven's music. In contrast to Schuppanzigh, Weiss was described as "tall and lean." Although he took part in the premieres of most of the quartets from Op. 59 on, we have not one evaluative word about his playing. Little more is known about the cellist Linke, except that he was lame from birth as well as an orphan. After the breakup of the Razumovsky Quartet he was retained by the aristocratic

13. Hanslick, *Geschichte,* 71; 229 n.

14. Johann Friedrich Reichardt, *Vertraute Briefe geschrieben auf einer Reise nach Wien und den österreichischen Staaten zu Ende 1808 und zu Anfang 1809,* 2 vols. (Amsterdam, 1810), 1:204–5.

Erdödy family, and it was for him that Beethoven wrote the two Cello Sonatas, Op. 102. An entry in a conversation book from early January 1825 reports on a performance of one of the Op. 59 Quartets (perhaps no. 1): "Linke played splendidly, / the cello is kept very busy / he was enthusiastically applauded."[15]

In general terms we need to remember that Schuppanzigh and his colleagues were much influenced by the brilliant but objective style of French violin playing that was dominant throughout western Europe from about 1780 to 1830. The dedication by Beethoven of his A-major Violin Sonata, Op. 23, to a leading French violinist, Rodolphe Kreutzer (1766–1831), was no accident. Kreutzer, along with Pierre Baillot (1771– 1842)—whose style was more elegant and refined than Kreutzer's—and Pierre Rode (1774–1830)—the most polished—formed a triumvirate that represented the peak of the classical French violin school. When the Italian Nicolò Paganini—whose virtuosity resonated throughout the nineteenth and into the twentieth century—played fancy passages in- volving harmonics or left-hand pizzicatos, it is said that Baillot hid his face.

The twelve string quartets (called *quatuors brillants*) of Rode, domi- nated completely by the first violin, contain none of the part writing that gives Beethoven's quartets their individual stamp. The three Frenchmen collaborated in 1803 to produce the first violin method for the Paris Conservatory.[16] Its influence was widespread and lasted until at least the middle of the century—though its limitations were apparent much ear- lier. On the one hand, the technical demands of the French school, in which multiple stops were restricted to moderate tempos and the upper range was limited to seventh position (hitting the ceiling at a^4—ten white notes shy of the top of the modern piano), fell far short of the emerging school of virtuosity headed by Paganini. On the other hand, the French method was inadequate to the highly complex phrase struc- ture and expressive language of Beethoven's quartets.

For example, Baillot, Rode, and Kreutzer's *Méthode* still describes mu- sical effects in terms of the three "species" of the "ancients": "tranquil

---

15. Karl-Heinz Köhler and Grita Herre, eds., *Ludwig van Beethovens Konversations- hefte,* 9 vols. (Leipzig, 1968–89), 7:67.

16. Pierre Baillot, Pierre Rode, and Rodolphe Kreutzer, *Méthode de violon* (Paris, 1803). Rode published his own method in 1834, which demonstrates how long the influence of the French school endured.

music, active music, and enthusiastic music."[17] A footnote traces the philosophical roots of this tripartite division back to Aristotle, Plutarch, Quintilian, and Euclid. However Beethoven's quartets might be grounded in narrative discourse, it was no longer the rhetorical framework of the Greeks. We can safely assume that each new quartet of Beethoven challenged its performers to expand their technical and expressive horizons.

In Schuppanzigh's absence, the Hungarian violinist Josef Böhm (1795–1876) put together a popular quartet around 1819 that included Karl Holz (1798–1858)—Beethoven's close associate from 1824 to 1826—as his second violinist. Böhm patterned his early style on his French teacher Rode, but in the course of a lengthy and distinguished career in Vienna he founded a new school of violin playing based squarely on the chamber works of Haydn, Mozart, Beethoven, and Schubert. He was the primary teacher of two of the most influential quartet players of the nineteenth century, Georg Hellmesberger (1800–1873) and Joseph Joachim (1831–1907). Rather than for his brilliance, Böhm was praised by Joachim for "an art of phrasing that enabled him to realize anything that he envisioned or felt"—a capacity addressed only scantily by the French school.

Our most detailed knowledge about the performance of quartets during Beethoven's lifetime concerns the late quartets—in no small measure because of the controversy surrounding their initial readings. With Schuppanzigh's return from St. Petersburg, and with Böhm's departure on a concert tour, Schuppanzigh again reconstituted his quartet, with Holz as the only new face since the Razumovsky days. Concerning an upcoming subscription concert in January 1825, Schuppanzigh wrote in a conversation book: "If he [Beethoven] is inclined to give me a work for a performance, that is, a work that I can perform for the first time, then that will make an enormous difference in my current subscription concert. . . . In E-flat major [Op. 127]. . . . Then he permits me to be the one to make it known [?]"[18] As was all too typical in Beethoven's career, the work was not ready for rehearsal in time for either a first or a second concert, nor was it ready for rehearsal until a few weeks before the actual premiere on 6 March. Mindful of this, Beethoven had the

17. Ibid., 159.
18. Köhler and Herre, eds., *Beethovens Konversationshefte*, 7:82–83.

four players sign a half-humorous, half-serious document in which each pledged to "do his best, to distinguish himself and to vie with each other in excellence." The reviewer of the premiere characterized the work as "symphonically conceived" and "requiring study by the performers down to the smallest detail."[19] But others at the premiere criticized the performance directly. Böhm later described it: "The affair did not come off well. Schuppanzigh, who played first violin, was weary from much rehearsing, there was no polish in the performance, the quartet did not appeal to him, he was not well disposed towards the performance, and the quartet did not please."[20] On 26 March, Nicholas Zmeskall wrote in the aftermath to the Countess Theresa Brunswik: "Beethoven had finished a new quartet.—Schuppanzigh had already played it at his quartet subscription concert. But the Austrian miscarried and the Hungarian was triumphant. Schuppanzigh received the disgrace and Böhm the victory. Beethoven, furious at the disdain with which his latest work had been received, got angry and arranged for a performance by another friend of the art, and a brilliant success, delight, and admiration followed."[21]

Böhm described his own preparation for the performance as follows:

[The quartet] was rehearsed frequently under Beethoven's own eyes: I said Beethoven's *eyes* intentionally, for the unhappy man was so deaf that he could no longer hear the heavenly sound of his compositions. And yet rehearsing in his presence was not easy. With close attention his eyes followed the bows and therefore he was able to judge the smallest fluctuations in tempo or rhythm and correct them immediately. At the close of the last movement of this quartet there occurred a *meno vivace,* which seemed to me to weaken the general effect. At the rehearsal, therefore, I advised that the original tempo be maintained, which was done, to the betterment of the effect.

Beethoven, crouched in a corner, heard nothing, but watched with strained attention. After the last stroke of the bows he said, laconically, "Let it remain so," went to the desks and crossed out the *meno vivace* in the four parts.[22]

In July Beethoven wrote to nephew Karl from Baden, ascribing the failure at the premiere to the fact that "Schuppanzigh, owing to his corpulence, now requires more time than he did formerly to master a work

19. *AmZ* 27 (1825): col. 246.

20. Joseph Böhm, quoted in Thayer-Forbes 1967, 940.

21. Nicholas Zmeskall, quoted in Frimmel, *Beethoven Handbuch,* 2:53.

22. Böhm, quoted in Thayer-Forbes 1967, 940–41. The original parts that might have verified Böhm's account have disappeared.

quickly. . . . For although Schuppanzigh and two others draw pensions from persons of princely rank, the quartet is no longer the same as it was when all the players were constantly together. On the other hand, the quartet has been performed splendidly six times by other artists and received with the greatest applause."[23] Nevertheless, Schuppanzigh took part—with Beethoven's apparent blessing—in the premieres of both Op. 132 and Op. 130 (both with the fugue, Op. 133, and with the new finale). Doubtless recalling the premiere of Op. 127, the critic at Schuppanzigh's performance on 21 April 1826 of the A-minor Quartet, Op. 132, reported that it was "comprehended much more and received incomparably more warmly."[24]

Although, as Maynard Solomon points out (p. 68), the B-flat quartet fared less well at its first performance, the beef was with the music rather than the performance. Indeed, so long as listeners struggled to make the barest sense of what they heard, the nuances of performance were a dispensable luxury. Whatever the virtues or defects of Schuppanzigh's playing, his two seminal contributions to the art of quartet playing—the pioneering of the permanent string quartet and the presentation of regular series of chamber concerts—changed the landscape of quartet playing forever.

With Beethoven's death in March 1827, the fate of the quartets was placed squarely in the hands of posterity. While the earlier works were now universally embraced, the late quartets unnerved even Beethoven's most devoted admirers. In a lengthy review of Op. 131 written fifteen months after Beethoven's death, Friedrich Rochlitz concedes in his opening sentence that "it is difficult and hazardous to write about Beethoven's last great works."[25] Five years after its founding by Robert Schumann in 1834, the *Neue Zeitschrift für Musik* printed a lead, three-part series entitled "On Beethoven's Late Quartets: An Introduction," starting from the author Hermann Hirschbach's admission that "judgments concerning these works are the most disparate that one could possibly imagine."[26] Yet in spite of the controversy surrounding the later works, the

23. Ludwig van Beethoven to Karl van Beethoven, in Emily Anderson, ed., *The Letters of Beethoven*, 3 vols. (London, 1961), letter 1394. Hereafter, citations to letters from this publication will appear in the form Anderson Letter 00.

24. *AmZ* 27 (1825): col. 21.

25. Ibid., 30 (1828): col. 485.

26. *Neue Zeitschrift für Musik* (hereafter *NZfM*), Jg. 7 (1839): 5.

interaction between the quartet repertoire bequeathed by Beethoven (not to mention Haydn, Mozart, and Schubert) and social and economic developments throughout Europe and America rapidly transformed the nature of chamber music performance and consumption.

Quartet playing was championed immediately after Beethoven's death by a select group of artists. The most distinguished among these early proponents was the Berlin composer and violinist Karl Möser (1774– 1851). After serving as a youth in Friedrich Wilhelm II's private quartet, he traveled to London where he met Rode and Giovanni Battista Viotti (though an Italian, in many ways the founder of the nineteenth-century French violin school), who greatly influenced his style of performance. By 1812 he had been appointed Konzertmeister of the Berlin Hofkapelle. By the next year he was offering regular quartet evenings, which from about 1816 he alternated with symphony concerts. After his ascension in 1825 to director of the Hofkapelle, Möser's orchestral and chamber music series—which lasted until 1843—became the hub of Berlin musical life. He was not afraid of audacious programming:

1828. We heard in the sixth event of the second Möser Quartet Cycle—aside from a very humorous quartet of the eternally youthful and cheerful Haydn— a Quartet in E-flat Major of Ludwig Spohr, less completely realized than a very difficult new quartet of Beethoven in A minor, Op. 132, which, in spite of individual beautiful thoughts, did not please in its total effect, owing principally to the exhausting length of the movements and the overly rhapsodic development.[27]

In subsequent chamber concerts over the next two seasons Möser programmed Op. 18 nos. 1 and 6, Op. 59 nos. 2 and 3, Op. 74, and Op. 95. For a brief period in Berlin, Möser enjoyed competition from the brothers Adolf (violin) and Moritz (cello) Ganz. They took a much more flexible approach to programming (and time of day!):

27. *AmZ* 30 (1828): col. 363. This and subsequent dated entries are drawn from popular music journals such as the *AmZ,* the *NZfM* (the most influential German music journal of the mid-nineteenth century), and, in America, *Dwight's Journal of Music.* These journals appeared weekly or biweekly in brief eight- to twelve-page formats. Their contents were beamed at serious amateurs. They usually included a lead article (like the series on the late quartets cited above) as well as reviews of recent publications (usually organized in groups, such as keyboard music) and performances (invariably organized by cities, since they were submitted by the generally anonymous local correspondents). Far-flung German correspondents extended their coverage to London and Paris as well. However cryptic, they are perhaps our most important source of information about contemporary musical life; their wisdom has scarcely been tapped by cultural historians.

1832. In two morning programs the Ganz brothers performed a Quintet by Feska, Scottish songs by Beethoven, . . . a piano quartet by C. M. von Weber, a fragment from the newest quartet of Beethoven in C-sharp minor, Op. 131 (rather incomprehensible), [the song] "Sehnsucht" [Longing] by Schubert, . . . a quartet by Dotzauer, . . . and finally a beautiful Piano Quartet in B Minor by Felix Mendelssohn Bartoldy.[28]

Apparently, concealing even a slice of late Beethoven (perhaps the opening fugue?) amidst a musical potpourri did little to enhance its palatability. Works that we regard today (after nearly a century of organicist theorists like Heinrich Schenker) as indissoluble or tamper-proof were viewed much differently by the nineteenth century. This extended especially to arrangements. In one of his orchestral concerts from the same 1832 season, Möser performed Ignaz von Seyfried's orchestral transcription of Mozart's Fantasy and Sonata in C Minor for Piano, K. 475 and 457. And what of this enthusiastic letter written on 15 April 1832 by none other than Frédéric Chopin in Paris back to his friend Joseph Nowakowski in Warsaw?

I wish I could give you my ticket for the Conservatoire concert. That's something that would exceed your expectations. The orchestra is unsurpassable. Today they are giving Beethoven's symphony with choir and one of his quartets played by the massed strings of the orchestra—violins, violas and 'cellos: fifty string players all told. This quartet [which?] is being repeated by special request. They did it at the previous concert. You could have imagined that no more than four instruments were playing, yet the tone of the violins could be compared to a Castle, the violas to a Bank, and the cellos to a Lutheran Church.[29]

There were, to be sure, dissenting voices. During the 1837 Dresden season an F. Kummer presented Beethoven's E-flat Quartet, Op. 74, as an orchestral symphony:

1837. Mr. Chamber Musician F. Kummer undertook an assignment that, if he had looked it squarely in the eye, would sooner have scared him away. . . . It was neither a symphony nor even anything Beethovenian. As an accomplished musician it cannot have escaped Mr. F. Kummer's attention that Beethoven's

28. Ibid., 34 (1832): col. 332.
29. Arthur Hedley, *The Life of Chopin* (London, 1974), 111. This tradition continued into the twentieth century with Karl Richter and Wilhelm Furtwängler's orchestral arrangements of Op. 133, Arturo Toscanini's of Op. 135 (second and third movements), and, most recently, Leonard Bernstein's arrangement and recording of the complete Op. 131 with the massed strings of the Vienna Philharmonic.

symphonic style relates to his quartet style as an enamel painting relates to a life-size oil painting. Had Beethoven wished to make this work a symphony he would have written it differently. One can—as Beethoven actually did—write a grandiose, even heroic quartet, but no symphony will come from it. Even the most clear thought in a symphony must be conceived broadly and from the variety of the full orchestral palette. The periods [phrases] are longer and the entire color scale is different, just as the *piano* and *forte* in a quartet is different from those in the symphony, not just quantitatively in terms of the number of instruments but qualitatively according to the idea. . . . It is as if one had erected a picture gallery for a room that, for purposes of exhibition, was placed out of doors in a magnificent square on a tall base with a wide cornice and stairs, at a height reserved for colossal monuments.[30]

Under Möser's sponsorship in Berlin, the early Beethoven quartets soon became familiar repertory pieces:

1833. Beethoven's first and fourth quartets [Op. 18 nos. 1 and 4] make no less an impression than before, [especially] in a superbly bowed and precise performance.

By now, anonymous correspondents were more confident of judging the quality of a performance:

1833. The four Müllers [all brothers!] from Braunschweig played two quartets, the first by L[udwig] Spohr, the other by Beethoven (in C with the fugue [Op. 59 no. 3]). One bowing, one accent, one breath, one soul.—Spohr and all listened in enchantment, even with genuine enthusiasm. That's what quartet playing is all about!

Indeed, the remarkable Müllers seem to have dazzled their early audiences precisely because of the results that playing together regularly made possible:

1833. We struggle to find words to mirror the indescribable enthusiasm that the Müller brothers from Braunschweig elicited among the true friends of music! This unique occurrence in the history of music, that four males from a single marriage have striven so unselfishly toward an exalted goal, deserves recognition in itself; that they have attained the highest, that they have brought the richest treasures of the quartet literature in the fullest measure to the initiated, but have also made them accessible to lay persons, fills us with admiration.—It is practically unbelievable, with what precision and synchronization this quartet per-

30. *AmZ* 39 (1837): cols. 29–30.

forms; the heavenly *pianos,* as if distant organ tones were sounding; the *mezzo forte;* the *crescendo* and *decrescendo,* as if with one bow, and even in pizzicato passages, which is nearly unbelievable; the *forte,* in which the first violin never drowns the others or dominates unreasonably—all of this is indescribable and can only be experienced when one has the luck to hear, to marvel, to admire. . . . It should not go unmentioned that they are all in possession of first-rate instruments. . . . [Beethoven's] passionate E-minor Quartet [Op. 59 no. 2] aroused the greatest delight of all, really exceeding anything else;—what an infinite world, what inexpressible treasures reside in this musical creation; one forgets entirely that one sits in front of only four instruments—for the feeling soul there is nothing more to be desired!—Here one encounters the essence of the word "rapture," which is invoked so frequently without justification.[31]

Even though quartets were performed before a public, the emphasis was still on intimacy and expression rather than virtuosity or power:

1833. The elder Herr Müller . . . possesses a very soft, less conspicuous tone, great technical facility, completely pure intonation, light bowstrokes, deep feeling, and an appropriate endowment of comprehension of the spirit of compositions of the most diverse character. . . . The second violinist as well as the violist follow the first violinist exactly and discreetly, without thereby renouncing the individuality of their voice leading. The cellist, however, stands out as excellent in tone, aplomb, character, and complete freedom in every ornament, pretension, or affectation of performance. These four players therefore fulfill nearly in truth the ideal of a thoroughly complete quartet, even if they were less virtuosos on their instruments than they are.[32]

Of their virtuosity there was no doubt. Fifteen years later a critic described their Berlin performance of the finale of the Quartet in C Major, Op. 59 no. 3, as "*prestissimo* with a nearly inconceivable rapidity, and simultaneously performed in the most precise manner."[33] Yet the Müller Quartet aroused such interest precisely because it was so unusual. The situation in a medium-size German town of less than 30,000 inhabitants was far more typical:

1843. From Magdeburg. The Quartet Evenings. With true joy our musical public has greeted the beginning of the quartet evenings that Messrs. Uhlrich, Fischer, Wendt, and Kabysius have arranged for this winter. The prejudice that string quartets are only for the musically knowledgeable is disappearing steadily,

31. Ibid., 35 (1833): cols. 25; 497; 785.
32. Ibid., col. 821.
33. Ibid., 50 (1848): col. 548.

and the participation among us in this species of chamber music is as lasting as
it is lively. . . . The program included, as it should always be at a performance
of a quartet cycle, works of Haydn, Mozart, and Beethoven.[34]

The view that chamber music was an art form for connoisseurs persisted.
Yet Magdeburg appears to have been exceptional. In 1846 the same reviewer noted: "When we read concerning other localities that the public
for string quartets is small but select, we must assert to Magdeburg's
credit that people here flock to quartet evenings as if there were some
inner need to hear such music."[35] The naming of the four performers
suggests that the ensemble was an ad hoc one brought together specifically for these concerts.

   Indeed, this practice became institutionalized in the growing number
of cities that boasted permanent orchestras:

1836. Mr. Ferdinand David has now been named to the position of concert
master to replace the deceased August Matthäi, and on the 25th of February he
appeared for the first time as a solo violinist. In concert with Ulrich, Queiser,
and Grabau he arranged three subscription quartet evenings, which were attended in large numbers and added to his flock of admirers. All four performers
so applied themselves consistently with diligence and love to the matter of performing the works at hand that their interpretations gave lasting pleasure and
must really be reckoned among the excellent achievements in this art. On the
16th of January we heard . . . Beethoven's Quartet in C Major, Op. 59 no.
3, which was repeated on the second quartet evening of the 23rd by popular
demand.[36]

1844. The Quartet Entertainments in the Hall of the Gewandhaus in Leipzig.
To the highest artistic pleasures offered by the previous winter season belong
indisputably the evenings which, though in a modest-sized but therefore more
select auditorium, brought to light masterpieces that are less suited to larger
concerts. . . . First we occupy ourselves with the . . . string quartets that were
performed entirely by concertmaster David with Klengel, Hunger, and Wittmann. It is difficult to decide whether the performers celebrated their mastery
most in the C-minor quartet of Beethoven [Op. 18 no. 4], the G-major quartet
of Haydn [presumably Op. 33 no. 5 or Op. 77 no. 1], or the G-major quartet of Mozart [presumably K. 387].[37]

34. *NZfM* Jg. 10 (1843): 176.
35. Ibid., Jg. 13 (1846): 60.
36. *AmZ* 38 (1836): cols. 133–34.
37. *NZfM* Jg. 11 (1844): 103–4.

The series inaugurated at the Gewandhaus became one of the best known throughout Europe and served as a model for many others. First, it enshrined the practice of presenting chamber music in formal concert halls. The Old Gewandhaus, built in 1780, seated only 400 listeners, which was viewed as ideal for chamber music but grossly inadequate for orchestral concerts—even though they sometimes crammed in a thousand people. A report on a morning chamber concert in 1836 in which Mendelssohn participated described the hall as "extraordinarily full, as is usually the case for the evening subscription [orchestral] concerts."[38]

During the 1860s the city began to raise money for a new hall, and construction finally began in 1882. The hall that opened in 1884 acknowledged formally the split that had taken place around mid-century. The large, double-square orchestral hall (almost 40 meters long, 20 meters wide, and 15 meters high) seated 1,560 persons downstairs, with balconies around the perimeter to accommodate a few hundred more. The small concert hall, nestled at the end of the complex, was identical in proportions but seated only 640.

Second, the Gewandhaus concerts consolidated the practice of assembling a string quartet from the four principal players in the local orchestra, headed in Leipzig by Ferdinand David (1810–73), one of the most influential German violinists of the nineteenth century. The fact that David's three accomplices in 1844 are all different from those in 1836 simply reflects the changes in orchestral personnel. Nor did its members devote most of their time to chamber music. Their major effort was usually a November through March series of five or six concerts. Although quartets might form the backbone of these concerts, the same players served as a core group that also performed in string and piano trios, piano quartets, string and piano quintets, and all the way up to the octets of Mendelssohn and Spohr.

David was born in Switzerland and studied as a teenager with Spohr. He met Mendelssohn in the late 1820s and spent the early 1830s leading a string quartet under aristocratic patronage (a model that survived from the Razumovsky days). In 1836 Mendelssohn invited him to be the concertmaster of the new Gewandhaus Orchestra, a position he occupied until the end of his life. With the opening of the Leipzig Conservatory in 1843, David was head of the string department and counted Joachim among his first students.

---

38. *AmZ* 38 (1836): col. 273.

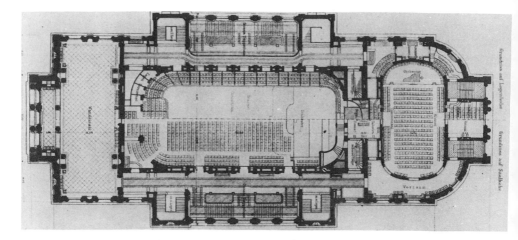

Built from 1882 to 1884, the Neues Gewandhaus in Leipzig formalized a clear separation between a large central hall for orchestral and choral music and a more intimate hall (on the right in the illustration) for chamber music. From Michael Forsyth, *Buildings for Music: The Architect, the Musician, and the Listener from the Seventeenth Century to the Present Day* (Cambridge: MIT Press, 1985), 211. (Reproduced by permission of the MIT Press.)

David contributed substantially to the conservatory curriculum, which was divided into the fields of performance, pedagogy, theory, and history, the fields that still make up the curricular grid at most American conservatories. His influential *Violinschule* of 1864 summed up two decades of teaching. Unlike the trio of French violinists at the turn of the century, David was not a virtuoso and reflected a more serious attitude toward chamber music. Illustrations such as those showing the holding of the violin bow demonstrate that the relatively light "old German grip" lasted well into the second half of the nineteenth century.

In some musical centers it took only one dramatic event to trigger a proposal for reforming the consumption of chamber music:

1845. Bremen. There is a fundamental contradiction between a quartet and performing it in an overflowing hall some 200 feet long before nearly 3000 people. . . . Besides his quartets Beethoven created a great many precious works that are not suitable for presentation before a large audience. It would not be a bad development if the current artists and their honored guests had a space designated exclusively for them, in which they could meet outside of public

In his *Violinschule* (Violin Method), Ferdinand David advocated what is now called "the old German grip," in which the bow is held relatively lightly. Frontispiece to David, *Violinschule* (Leipzig: Breitkopf & Härtel, 1864).

festivities. In it would be a fortepiano, quartet instruments, as well as a collection (as complete as possible) of Beethoven's works, which those who were present could then use according to their own choice and for their own pleasure and joy.[39]

Along with efforts to recapture the original spirit of chamber music, there were efforts to establish permanent quartets. They rarely succeeded:

39. Ibid., 47 (1845): col. 591.

1839. Frankfurt am Main. Reifstahl's quartets receive more and more approbation. It is certainly a good indicator of the taste of our public that music as serious as quartet music wins more supporters from year to year. There have already been several attempts made here by Spohr, later Guhr, and finally by the Herrmann brothers to found a quartet, yet Herr Riefstahl appears to be the only one to succeed.[40]

In smaller towns it was often necessary to piece together a quartet from several professions; the Breslau correspondent of the *AmZ* reported in 1841 that its quartet was made "permanent" by the use of a Gymnasium (high school) instructor as the second violinist and a cantor as the cellist—adding with evident pride that each performance was preceded by no fewer than two rehearsals.

Just as common was the practice of leading virtuosos when on tour:

1842. Berlin. After the popular violinist [Heinrich Wilhelm] Ernst put on eight concerts with various participants, he presented, with the support of Kappellmeister Mendelssohn and the concertmaster Ries, Leopold, and Moritz Ganz, two quartet evenings. . . . If Mr. Ernst rushed the *Allegro* tempos, these were compensated for by the refinement and elegance of his delivery, especially praiseworthy in the *Adagios*.[41]

Leipzig musicians were already staking out a position as spokespersons for what we have come to know as "the canon"—a select group of works by deceased composers viewed as timeless masterpieces, always with a conservative bias. For example:

1846. Leipzig Music Life. . . . The first entertainment brought us . . . Op. 131 in C-sharp minor by Beethoven—so far as we know, the first public performance [in Leipzig], . . . given under the leadership of Mr. Leonard from Paris, who has already been mentioned frequently in these pages and to whom we owe thanks for undertaking this assignment.[42]

If it took twenty years for Op. 131 to reach performance in Leipzig, within fifteen years of Beethoven's death the quartets of Haydn, Mozart, and Beethoven through Op. 74 had become the centerpiece of most quartet programs. By the mid-1830s this triumvirate is referred to routinely in popular publications as "the three classical masters" and their

40. Ibid., 41 (1839): col. 71. His success, too, it seems, was brief.
41. Ibid., 44 (1842): col. 436.
42. *NZfM* Jg. 13 (1846): 32.

creations as "master quartets." While few may remember that a quartet by Bernard Romberg was also premiered by Schuppanzigh's quartet at the first performance of Beethoven's A-minor Quartet, Op. 132, the focus on "new music" diminished steadily as the century wore on. The gradual transformation of the quartet audience from a select group of intrepid explorers to a larger group of defenders of tradition has many roots in the cultural soil of the nineteenth century, but none was stronger than the shift we have described in quartet performance from the informal gathering to the middle-class concert hall. In one sense, the very commercial success of the string quartet inhibited its future development.

Even at mid-century the consistent playing together of a group was still deemed worthy of mention:

1847. Danzig. . . . The quartet entertainments by Deneke have benefited from long-term participation. . . . The quartet players . . . have gained steadily in ensemble, and their level of performance often reaches to excellent.[43]

The part-time group remained the rule—though perhaps taken to extremes in this remarkable program:

1849. Leipzig. . . . We heard: Quartet in B-Flat Major by Haydn, Quartet in D Major by Mozart, and finally the Quartet in F Major, Op. 59 [no. 1], by Beethoven, the first performed by David, Joachim, Herrmann, and Wittmann; the second by Joachim, Klengel, and the others; and the third by Ernst, David, Joachim [playing viola], and Rietz.[44]

In order to expedite preparation and to offer players sufficient involvement, several "quartets" were assembled. In this particular evening, the young Joseph Joachim played first violin, second violin, and viola! Regardless of the group, the level of playing was by no means uniformly high, as this earlier review of David's group shows:

1848. Leipzig. . . . The performances from the perspective of the performers were in general satisfying. A few mishaps we would wish to ascribe to the usual accidents or to unfortunate tuning.[45]

Just how important pioneers like Möser were for the large-scale public acceptance of Beethoven's quartets is shown by this review written ten years after Möser's retirement:

43. Ibid., Jg. 14 (1847): 193.
44. Ibid., Jg. 16 (1849): 51.
45. Ibid., Jg. 15 (1848): 65.

1853. Berlin. . . . As in earlier years, Messrs. Zimmerman, Ronneburger, Richter, and Espenhahn sponsored six concerts in the small (Cäcile) hall of the Sing-
akademie. To judge from the small but loyal remnant of listeners, one would
almost conclude that this species of music counts fewer adherents in Berlin, and
in fact this meager participation would be hard to explain against the backdrop
of the superb performances were it not for the many private circles in which
string quartets are played (I cite here, for example, the quartet gatherings that
take place every two weeks at the court chamber musician Hahnemann's
dwellings).[46]

The distinction of the first permanent, named quartet seems to go to
the one founded in 1849 by the Austrian violinist Joseph Hellmesberger
(1828–93), himself the son of the distinguished violinist Georg Hellmesberger. The group appeared first in public the day after Hellmesberger's twenty-first birthday, making its last appearance in 1893, a few
months before Hellmesberger's death at age 65. In strong contrast to the
elegant French style, Hellmesberger's quartet played in an unabashedly
subjective and emotional manner that seemed to have been especially
well suited to the late quartets of Beethoven. Hellmesberger still needed
to work as an orchestral leader; he was also the teacher of several famous
musicians, including the violinist Leopold Auer and the conductor Arthur Nikish. More than thirty years after Beethoven's death, Hellmesberger brought the Viennese to grips with the late quartets:

1859. Letters from Vienna. . . . I begin with Hellmesberger's Quartet, whose
first cycle is now underway. . . . The masterworks of [Beethoven's] last period:
the C-sharp minor (Op. 131) and E-flat major (Op. 127) quartets, as well as the
first public performance here of the *Grosse Fuge* (Op. 133) [were featured]. It is
Hellmesberger's great service to have made this prophetic and progressive artist
so popular among us. . . . The crowning contribution of this quartet [is] that
even a many-faceted structure, Beethoven's quartet fugue, was listened to so
attentively by the entire audience and after its completion greeted so warmly
and with so much applause. For even a very practiced score reader will require
many repetitions to grasp this musical pyramid. . . . Finally, the sounding of
both fugue themes, the one simple and the other in double counterpoint, was
crowned with resounding bravos. That says a great deal.[47]

After about 1870, mention of quartet performances in the *AmZ* and
NZfM becomes increasingly rare, overshadowed by coverage of operatic

46. Ibid., Jg. 20 (1853): 219.
47. Ibid., Jg. 26 (1859): 208.

and pianistic events. Attention also shifts to named quartets that now tour professionally full-time. More attention is devoted to group characteristics, which reviewers increasingly ascribe to national traits:

1892. A strong desire, great understanding, a loving quest after the highest artistic goals, the selfless renunciation of individual personality when it concerns the great, noble whole—these are the characteristics that mark the Frankfurt Quartet as the best in Germany and make them worthy ambassadors of the great masters Beethoven, Haydn, and Mozart. . . . In Mr. Heermann's artistic individuality lies something specifically German. His playing is clear, warm, sure, quietly serious, and deeply spiritual. It neither dazzles nor distracts, rather it accumulates and uplifts. In spite of his extraordinary technique, one forgoes with Herr Heermann the virtuoso for the artist, and even frequently the artist for the work.[48]

These were indeed the characteristics that now marked Austro-German quartets such as the Frankfurt or the Cologne or the ensembles led by Joseph Joachim and Arnold Rosé (1863–1946). It had taken almost a century of playing the quartets to move from the French classical style to an expressive style that quietly incorporated the advances of Paganini without surrendering to its exhibitionist excesses.

Joachim lived long enough to make a few early recordings, from which we learn that the continuous vibrato introduced by Fritz Kreisler (1875–1962) in the early twentieth century was virtually unknown in the nineteenth century. But that chapter belongs properly to another essay.

What was the fate of the quartets outside of German-speaking lands? In England the founding of the Beethoven Quartet Society enabled the quartets to serve as a bridge between musicians and the aristocracy:

1846. London. . . . Yet to mention is the Beethoven Quartet Society. For several seasons a quartet society has existed here, whose founder and chief patron was F. M. Alsayer, Esq. This society has as its chief mission the careful study of the late quartets of Beethoven. Both amateurs and professionals are invited. Last year the society hit upon the notion of widening this circle, and so the Beethoven Quartet Society came into existence. Besides aristocratic supporters they have admitted a large number of professional performers. The performing musicians are Sivori, Sainton—who alternate between first and second violin—Hill on viola, and Rousselot on cello. There are many rehearsals; the performances are masterful. In the course of the season they will sponsor eight events, in

48. Ibid., Jg. 59 (1892): 19.

which all the quartets of Beethoven and several of Mozart and Haydn will be performed.

Ferd. Präger[49]

Rehearsals were open to both nonperforming members and to performers who did not play on these occasions. If surnames are a reliable guide, then only the violist Hill seems to have been a native Englishman.

A similar society sprang up even earlier in Paris. Its champion was Pierre Chevillard, a Belgian cellist who entered the Paris Conservatory at the age of 9 and graduated at 16 with its first prize. In 1831 he became the principal cellist at the Théâtre Italien in Paris. But his passion lay elsewhere, and in 1835 (when Chevillard was only 24) he founded the Society for the Last Quartets of Beethoven. The group rehearsed and played privately for some time, undergoing a number of personnel changes. Finally, in 1849 it coalesced around regular players and made its first public performance at the Salle Pleyel (a small Paris hall operated by the piano manufacturer Camille Pleyel).

Their 1855–56 tour of France and Germany was a great success, arousing the admiration of Berlioz. The French were among the first to adopt the idea of a permanent quartet that devoted itself to a specific portion of the repertoire. The electrifying effect the group had on audiences suggests that their brand of tight ensemble was still very unusual:

1856. The Beethoven Quartet Society in Paris. . . . As is known, a native quartet of artists that has dedicated itself principally to the late quartets of Beethoven recently made a small excursion across the Rhein. . . . They are . . . the Messrs. Chevillard, Mas, Sabatier, and Maurin. . . . At the previously announced third concert the hall was packed to the gills. The expectations, considering what we had already read and heard, were the highest—and were nevertheless exceeded. Beethoven's great quartet (Op. 130) opened, and already in the second movement (*Presto*) a repeat was loudly demanded [clapping between movements was common throughout the nineteenth century]. We know of no other example where, in a long six-movement quartet of Beethoven (not to mention one of the impenetrable late ones), a repeat has been demanded. The quartet players captured the attention of the entire auditorium and played with it at will. Now it was moved to shuddering and tears; now it was charmed and smiled contentedly. In short, the effect was unheard of.[50]

49. Ibid., Jg. 13 (1846): 199.
50. Ibid., Jg. 23 (1856): 47–48.

In the course of what is an even longer essay, the reviewer, August Gathy, describes Beethoven's last period as his "third or sick [kränklichen] period," reserving his harshest criticism for the "unendurable length" of the Song of Thanksgiving from Op. 132. But he also describes how the group's local Parisian popularity led to their first public appearances:

Since after a short time the room in which the rehearsals took place was filled to overflowing, and gradually the adjoining rooms as well, and before long the entire dwelling of Chevillard was crammed to the gills, and a not insignificant core of admirers of this music had formed who understood both its value and its enjoyment, the quartet felt emboldened, in response to the persistent requests of its partisans, to dare to take its achievements before the public. . . . Their first appearance was a triumph, and every following appearance brought a capacity house and enthusiastic participation.[51]

In America, the closest parallel to the *AmZ* and the *NZfM* was *Dwight's Journal of Music,* founded in Boston in 1852 by a rock-ribbed, puritanical Yankee named John Sullivan Dwight (1813–93). Dwight's journal lasted thirty years; it strove to be "impartial, independent, catholic, conciliatory," but it largely represented the middle-class, canon-centered, anti-Wagnerian side of American music criticism. Its lead articles were often translations of essays by Germans like Rochlitz and E. T. A. Hoffmann, but it also reviewed local (largely Boston) events with its own correspondents.

In addition to the Handel and Haydn Society, which continues to this day, Boston was also home to a chamber music society known curiously as the Mendelssohn Quintette Club—suggesting an even more conservative orientation than European cities such as Vienna. Patterned after its British models, the club invited memberships from musicians and nonmusicians alike. It put on several concerts a season, open primarily to members. It was a gathering place for the upwardly mobile:

1855. The third chamber concert, Tuesday evening, was the best (so far) of the season, as well as the most largely attended. The Chickering [run by Jonas Chickering, a noted Boston piano builder] saloon [*sic!*] was more than full. Mendelssohn's second Quintet (in B-flat, Op. 87), one of his most brilliant and entertaining works, full of fancy and variety, was played with admirable spirit, delicacy, and fineness. Certainly the Quintette Club have never played so well

51. Ibid., Jg. 23 (1856): 49.

as they do this winter. Such an opening of the evening was worthy of such a close as the great ninth Quartet of BEETHOVEN, in C (the third of Op. 59), a work as great among his quartets (at least those everheard [*sic*] in our country) as his B-flat Trio among his Trios. It is wonderfully original, imaginative, and exciting, as well as wonderfully difficult, especially for the first violin, which has to shoot continually into the region of the very highest tones, where any swerving from the purest pitch would be most noticeable. We cannot but congratulate our friend FRIES upon the ease and certainty with which he kept his footing there. . . . The fugue in the finale, with its long and figurative theme, swiftly and delicately winding in and out through all the parts, like the most intricate and exquisite embroidery, is strangely interesting, and its clear rendering was quite a triumph. The Club must certainly repeat that quartet.[52]

The innocence and freshness of this report suggest not only that the Americans lagged behind the Europeans in their digesting of the Beethoven quartets but that they were free of many of the prejudices that haunted its more traditional ancestors. We can probably assume safely that "friend FRIES" was a transplanted German.

It may be fitting to close with a quotation that suggests the loyalty with which Bostonians attended chamber music through this nation's most tumultuous period.

1861. It is hard to realize that we are in the midst of civil war.—that we are fighting the fight, perhaps the final one, of Civilization against a treacherous and arrogant pro-Slavery rebellion, with all its backward and Barbarian proclivities, when we can come together in peace and comfort, just as in the unsuspecting days, to meet the familiar music-loving faces, and listen to a concert of the Mendelssohn Quintette Club. Nothing perhaps in Boston could show so little change to one who went away not dreaming of what the year was to bring forth for us politically, as that quiet scene in Chickering's Hall, on Wednesday evening. There they were, the constant old habitués, the faithful ones, whose presence has been identified with the Quintette concerts from the beginning and throughout their twelve years' history—at least enough of them there were to make it seem the same sphere and the same life, until one began to look for others who were not there. . . . There was about the old average number of people—a couple of hundred or so—with the hum of cheerful expectation, with the curious scrutiny and glad counting of each new comer.[53]

52. *Dwight's Journal of Music* 7 (1855): 94.
53. Ibid., 19 (1861): 278.

The program opened with Beethoven's Quartet in D Major, Op. 18 no. 3, which the reviewer characterized as "not . . . quite so familiar here, as some others of the set of six included in Op. 18."

By the end of the nineteenth century, the world of the Beethoven quartets had—from the performer's perspective—been largely professionalized. Most major urban centers sported regular chamber music series presented in public halls. The touring professional quartet had come into its own, largely displacing the ad hoc groups so common in Beethoven's day. Yet as we entered the electronic age there were ironies to ponder. The first string quartet to record extensively—the Flonzaley Quartet—was established in 1902 by an American banker for private performances in his own home. Shades of Count Razumovsky!

But for the quartet audience there has been the increasing responsibility of a canonic tradition that not only invites study but needs defending. If modernists such as Arnold Schoenberg could still point to passages in the late quartets that supported their radical agendas, the seventeen quartets have increasingly borne the burden of the great classical tradition that—argued critics and theorists such as Hanslick and Schenker—died with Brahms. Although in early twentieth-century America appreciation of the Beethoven quartets often carried an uncomfortable connotation of social elitism, several generations of listeners learned about the quartets at their parents' knees (or sitting on their laps at concerts). As we approach the end of the twentieth century, we have for the first time a generation of young Americans for whom works such as Op. 18 no. 1—much less Op. 131—are as new (newer if one considers general knowledge of the style) as they were to Ignaz Schuppanzigh. The challenge, as always, will fall most heavily on those performers with the same burning desire to make new friends for the quartets that Karl Möser felt more than a century and a half ago.

Within a decade of Beethoven's death, romanticized likenesses of him began to appear. This lithograph of "Beethoven Composing the 'Pastoral' [Symphony] by a Brook" was published in 1834 in the Almanac of the Zürich Musikgesellschaft. (Reproduced by permission of the Beethoven-Archiv, Bonn.)

Beethoven:
Beyond Classicism

MAYNARD SOLOMON

It is common knowledge that Beethoven was a founder of the romantic movement in music and that his works influenced most of the romantic composers and were the models against which nineteenth-century romanticism measured its achievements and failures. However, the issue of Beethoven's place in the turn from classicism to romanticism has not only been the subject of some controversy but has undergone several extreme pendulum swings over the course of time. The issue is by no means settled, and this may be a good time to take stock of it, for it has an important bearing on whether we perceive and perform works such as the quartets primarily as outgrowths of eighteenth-century traditions and performance practices or as auguries of fresh traditions in the process of formation.

The initial articulation of Beethoven's romanticism was in large part the work of nineteenth-century composers and literary figures: it was through the writings of E. T. A. Hoffmann, Bettina Brentano von Arnim, Lamartine, Hugo, Berlioz, and Wagner that Beethoven came to be viewed as the originator of the romantic movement in music and as its most representative and influential composer. However, even during the nineteenth century, informed musical opinion increasingly came to stress Beethoven's adherence to classical techniques and principles of structure, so that, by the end of the century, the influential theorist and historian Hugo Riemann defined the romantics as those composers who "came after Beethoven."[1] For others the issue became a standoff, at best. "In

1. Hugo Riemann, *Dictionnaire de musique* (Paris, 1931), 1132.

[Beethoven's] works," wrote Tovey's teacher, Hubert Parry, "the classical type of sonata found its ripest perfection, and the romantic impulse, which finally superseded the sonata, found its first decisive expression."[2]

Nevertheless, Victor Hugo and Richard Wagner were rather more influential than were the sober music historians, and Beethoven's romanticism was widely taken for granted, a perception that has persisted in much popular literature on music. But the loose and poetic formulations of the French and German romantics appeared to dissolve under the first sustained examination. This took place in 1927, the centenary year of Beethoven's death, with the publication of Arnold Schmitz's *Das romantische Beethovenbild,* which thoughtfully reconstructed the evolution of the romantic image of Beethoven and subjected the musical and biographical evidence of his romanticism to close and skeptical scrutiny. Together with several chapters of Ludwig Schiedermair's somewhat earlier *Der junge Beethoven* and a subsequent massive study by Jean Boyer, *Le "romantisme" de Beethoven,* Schmitz overturned the accepted notion of Beethoven's romanticism and established the dominant modern view of him as the inheritor of twin traditions—ideologically those of the Enlightenment and musically those of European, especially Viennese, classicism.[3] Beethoven was seen in both instances as the child of these eighteenth-century traditions rather than as one who departed from them in some radical or disruptive way.

It was not difficult to uncover Beethoven's roots in the eighteenth century. He grew to maturity in the Habsburg dominions, which were imbued with the spirit of the German *Aufklärung,* a movement fed from one side by Kantian philosophy and from another by the ideological outlook of enlightened despotism in its highly rationalist manifestation. Beethoven was proud of his dedication to the central tenets of the Habsburg Josephinian Enlightenment—its idealization of reason, its furtherance of reform, its critique of superstition, its altruistic commitment to virtue. And, of course, there is much evidence of his pride in belonging to an ongoing musical tradition. "Portraits of Handel, Bach, Gluck, Mozart and Haydn in my room," he wrote in his intimate diary in 1815, "they can promote my capacity for endurance."[4] It is scarcely surprising

2. C. Hubert H. Parry, *Style in Musical Art* (London, 1911), 326.

3. Arnold Schmitz, *Das romantische Beethovenbild* (Berlin and Bonn, 1927); Ludwig Schiedermair, *Der junge Beethoven* (Leipzig, 1925); Jean Boyer, *Le "romantisme" de Beethoven* (Paris, 1938). See also William S. Newman, "The Beethoven Mystique in Romantic Art, Literature, and Music," *Musical Quarterly* 69 (1983): 354–87.

4. Ludwig van Beethoven, quoted in "Beethoven's Tagebuch," in Maynard Solomon, *Beethoven Essays* (Cambridge, Mass., 1988), 258 (No. 43).

that Beethoven scholarship has been able to accumulate voluminous materials on his sources and influences; or that it has succeeded in demonstrating that a thoroughly assimilated, lucid, and highly structured classicism persists even in his most adventurous works.

Schmitz used several effective strategies. He showed that romantic conceptions of Beethoven were riddled with misconceptions and errors. And he readily disparaged the extravagant programmatic interpretations of Beethoven's music by enthusiastic romantic writers and musicians. Mainly, however, his strategy was to present a simplified view of romanticism, portrayed as an irrational and morbid movement, one irrevocably hostile to form. By these yardsticks, Beethoven surely was no romantic, for he linked art with science as redemptive activities, he neglected no opportunity to praise the powers of reason, he scorned the gravitation of Viennese romantics to a highly eroticized, mystical Catholicism, and he dissociated himself from the dogmas of the Church in both its conventional and revivalist forms. And Beethoven's works themselves are the clearest demonstration of his unshakable adherence to the sonata principle.

Just as some romantics purveyed a myth of the "shallow Enlightenment," chroniclers of romanticism such as Schmitz purveyed an unmediated conception of an "irrational romanticism," a conception whose criteria were primarily derived from the more nocturnal characteristics of late romanticism. That the early romantics were drawn to the mysterious, the fantastic, and the irrational, is, of course, not in question; but early romanticism strove to maintain a precarious balance between reason and the darker currents of existence. Its main quarrel was not with Kant or Lessing but with a diluted and dogmatic pseudo-rationalism. As Friedrich Schlegel observed in one of the *Lyceum* fragments of 1797, "What's commonly called reason is only a subspecies of it; namely, the thin and watery sort."[5] Romanticism resisted those barren blueprints of reality that foreclose the claims of the imagination, what Harold Bloom called "those premature modes of conceptualization that masquerade as final accounts of reason in every age."[6]

So persuasive was Schmitz's critique—and so congruent was it with the historicizing temper of early twentieth-century *Musikwissenschaft*—that the romanticist position was virtually bereft of significant defenders.

5. Friedrich Schlegel, *Friedrich Schlegel's Lucinde and the Fragments,* trans. Peter Firchow (Minneapolis, 1971), 155.

6. Harold Bloom, *The Ringers in the Tower: Studies in the Romantic Tradition* (Chicago and London, 1971), 323.

To cite a few examples, among many: "The deeper we delve into the essence of Beethoven's music," wrote Riezler in 1936, "the more obvious it is that it belongs to the classical world, and the more clearly it is divided from the romantic."[7] "To count him among the Romanticists," wrote Lang in 1940, "amounts to a fundamental misreading of styles, for Beethoven grew out of the eighteenth-century. . . . What he did was to make a new synthesis of classicism and then hand it down to the new century."[8] Most of the other leading critics of the first half of the twentieth century—including even so unlikely a figure as the supposed archromantic Romain Rolland—followed Schmitz's lead. Even where music historians saw in Beethoven impulses toward romanticism, or romantic experiments and gestures, or foreshadowings of romantic developments, they tended to regard him as responding in a fragmentary, unsystematic way to an emergent movement from which he himself remained aloof.

The most influential recent elaboration of the classicist position is in Charles Rosen's *The Classical Style* (1970) and *Sonata Forms* (1980). Surveying Beethoven's stylistic evolution with his customary insight and sensibility, Rosen suggests that Beethoven's earlier Viennese compositions were written "now in a proto-Romantic style and now in a late and somewhat attenuated version of the classical style" but that he soon "returned decisively to the closed, concise, and dramatic forms of Haydn and Mozart, expanding these forms and heightening their power without betraying their proportions." For Rosen, Beethoven's harmonic practice "enlarged the limits of the classical style beyond all previous conceptions, but he never changed its essential structure or abandoned it . . . even while using it in startlingly radical and original ways." Contrary to most historians, Rosen finds "no line that can be drawn" between Beethoven's "first and second periods"; he suggests that the *Eroica* Symphony's innovative significance lies in extending "the range of hearing in time" and in carrying classical procedures "to the outer limits beyond which the language itself would have had to change."[9]

Rosen observes that Beethoven occasionally experimented with romantic tonality and proportions, especially in several works written during the years of transition to the late style. But he regards these romantic ventures either as unworthy or, in the case of *An die ferne Geliebte*, Op. 98, the song cycle that "stands as the first example of what was the most original and perhaps the most important of romantic forms," as "a sport

---

7. Walter Riezler, *Beethoven* (London, 1938), 106.
8. Paul Henry Lang, *Music in Western Civilization* (New York, 1940), 752.
9. Charles Rosen, *The Classical Style* (New York, 1970), 380–81; 384; 389; 393; 350.

among his forms." The *Diabelli* Variations, Op. 120, is seen as "an investigation of the language of classical tonality," and, in his late music, Beethoven's most "startling innovations" are regarded as taking place "comfortably within the sonata style."[10] Beethoven, then, is best understood
as one who extended the musical styles and structures of others—Haydn
and Mozart—and who exercised only marginal influence on the immediately succeeding musical generation because of the highly organized
classical style in which he worked: "The Romantic style did not come
from Beethoven, in spite of the great admiration that was felt for him,
but from his lesser contemporaries and from Bach."[11]

Lest we misunderstand his powerful argument, one worked out with
considerable flexibility and in full awareness of the counterindications,
Rosen presents his conclusion aphoristically: "I have treated Beethoven
throughout as if he were a late eighteenth-century composer," he writes
in *Sonata Forms*.[12] Joseph Kerman has taken strong exception to this
view, for it contradicts his modernist perspective of Beethoven's musical
evolution. He sees Rosen as making sonata form wholly dependent on
the classical style, with failing to "see how the form can be squared
with the evolving style or styles of musical romanticism." Citing Rosen's
statement that, despite the emotional and ideological climate of Beethoven's music, he is "intelligible only as a part and extension of the
eighteenth-century tradition of sonata style," Kerman observes: "In a
symphony called 'heroic' the emotional climate cannot, I believe, be
separated off from form and style as clearly as Rosen would like"; for
Kerman, "the ideological content skews the form."[13] The power of
sound and the affects of utterance, though resistant to measurement by
conventional analytical tools, ought not to be orphaned by criticism.[14]

Rosen's brief for Beethoven's classicism tacitly—and rather precari-

---

10. Ibid., 403; 379; 445; 384.

11. Ibid., 385; see also p. 379.

12. Charles Rosen, *Sonata Forms*, rev. ed. (New York, 1988), 354.

13. Joseph Kerman, Review of Charles Rosen, *Sonata Forms*, in *New York Review of Books*, 23 October 1980, 51; 53. Kerman may (or may not) be surprised to find himself allied with Richard Wagner, who also emphasized that sonata form is scarcely identical with, let alone exhausted by, the classical style. Wagner perceived that the "same structure" could be found in Beethoven's last works as in his first: "But let us compare these works with each other," he exclaimed, "and wonder at the entirely new world which meets us there, almost in precisely the same form!" (*Beethoven* [New York, 1871], 52).

14. See Leo Steinberg, *Other Criteria: Confrontations with Twentieth-Century Art* (London, Oxford, and New York, 1972), 63–66 and 78–79, and Hans Heinrich Eggebrecht, "Beethoven und der Begriff der Klassik," in *Beethoven-Symposion, Wien 1970: Bericht*, ed. Erich Schenk (Vienna, 1971), 59.

ously—depends on his definition of classical form as the contrast between dramatic tension and stability that finds its reconciliation in "the
symmetrical resolution of opposing forces." But this is a dialectical description that Rosen himself suspects to appear "so broad as to be a
definition of artistic form in general." [15] Of course, no global definition
of either classicism or romanticism has ever proven wholly satisfactory.
Theorists have always been disconcerted to discover that the properties,
tropes, and conventions thought to be uniquely characteristic of a given
style period are also present in other style periods. Classical, romantic,
baroque, mannerist, modern—every style period has been thrown into
question. A striking example of style-period deflation is what Panofsky
called the "Renaissance-Dämmerung," the increasing tendency by early
twentieth-century medievalists "to contest the very existence of the Renaissance, either *in toto* or in part." [16] In music history, some have concluded from the evidence of cultural continuity that there is no disjunction between classicism and romanticism.

Codifying positions formulated earlier by Lang and others, Friedrich
Blume held classicism and romanticism to be a unity in music history,
"two aspects of the same musical phenomenon just as they are two aspects of one and the same historical period." [17] Within the unified style
period that Blume dubs "the Classic-Romantic," Beethoven "occupies
but one of the many intermediate positions in the continuing development of this antinomy." Therefore, the question whether Beethoven
"should be counted among the Classics or the Romantics, becomes
meaningless," for "he was simply both in his own personal way, just as
all creative musicians were." [18] Although stressing continuity rather than
change, Blume is keenly aware of the special characteristics and novelties
of musical romanticism. So it remains an open question whether he
actually succeeded in abolishing the traditional classic–romantic dichotomy or merely in displacing it into two phases of a more extended historical period.

15. Rosen, *Classical Style,* 74–75; 83.

16. Erwin Panofsky, "Artist, Scientist, Genius: Notes on the 'Renaissance-
Dämmerung,'" in *The Renaissance: A Symposium, February 8–10, 1952* (New York,
1953), 78.

17. Friedrich Blume, "Romantik," in *Die Musik in Geschichte und Gegenwart,* 17 vols.
(Kassel, 1949–86), 11: col. 802; trans. in Blume, *Classic and Romantic Music: A Comprehensive Survey* (New York, 1970), 124. Dahlhaus similarly remarks upon "the simultaneity of
the Classical and Romantic" (Carl Dahlhaus, "Musik und Romantik," in *Musik-Edition-
Interpretation: Gedenkschrift Günter Henle,* ed. Martin Bente [Munich, 1980], 136).

18. Blume, *Classic and Romantic Music,* 129; 127.

Most of us continue to see a universe of differences between the classical and the romantic, discriminations that we can sense even if we cannot describe them in such a way that they can be mapped and fully analyzed.[19] Still, for those who are vexed by apparently insolvable terminological disputes, Blume's point of view is an attractive one. However, it is because the issues far transcend terminology and nomenclature that the debate over Beethoven's romanticism has thus far been so extraordinarily fruitful. The anti-romantic view of Beethoven and his music has enabled us to strip away many of the accretions and falsehoods of extravagant heroizing biographies; it has given us a more accurate insight into Beethoven's political and ideological outlook, uncovered the complexities of his attitudes toward authority, revealing the irreconcilable tension in his personality between obedience and rebellion. And, in viewing the Beethoven style as a personal fusion of preexistent styles, traditions, and procedures rather than as a demonic or divinely inspired creation *ex nihilo,* it has placed the evolution of his musical style in clearer perspective.

On the debit side, the unrelenting view of Beethoven as a classicist has tended to close off serious consideration of his intellectual and musical receptivity to post-classical and post-Enlightenment ideas and imagery. In addition, it has tended to limit the investigation of his artistic individuality to a relatively small number of formal and technical issues at the expense of the expressive content of his music and the symbolic implications of his works. Especially, it has given rise to the tendency to see Beethoven as an inheritor of tradition rather than as an active force in cultural history. A strategy of selective simplification has enabled classicizing scholars to collapse Beethoven's innovations into their sources, thereby minimizing his uniqueness while simultaneously magnifying the originality of his predecessors, whose own sources in tradition are rarely scrutinized. For example, surveying Beethoven's middle-period quartets from a historicizing standpoint, Haydn scholar James Webster asserted that "many aspects of Beethoven's supposed originality" in the quartets "were not entirely original"; citing various examples of anticipations of Beethoven's techniques by Haydn and, to a lesser extent, Mozart, he

---

19. There may be some truth in Baensch's claim that such concepts as classic and romantic, Apollonian and Dionysian, tragic and comic are "basically nothing but vague collective terms for feelings we find qualitatively related, though we cannot further demonstrate this relationship by anything in the feelings themselves, and cannot reduce it to distinct characteristics." Otto Baensch, "Art and Feeling," in *Reflections on Art,* ed. Susanne Langer (New York, 1961), 33.

concluded that, apart from "a few individual movements," many of "the ostensibly pathbreaking features in these works have ample precedent in the tradition."[20] The "titanic" Beethoven thus yields to a more subdued, even a tame Beethoven.

To emphasize in Beethoven the traditional rather than the modern, the compliant rather than the disruptive, the origins of his style rather than its originality, has had unexpected consequences. For the issue of Beethoven's classicism versus his romanticism, whatever its intrinsic merit, has served as a condensed metaphor for the way we perceive his music. The apparently abstract issue turns out to be the surface of an array of aesthetic and ideological subtexts. Thus, refuting Beethoven's romanticism enabled Schmitz to conclude that Beethoven "never created the calling of the free musician in a revolutionary sense. . . . He did not revolutionize the art of music, invented no new artistic methods, laws, or forms, or dispensed with the traditional rules of music either for himself or for others."[21] Here, Schmitz was adding his voice to a continuing theme of conservative German cultural criticism, a theme already sounded by Wagner, who, at least on one occasion, refused to see Beethoven as a revolutionary composer: "The German nature . . . remodels the form from within, and is thus relieved of the necessity of externally overthrowing it. Germans, consequently, are not revolutionary, but reformist."[22] In our own time, classicist and formalist views of Beethoven converge with archaizing trends in performance practice and various commercializations of Beethoven's works to anesthetize the impact of his music.

Such conservative perceptions of Beethoven would have come as a great surprise to both his supporters and his adversaries in his own time. Contemporary critiques of Beethoven were typically written from the standpoint of what we would now call classicism—though it was not yet defined as such—reproaching him for perceived violations of normative precepts of order, unity, balance, and decorum. The early report of Haydn's dissatisfaction with his pupil's Trio, Op. 1 no. 3, may bear on this point, but the professional reviewers were the first to sound this

20. James Webster, "Traditional Elements in Beethoven's Middle-Period String Quartets," in *Beethoven, Performers, and Critics: The International Beethoven Congress, Detroit, 1977,* ed. Robert Winter and Bruce Carr (Detroit, 1980), 99; 103.

21. Schmitz, *Das romantische Beethovenbild,* 178.

22. Wagner, *Beethoven,* 52. Translation amended.

note in print.[23] From the late 1790s they showed extreme sensitivity to Beethoven's departures from tradition, especially to his extended tonal trajectories and harmonic idiosyncrasies.

In the first volume of the Leipzig *Allgemeine musikalische Zeitung* (*AmZ* hereafter), the Violin Sonatas, Op. 12, were said to reveal Beethoven's "search for rare modulations, an aversion to customary [harmonic] relationships"; the reviewer concluded that "Beethoven goes his own path; but what a bizarre and thorny path it is!"[24] Later, in a notorious review, the *Eroica* Symphony was described as "losing itself entirely in lawlessness," containing "too much that is glaring and bizarre, which hinders greatly one's grasp of the whole."[25] A subsequent review of the same work suggested that it urgently required abbreviation as well as "more light, clarity and unity."[26] The *Allegro assai* of the Piano Sonata, Op. 57, was found to be filled with "oddities and bizarreries" (*Wunderlichkeiten und Bizarrerien*); Beethoven, noted the critic, "has once again unleashed many evil spirits."[27] Expectedly, many of Beethoven's later works were described in similar terms, with the Cello Sonatas, Op. 102, held to be "most singular and most strange."[28]

Reviews of Beethoven quartets fairly represent the classicist perspectives of Beethoven criticism during his lifetime. In August 1801, the *AmZ* took note of the first installment of the Op. 18 quartets, which had appeared in Leipzig two months earlier, stressing their learned style and difficulty of execution: "Among the works that have recently appeared . . . three quartets give a conclusive indication of his artistry; however, they must be played frequently, since they are difficult to perform and are in no way popular."[29] The Op. 59 quartets received only a few inauspicious lines in *AmZ;* the reviewer found them "very long and difficult" and predicted that, with the possible exception of the C-major quartet, they "will not be intelligible to everyone."[30] By 1811, an *AmZ*

---

23. In the following, I cite reviews in the *Allgemeine musikalische Zeitung* (hereafter *AmZ*) as both typical and exemplary of Beethoven criticism up to ca. 1815. After 1815, devotees of Beethoven and of romantic aesthetic attitudes were in charge of such publications as *Wiener AmZ,* Schott's *Cäcilia,* and Schlesinger's *Berliner amZ* (*BamZ*).

24. *AmZ* 1 (1798–99): col. 571.

25. Ibid., 7 (1804–5): col. 321.

26. Ibid., col. 501. A later review withdrew the critique, finding the "greatest unity, with clarity and purity alongside the greatest complexity" (ibid., 9 [1806–7]: col. 497).

27. Ibid., 9 (1806–7): col. 433.

28. Ibid., 20 (1818): col. 792.

29. Ibid., 3 (1800–1801): col. 800.

30. Ibid., 9 (1806–7): col. 400.

critic, whatever his view of Op. 18 might have been a decade earlier, had now come to regard Beethoven's first six quartets as classical models, distinguished by "unity, utmost simplicity, and adherence to a specific character in each work . . . which raise them to the rank of masterworks and validate Beethoven's place alongside the honored names of our Haydn and Mozart."[31]

In contrast, however, the critic saw the Razumovsky quartets as "indulging without consideration in the strangest and most singular whims of [Beethoven's] ingenious imagination," and the Quartet, Op. 74, which Breitkopf & Härtel had published in November 1810, as a powerful blend of the bizarre and the fantastic, an amalgam of heterogeneous elements pervaded by a somber and even lugubrious spirit. He reproached Beethoven for trying to express in this quartet sentiments alien to what he conceived to be the nature of the genre, one "which indeed is capable of sweet earnestness and lamenting melancholy but which should not have the goal of celebrating the dead or of picturing feelings of despair; rather, it ought to gladden the heart through the mild, comforting play of the imagination."[32] Clearly, the issue of classical decorum had now spilled over from its customary concern with issues of formal symmetry, balance, and proportion to disclose its underlying preoccupation with music's expressive content and rhetorical subject matter.

Naturally, Beethoven's late quartets met with great resistance, although by now his reputation was such that many reviewers merely alluded to the difficulty of understanding, performing, and appraising his music, tasks which they were grateful to leave for their successors. Critics balanced their attacks on Beethoven with obligatory bows to his genius. For example, the *AmZ* reviewer of the B-Flat Quartet, Op. 130, described the odd-numbered movements as "grave, mysterious, somber, although also certainly bizarre, harsh, and capricious," and the second and fourth movements as "full of mischief, gaiety, and cunning." But the trite charge of bizarrerie was found insufficient to describe the same critic's disorientation on hearing the *Grosse Fuge,* which was found to be "incomprehensible, like Chinese," a "confusion of babel"; and, in a phrase that would have delighted the Dadaists, the concert as a whole was held to be one that "only the Moroccans might enjoy."[33]

The classicist critique of Beethoven in his own time was scarcely lim-

31. Ibid., 13 (1811): col. 349.
32. Ibid., cols. 349–51.
33. Ibid., 28 (1826): cols. 310–11.

ited to music journalists. Those who resisted Beethoven's music made up a brilliant constellation of his contemporaries, including, on occasion, such writers as Goethe, Hegel, and Grillparzer, and such composers as Haydn, Zelter, Weber, Spohr, Cherubini, and even Beethoven's greatest—but, for a time, most reluctant—disciple, Franz Schubert. Spohr dismissed the Fifth Symphony with the remark: "Though with many individual beauties, yet it does not constitute a classical whole."[34] Weber felt certain that Beethoven could rise to true greatness "if he would only rein in his exuberant fantasy."[35] The young Schubert's rejection of Beethoven turned precisely upon the issues of classical unity and restraint: a reference to Beethoven in his diary disclaimed the "eccentricity which joins and confuses the tragic with the comic, the agreeable with the repulsive, heroism with howlings and the holiest with harlequinades, without distinction. . . ."[36] In a similar vein, Hegel (who, like Schubert, avoided mentioning Beethoven by name) compared the "bacchantic thunder and tumult" of modern music with the "tranquility of soul" to be found in the compositions of the great masters, of whom he mentions none later than Mozart and Haydn. In their music, by way of contrast to Beethoven's, "the resolution is always there; the luminous sense of proportion never breaks down in extremes: everything finds its due place knit together in the whole. . . ."[37] Only a few years after his moving oration at Beethoven's funeral, Grillparzer wrote in his *Tagebuch* an indictment of Beethoven's "unfortunate" influence, with particular stress upon the composer's transgressions of "all conception of musical order and unity," his "frequent infractions of rules," and his replacement of beauty by the "powerful, violent, and intoxicating."[38]

In all of these critiques Beethoven's music was measured against an implicit classical standard whose ideals included lawfulness, objectivity, and moderation; and he was denounced for his excessive fancy, his mingling of styles and affects, his infringement of traditional rules. Even

34. Ludwig Spohr, *Autobiography*, 2 vols. (London, 1865), 1:213.

35. Carl Maria von Weber, letter of 1 May 1810 to Hans Georg Nägeli, in Ludwig Nohl, ed., *Letters of Distinguished Musicians,* trans. Lady Wallace (London, 1867), 209.

36. Franz Schubert, diary entry of 16 June 1816, in Otto Erich Deutsch, ed., *Schubert: A Documentary Biography* (London, 1946), 64.

37. Georg Wilhelm Friedrich Hegel, *The Philosophy of Fine Art,* trans. F. P. B. Osmaston, 4 vols. (London, 1920), 3:406. See also 3:353, 417.

38. *Grillparzers Werke,* ed. August Sauer, part 2, vol. 9: *Tagebücher und literarische Skizzenhefte III* (Vienna and Leipzig, 1916), 171–72; Gustav Pollak, *Franz Grillparzer and the Austrian Drama* (New York, 1907), 427–28.

Beethoven's students and disciples were placed on the defensive by his perceived iconoclasm. Ignaz Moscheles described how he eventually reconciled himself to Beethoven's "unlooked-for episodes, shrill dissonances, and bold modulations" and admonished that Beethoven's "eccentricities . . . are reconcilable with *his* works alone, and are dangerous models to other composers."[39] Similarly, Carl Czerny wrote that the "so-called irregularities of harmony found in certain of Beethoven's works can be justified and explained on aesthetic grounds. . . . They are suitable only in those places where Beethoven used them"; but he disclaimed such passages as the dissonant horn entrance preceding the recapitulation in the first movement of the *Eroica* Symphony and the development of the *Thème russe* in the scherzo of the Quartet, Op. 59 no. 2: "They are the children of an ingenious love of mischief and a bizarre frame of mind, which often got the better of him."[40]

Of course the later Beethoven also had his romanticist defenders, who freely acknowledged and rejoiced in his subjectivity, in the free play of his imagination, and in his new organizing conceptions of musical form. Writing in Schlesinger's romantic journal, the *Berliner allgemeine musikalische Zeitung,* Ludwig Rellstab praised the "exaltation and fervor" of the Quartet, Op. 127, seeing in it the soul of "the genius who desires only self-realization," whose struggle to express his sufferings evoked "the manly anguish of a Laocoon."[41] In the same journal Adolph Bernhard Marx predicted that future generations would easily learn to comprehend the quartets, Opp. 132 and 135, "in the same way that our contemporaries no longer have difficulties" with Haydn quartets.[42] Fétis realized that Beethoven's aims represented a definitive break with those of his predecessors: "He had a different object than to charm the ear by the successive development of some principal phrase, by happy melodies or by beautiful harmonic combinations." Beethoven, he concluded, "found the ordinary forms of music too symmetrical, too conventional, and too proper" adequately to encompass his thought.[43]

It follows that, during his own time, Beethoven was widely regarded as a radical modernist, whose modernism was seen sharply to distinguish

39. Anton Schindler, *Life of Beethoven,* ed. Ignaz Moscheles (Boston, [1841]), vii–viii.

40. Carl Czerny, *On the Proper Performance of All of Beethoven's Works for the Piano* (Vienna, 1970), 16.

41. *BamZ* 2 (1825): 166.

42. Ibid., 5 (1828): 467.

43. *Revue musicale* 4 (1830): 279–86, 345–51, cited in Stefan Kunze, ed., *Ludwig van Beethoven: Die Werke im Spiegel seiner Zeit* (Laaber, 1987), 581.

him from the classical standards established, in the main, by Mozart and Haydn. Of course, they too had their share of hostile notices before they were elevated to canonical status; but the classicizing critiques of Beethoven were too intense and pervasive to be regarded as merely the usual, provisional resistance to modifications of cultural traditions. His contemporaries—including many of his advocates—saw him as subverting classical principles and procedures, as radical, iconoclastic, and eccentric. They did not regard him as an eighteenth-century composer.

The question naturally arises whether this modernism can be defined as romanticism. No simple answer is possible, for the classic–romantic dichotomy in the arts, like the Enlightenment–romantic polarity in philosophy, appears *post festum*. None of the early romantic poets in England had a self-awareness of belonging to a romantic movement; in Germany, even the Schlegels, observed René Wellek, "were not conscious of forming or founding a romantic school."[44] But most of those whom we now call romantics did have a sense of participating in an important modernist project, one with serious ideological overtones—whether aesthetic, philosophical, political, or religious.

And, paradoxically, this sense coexisted—indeed was inextricably blended—with an unswerving devotion to the ideals of classicism. The early German romantics rarely repudiated Hellenic concepts of order, measure, and harmony or classical notions of aesthetic coherence, proportion, and decorum, even when their writings were most transparently dedicated to the overthrow of these concepts. They did not consider themselves antithetical to classicism; rather they aspired to be its heirs. That is why the first definitions of romanticism are not manifestos of dissidence but of adherence to a dynamic tradition. "Romantic poetry is a progressive, universal poetry," reads Friedrich Schlegel's *Athenæum* fragment 116 (1798), in which the term "romantic" was applied to the new poetry for the first time; but, he continues, it is a poetry that "opens up a perspective upon an infinitely increasing classicism."[45]

The interpenetration of classical and romantic characteristics in Beethoven was first recognized by E. T. A. Hoffmann, in his 1810 review of the Fifth Symphony. He acknowledged that Beethoven's works were usually viewed as the "products of a genius who ignores form and dis-

44. René Wellek, *A History of Modern Criticism: 1750–1950,* 7 vols. (New Haven and London, 1955–91), 2:1.
45. Schlegel, *Friedrich Schlegel's Lucinde and the Fragments,* 175.

crimination of thought and surrenders to his creative fervor and the passing dictates of his imagination."[46] However, by way of refutation, his
essay offered a lengthy analysis of the Fifth Symphony's thematic and
structural unity.[47] Hoffmann's achievement was to define as romantic the
profoundly modern elements of Beethoven's music and, in the same
breath, to reconcile those elements with the attitudes, styles, and forms
of classicism. Casting his net perhaps wider than was necessary, he designated Mozart, Haydn, Bach, and Palestrina as romantic, but he allowed
for a variety of romanticisms, thus giving the widest latitude to each
composer's individuality. He pictured Beethoven's adherence to the rules
as the riskiest kind of musical romanticism, one that sought to bind in
aesthetic form fearful and perilous subject matter: "Beethoven's music,"
he wrote in what was to become one of the most famous passages in the
history of music criticism, "sets in motion the machinery of awe, of fear,
of terror, of pain, and awakens that infinite yearning which is the essence
of romanticism."[48]

German idealist aesthetics was well aware of the hazards of the unbri-
dled romantic imagination, which, as August Wilhelm Schlegel acknowledged, had a "secret attraction to a chaos which lies concealed in
the very bosom of the ordered universe, and is perpetually striving after
new and marvelous births."[49] Schiller, too, had earlier warned: "The
danger for the sentimental [i.e., romantic] genius is, . . . by trying to
remove all limits, of nullifying human nature absolutely . . . [and] passing
even beyond possibility."[50] Thus, Hoffmann's defense of Beethoven was

---

46. E. T. A. Hoffmann, Review of Beethoven's Fifth Symphony, *AmZ* 12 (1809–10):
col. 633, trans. in David Charlton, ed., *E. T. A. Hoffmann's Musical Writings: "Kreisleri-
ana," "The Poet and the Composer," Music Criticism,* trans. Martyn Clarke (Cambridge,
1989), 238. For an overview of Hoffmann's Beethoven criticism, see Peter Schnaus,
E. T. A. Hoffmann als Beethoven-Rezensent der Allgemeinen musikalischen Zeitung, Frei-
burger Schriften zur Musikwissenschaft, vol. 8 (Munich and Salzburg, 1977).

47. Extending Hoffmann's position, A. B. Marx proposed that Beethoven composed
each of his works according to a "specific conception" or "fundamental idea" (*Grund-
idee*) that underpinned "the connectedness, unity, and harmony of its apparently discor-
dant features" (*BamZ* 6 [1829]: 169).

48. Hoffmann, Review of Beethoven's Fifth Symphony, *AmZ* 12 (1809–10): col.
633, trans. in Charlton, ed., *Hoffmann's Musical Writings,* 238.

49. August Wilhelm Schlegel, *Über dramatische Kunst und Litteratur,* 2d ed., 3 vols.
(Heidelberg, 1817), 3:14–15; *A Course of Lectures on Dramatic Art and Literature,* trans. John
Black, rev. the Rev. A. J. W. Morrison (London, 1846), 343.

50. Friedrich Schiller, "On Naive and Sentimental Poetry," in *The Works of Friedrich
Schiller: Aesthetical and Philosophical Essays,* ed. Nathan Haskell Dole, 2 vols. (New York,
1902), 2:44.

a bold one in that it did not minimize Beethoven's attraction to chaos. Rather, he declared that Beethoven's music enters "the realm of the colossal and the immeasurable," opening upon a labyrinthian cosmos, highly individual, utterly fantastic, and giving free play to extreme emotions such as terror, longing, and ecstasy. Uncompromising, Hoffman saw Beethoven's revolutionary imagination as wholly consistent with his genius for classical form.[51]

Beethoven is *sui generis*. He never joined any movement, despite his early, loose affiliation with Freemasonry, his youthful passion for the French Revolution's ideals, his tilt toward German nationalism after 1804, his lifelong adherence to the reformism of Austrian Emperor Joseph II. Mozart joined the Freemasons; after several rebuffs, Haydn at last gained membership in the Tonkünstlersocietät; Schubert was elected to the Gesellschaft der Musikfreunde. But Beethoven remained aloof. Similarly, whatever the power of romanticism's pull upon his imagination, he never became an adherent of any specific romantic tendency. Nor, even apart from his rejection of the irrational and the sentimental, could he consciously yield to several of romanticism's most dangerous blandishments—its often undisguised eroticism, its mystical view of death as the doorway to life, its tendency to convert systematic thought into aphorism.

Of course, these were Beethoven's preoccupations too, but he tried to insist on their strict control and sublimation: his lovers are never united, except, at the close of *Fidelio,* in conventional conjugal fidelity; "Joyfully I go to meet death," he wrote in his Heiligenstadt Testament, but this was hardly his "Hymn to the Night," for he added, "Should it come before I have had an opportunity to develop all my artistic gifts then . . . I certainly would like to postpone it";[52] and though his Bagatelles, Op. 126, and many of the individual *Diabelli* Variations are supreme embodiments of the romantic aphorism, Beethoven urgently forges them into larger designs—a "Cycle of Bagatelles" and, in the *Diabelli* Variations, the most coherent variation cycle since Bach. Simi-

51. Dahlhaus sees both Hoffmann's theory of romantic symphonic music and Beethoven's "monumental style" as fully grounded in eighteenth-century aesthetics of the sublime, implying that neither Hoffmann nor Beethoven may be claimed exclusively by romanticism (Carl Dahlhaus, *Ludwig van Beethoven und seine Zeit* [Laaber, 1987], 100–105, 110; "E. T. A. Hoffmann's Beethoven-Kritik und die Aesthetik des Erhabenen," *Archiv für Musikwissenschaft* 38 [1981]: 79–92).

52. Ludwig van Beethoven, Heiligenstadt Testament, 6–10 October 1802, in *The Letters of Beethoven,* ed. Emily Anderson, 3 vols. (London, 1961), Appendix A.

larly, although *An die ferne Geliebte* opens the way to romanticism and is itself saturated in romantic imagery, the interlocking structure (and inseparability) of its component songs suggests that romantic openness impelled Beethoven toward ever more profound formal integration.

Writing to his publisher, Schott's Sons, Beethoven mischievously described the most radically structured of his late quartets, the seven-movement Quartet in C-Sharp Minor, Op. 131, as "stolen together out of various bits of this and that";[53] yet the carefully ordered series of subdominant relationships and the thematic integration of the corner movements show it to be a monument of large-scale design. Romanticism may have given Beethoven license to represent the forbidden and the boundless; but his will to form—his classicism, if you like—enabled him to set boundaries upon the infinite, to portray disorder in the process of its metamorphosis into order, to transform suffering, tragedy, and death into healing, hope, and affirmation, and to do this by sheer aesthetic power. It is in this larger sense that Rosen has offered a most persuasive model of Beethoven's development, a reconciliation of Beethoven's "startlingly radical and original ways" with his refusal to abandon classicism.

It is not my purpose to replace a classicizing historicism with a romanticizing historicism. And so, it may be time once again to sidestep the issue of Beethoven's romanticism and to revert to the more transparent issue of his modernism, which was so plainly recognized in his own time. Beethoven's unprecedented expressive, technical, and formal innovations, his simulation of narrative forms in instrumental music, his drive toward the denotative in music, his creation of new characteristic styles expressive of propulsive, heightened, and transcendent states could well have emerged without the stimulus of romantic philosophy, without the examples of romantic literature and art. After all, the drive to originality of expression was at the core of his creativity. As he remarked to Karl Holz in the afterglow of his late quartets: "Art demands of us that we shall not stand still," adding, "The imagination, too, insists upon its privileges."[54]

Certainly, Beethoven shared many of romanticism's fundamental preoccupations, creative tropes, and imaginative metaphors. His close kin-

---

53. "Zusammengestohlen aus Verschiedenem diesem u. jenem." Written on the autograph copy provided to the publisher, Schott's Sons. Georg Kinsky, *Das Werk Beethovens: Thematisch-bibliographisch Verzeichnis* (Munich-Duisburg, 1955), 397.

54. Elliot Forbes, ed., *Thayer's Life of Beethoven* (Princeton, 1964), 982.

ship to romanticism appears also in his choice of texts, in his attraction to issues involving extreme alternatives—death and resurrection, freedom and necessity, Arcadia and Elysium, the individual and the cosmos, yearning and fulfillment—and, not least, in his radical reformulation of the expressive capabilities of music. Thus, it may be safe to conclude that Beethoven's intellectual and spiritual interests are more centrally located in early romanticism than has previously been supposed, even if we make allowance for the possibility that his apparent receptivity to romantic conventions, metaphors, images, and designs may well be but a special case of his receptivity to the manifold forms of the imaginative, exemplifying his endless quest for materials useful to an urgent modernist project.

Such a quest, of course, may itself be an essential ingredient of romanticism, of its Faustian drive to transcend the given, its yearning for the unreachable, its rebellious temper. However, as those of Beethoven's contemporaries who were nurtured on Schiller's aesthetics understood, this drive is actually predicated upon the existence of the classical, which holds out unsurpassable models of the ideal—promises of liberation, of brotherhood, of reconciliation with nature, eternal life, fusion with the Godhead, the achievement of pure joy, the experience of beauty—in every potential embodiment. Schiller had proposed the tormenting but ecstatic dilemma of the modern artist: to represent in art an unreachable ideal, unreachable because "nothing can satisfy whilst a superior thing can be conceived" and because the ideal that had existed in paradise and will exist once again hereafter can never exist in the present moment.[55] Thus, it follows that the quest for the classical ideal is a task for Tantalus or for one endowed with the will, the restlessness, and the romantic temperament of a Beethoven.

55. Schiller, "On Naive and Sentimental Poetry," 2:52.

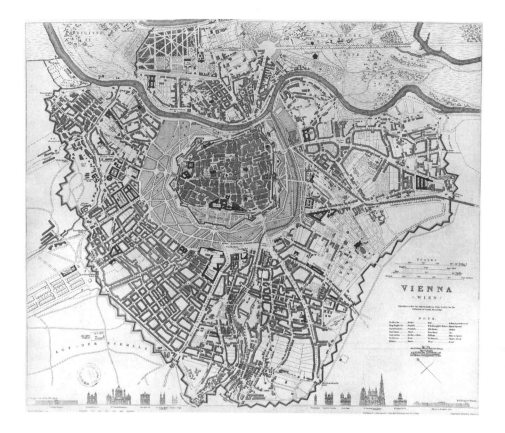

Vienna in 1833. The old medieval city (*center*) and the new Renaissance one were separated by an open space, the glacis of the city's earlier defense system. Twenty-five years later this open space was transformed into the famous Ringstrasse and its adjoining parks and public buildings. (From James Mickleburgh, *Index to the Principal Places in the World* [London, 1844]; photo courtesy of the University Research Library of UCLA, Special Collections)

The Patrons and Publics of the Quartets: Music, Culture, and Society in Beethoven's Vienna

LEON BOTSTEIN

It is amazing where the newest composers are heading, with technical and me-chanical dimensions raised to the very highest levels; their works end up no longer being music, for they go beyond the scope of human emotional re-sponses and one cannot add anything more to such works from one's own spirit and heart. . . . For me, everything just remains stuck in my ears.

> Johann Wolfgang von Goethe,
> conversation with Eckermann,
> 12 January 1827[1]

Möser's quartet evenings . . . are, when it comes to instrumental music, the most comprehensible to me: one hears four rational people talk among them-selves, one believes that one gains something from their discourse and becomes acquainted with the idiosyncrasies of their instruments.

> Goethe to Carl Friedrich Zelter, 1829

I doubt whether Haydn, Mozart, and Beethoven ever reexperienced their works in so clean, secure, and healthy a way as they are given here. . . . [Möser] so electrifies his fellow players that the hearer also does not know what is hap-pening to him. One believes that one is playing along; one understands the unfathomable, one is possessed—one does not know by what.

> Zelter to Goethe, 1829[2]

---

1. Translated from Fl. Frhr. von Biedermann, *Goethes Gespräche: Gesamtausgabe,* 5 vols. (Leipzig, 1910), 3:315.
2. Both excerpts translated from *Briefwechsel zwischen Goethe und Zelter 1799–1832,* ed. Max Hecker, 3 vols. (Frankfurt am Main, 1987), 3:233; 246.

To the Beethoven Enthusiasts

Like you, I have greatly admired Beethoven
However, with one difference.
Where your admiration first really begins
Mine has already ended.

Franz Grillparzer, 1870[3]

Who remains then to speak for the deepest drive of a nation transported into
profundity and therefore religious; who remains left to approach God—even if
with ponderous and hesitant words like Moses, the first of the prophets—who
remains but he: Beethoven?

Hugo von Hofmannsthal, 1920[4]

This collection of fragments provides a historical framework for reflect-
ing on the Beethoven quartets. The weight of past interpretations frequently burdens the hearing and playing of works possessed of a rich critical tradition. Each generation of listeners is caught between inherited
paradigms and the demand for a fresh aesthetic response. This essay attempts to illuminate anew the early nineteenth-century cultural and social contexts of the quartets through a reimagining of the past—its politics, theatrical traditions, literary passions, social structures, and patronage.

The first fragment, Goethe's remark to Eckermann, made just months
before Beethoven's death, evokes what a discerning listener in the late
eighteenth and early nineteenth century expected from music. Goethe
was an avid lover of music who acknowledged Beethoven's genius. The
admiration was reciprocated—Beethoven set Goethe to music (Op. 84
and Op. 112, for example), owned twenty-four volumes of Goethe's
works, and toyed with the notion of setting *Faust*. For Goethe, music
was an art allied specifically to nature through an inherent parallelism to
human emotions. Aesthetic judgments for music were measurable by
the human capacity for sentiment and feeling.

Music created an intimate imaginary discourse of feeling. In the act
of listening, an internal dialogue was generated; patterns of memory and
remembrance were triggered—"the awakening of reminiscences," as
Goethe put it.[5] The paradox and lure of music for Goethe and his contemporaries lay in the social (the listener and participant, the objective

3. Franz Grillparzer, *Sämmtliche Werke,* ed. August Sauer, 16 vols. (Stuttgart, 1887),
11:86.

4. Hugo von Hofmannsthal, *Reden und Aufsätze (1914–1924)* (Frankfurt am Main,
1979), 76, 78.

5. *Goethes Gespräche,* 3:234.

and observable) and yet secret (the intimate, capable of powerful personal appropriation) qualities of music. What troubled Goethe in 1827 was that newer music, including perhaps even some Beethoven, seemed to break the link between nature (e.g., emotion) and art, upsetting the special symmetries between music as an art and the profound nonmusical emotional experiences of which the cultivated listener was capable. Despite the surface brilliance of a new generation of virtuosos, music's aesthetic logic seemed at risk. "No art," Zelter wrote to Goethe in 1808, "can have a beneficial human effect if it wanders around in endless space, as arrogantly and formlessly as the newer music, which separates its most secret and highest charms from the whole and exposes them publicly to the common mob . . . to satiate their cheap curiosity."[6]

In 1807 and 1811 critics chose to characterize the Beethoven quartets as intended for "the educated friend of music," the "true friend of musical art."[7] Yet they appeared over a period marked by audience expansion, by intense ferment and reflection about art and music. After the French Revolution, the influence of the secular rationalism of the Enlightenment receded. It was supplanted by a renewed fascination with religion. The classical and the ideal of the objective were pitted against the "romantic" and the embrace of the subjective.

These conflicting tendencies between new and old created paradoxical links between culture and politics in the early nineteenth century. The old seemed allied with rationalism and liberalism; the new with political reaction, the disappearance of the *citoyen* of the 1790s, the emergence of the domesticated *Bürger,* and the revival of religion and the prestige of monarchical power after 1815.

Beethoven and the elite Viennese world for which he wrote the quartets were involved in this intense, multifaceted discourse. New audiences and forms of patronage evolved, accompanying the transition from the world of Beethoven, Hegel, and Goethe to that of Mendelssohn, Schlegel, Schleiermacher, and Schumann. Between 1800 and 1827, the years during which they were first published, the quartets mirrored a transformation of culture and society.[8]

6. Carl Friedrich Zelter, to Goethe, in *Briefwechsel zwischen Goethe und Zelter,* 1:245.

7. Stefan Kunze, ed., *Ludwig van Beethoven—Die Werke im Spiegel seiner Zeit: Gesammelte Konzertberichte und Rezensionen bis 1830* (Laaber, 1987), 72; 207.

8. See Carl Dahlhaus, "Bürgerliche Musikkultur" and "Metaphysik der Instrumentalmusik" in *Die Musik des 19. Jahrhunderts* (Wiesbaden, 1980). See also Maynard Solomon, "Beethoven, Sonata and Utopia," *Telos* 9 (Fall 1971): 32–47, and "Beethoven and the Enlightenment," *Telos* 19 (Spring 1974): 146–53, and the response by Robert Solomon, "Beethoven and the Sonata Form," *Telos* 19 (Spring 1974): 141–46.

The second and third fragments suggest the character of early nineteenth-century string quartet performances. By the end of the 1820s Vienna and Berlin offered professional renditions for a small listening audience. In 1823, Ignaz Schuppanzigh returned to Vienna from Russia and began a series of afternoon chamber performances at the inn "Zum roten Igel" on the Tuchlauben in Vienna's inner city. In 1824 his quartet played six Beethoven quartets in addition to quartets by Haydn and Mozart.[9]

By the 1820s the string quartet had achieved a unique status as a vehicle of cultural discourse. Goethe pointed to the essential conceit adopted by the musical connoisseur of Beethoven's generation. Rather than being merely distracted or entertained, as by a "divertimento," the listener could engage in rational internal discourse—conversation and perhaps even argument—while seeming to enjoy the quartets as "pure" music. Reason and the faculty of wisdom were at play for both sides, listener and player. The complex and subtle development of musical narrative and materials over the length of the quartet form—replete with highly varied sonorities—achieved its peak in Beethoven's work.

In contrast to Goethe, Zelter expressed the unfathomable in the quartet experience: its capacity to draw us into regions otherwise opaque, impenetrable by ordinary language. Using the modern metaphor of electricity (the players are "electrified"), Zelter invoked music's power to awaken the deep, seemingly nonrational aspects of human nature, a point decisively argued ten years earlier by Schopenhauer, who was an accomplished musical amateur. The string quartet was most effective in reaching beyond externals into inner consciousness.

Using Möser's superb quartet performances, Zelter defined the essence of deep listening. The symbiosis of player and listener must result in the illusion of "playing along." The experience Goethe described as comprehension and understanding was gained by *imagining* the act of creating the sounds. In the early nineteenth century, listening to chamber music was not considered passive activity. Authentic appreciation, Zelter felt, depended on the listener's capacity to imagine playing and reenacting what was heard. It was this habit of listening that enabled the listener to generate the extramusical meaning. The illusion of participation defined true appreciation and connoisseurship. During Beethoven's lifetime, this

9. Eduard Hanslick, *Geschichte des Concertwesens in Wien,* 2 vols. (Vienna, 1869), 1:203–7.

relationship between composer and audience, particularly for the quartet form, drifted from this model as musical literacy evolved. A different conception of listening and musical communication came into being.[10]

The fourth fragment, by Beethoven's acquaintance and would-be librettist Franz Grillparzer (1791–1872), Vienna's leading nineteenth-century literary figure, was written in the centenary year of Beethoven's birth. It hints at Grillparzer's own aesthetic beliefs, which mirrored widespread mid-nineteenth-century notions about Beethoven's later quartets (starting with Opp. 74 and 95, but primarily the last group, beginning with Op. 127) as aberrant and disjointed. At best, this view held, the late quartets were perverse echoes of the great Beethoven of the early and middle works.

However, by 1870 a shift in taste had begun to take shape. Younger audiences embraced the late quartets enthusiastically, a turn of events the aging Grillparzer felt obliged to tweak with his bit of doggerel. The late quartets ultimately became icons of modernism; examples of how Beethoven prefigured a progressive aesthetic, making a great leap over the history of the nineteenth century. By 1870, the myth of Beethoven as the revolutionary genius without equal was in full bloom. He embodied the qualities of freedom, inspiration, and creativity beyond the limits of everyday bourgeois convention. During the last decades of the nineteenth century enthusiasm among listeners for the late quartets constituted a display of genuine taste and the recognition of musical art as the highest expression of spiritual autonomy.

This late nineteenth-century sentiment was abetted by Wagner and his followers, particularly in Vienna. Beethoven was reconceived (in part through Wagner's own writings) as a forerunner of Wagnerian aesthetic ideals. Grillparzer loathed these trends, in part because, as a survivor of Beethoven's era, he feared that the Wagnerian myth would supplant the aesthetic ideals rooted in the culture of Europe before 1848 and best exemplified by early and mid-career Beethoven. Sure enough, Wagnerian notions of the quartets as harbingers of a novel and modern dramatic and narrative concept of musical space and time remain today.[11]

The fifth fragment, by Hugo von Hofmannsthal, Richard Strauss's collaborator and arguably the most musical of modern Austrian poets,

---

10. See Leon Botstein, "Listening through Reading: Musical Literacy and the Concert Audience," *Nineteenth-Century Music* 16 (1992): 129–45.

11. On Wagner's view of the quartets see Richard Wagner, "Beethoven," in *Gesammelte Schriften und Dichtungen,* 10 vols. (Leipzig, 1888), especially 9:96–97.

captures the essence of a twentieth-century enthusiasm for Beethoven. The composer, Hofmannsthal maintained, demonstrated that music was more powerful than speech. Hofmannsthal's contemporary Ludwig Wittgenstein argued in 1931 that Beethoven tackled "problems of the intellectual world . . . which no philosopher has ever confronted . . . in the obscure language of prophecy, comprehensible to very few indeed."[12] For Wittgenstein, an avid although conservative music enthusiast and brought up, like Hofmannsthal, in a Viennese culture that sought to sustain a link with the world of Beethoven's patrons and public, music was a discrete language, a form of life and communication. "Musical themes," Wittgenstein observed in 1915, "are in a certain sense propositions. And so the recognition of the essence of logic will lead to the recognition of the essence of music."[13] Later he suggested that "understanding a sentence is much more akin to understanding a theme in music than one may think."[14]

Hofmannsthal and Wittgenstein were obsessed with the incapacities of conventional language with respect to ethical truths and the crucial questions of life. In Hofmannsthal's comparison between Beethoven and Goethe, Schiller and Herder, Beethoven remained the true "prophet" of the nineteenth century, in whose work ethical truth and beauty are communicated adequately.

This modernist celebration of the Beethoven of the quartets as providing an alternative mode of expression in a world where ordinary and philosophic language falls short found ironic response in the work of another Viennese, Arnold Schoenberg. In his opera *Moses und Aron,* Schoenberg assigned the character of Moses (Hofmannsthal's Beethoven) only "Sprechstimme," a cross between speech and music. The composer abandoned the opera after two acts, leaving only a textual fragment of the third. Schoenberg left the work with the unrealized hope that music might ultimately communicate sacred and human truth where language had failed.

The legacy of these three twentieth-century Viennese intellectual giants—all of whom witnessed the 1902 secession exhibit in Vienna,

12. Ludwig Wittgenstein, *Culture and Value,* trans. Peter Finch, ed. G. H. von Wright (Chicago, 1980), 9e.

13. Brian McGuinness, *Wittgenstein—A Life: Young Ludwig, 1889–1921* (Berkeley, 1988), 127; see also pp. 19–34, 55–56, and 123–28.

14. Ludwig Wittgenstein, *Philosophical Investigations,* 2d ed., trans. G. E. M. Anscombe (New York, 1958), pt. 1, sec. 527, p. 143e.

with its Klimt friezes and Max Klinger's Beethoven statue—is the popular view of Beethoven as the heroic prophet of progressive modernity, the musical articulator not only of the Faustian human condition, but of the sublime and the truthful. The late quartets in particular account for this reputation. We continue to hear in them the most compelling balance between, on the one hand, the abstract and the descriptive, the autonomous, suggestive, and ineffable, and, on the other hand, the narrative, the concrete, and the expressible.

The Quartets in Viennese Society and Culture

Beethoven lived in Vienna from the end of 1792 until his death in 1827. The Vienna to which he moved was a walled city of 55,000, surrounded by districts with populations about four times that of the inner city. By the time Beethoven died, the "suburbs" of Vienna had grown to some 300,000 inhabitants, while the population of the inner city remained the same. Twelve gates led from the inner city to the outer districts, with a large open space called the Glacis in between (occupied today by the Ringstrasse). The central landmark of the inner city was St. Stephen's Cathedral, challenged visually only by Fischer von Erlach's Karlskirche (1739), which stood on a hill outside the walls, a magnificent symbolic synthesis of Catholicism, baroque theatricality, and the Habsburg dynasty that ruled Vienna throughout Beethoven's lifetime.

Unlike Rome, Paris, or London, Beethoven's Vienna contained few remnants of cultures before the eighteenth century. A century before Beethoven arrived, the city had been the scene of the triumphant defense of Western Christendom against the Turks. But the siege of Vienna and the victory of 1683 had left the city—except for St. Stephen's—essentially destroyed.[15]

Thus, eighteenth-century Vienna looked like a new city. The princely palaces, churches, and state buildings—even the inns and coffeehouses Beethoven frequented—were built mostly after 1690. The newness was reflected in the pervasive Italianate baroque style of many structures and, later, in the use of French neoclassicism, the dominant architectural style of late eighteenth-century Vienna. Among the greatest neoclassical structures was the palace built by Louis von Montoyer for Count Razu-

---

15. See Felix Czeike, *Geschichte der Stadt Wiens* (Vienna, 1981), chap. 4.

movsky, the accomplished amateur violinist for whom Op. 59 was written. Razumovsky maintained a standing string quartet headed by Ignaz Schuppanzigh, Beethoven's friend and colleague and one of Vienna's leading violinists.[16]

Beethoven's life spanned a period of intense political and economic activity in Vienna, called by some *Manufakturzeitalter*—"the age of manufacturing." As a result of political reforms in the 1780s, Vienna became a leading center of finance, bureaucracy, and trade. In the wake of this economic activity came the opening of new theaters, a hospital, a medical school, and princely palaces. After 1815 a second surge of development witnessed the creation of parks, a university library, a synagogue, the first steamship connections, and buildings such as the 1826 Schottenhof—the prototype for end-of-the-century apartment houses.

By 1805, the year of the first Napoleonic invasion, Vienna had developed a vitality, novelty, and spirit of progress that lured not only Beethoven but many other musicians, writers, scholars, artists, architects, cultivated aristocrats, successful merchants, and professional families. Most of the musicians in Vienna before 1800 were foreigners or immigrants from within the Habsburg realm who sought opportunity in the city's teeming social and economic environment.

The vast majority—perhaps two-thirds—of walled Vienna's population in 1790 was made up of servants or household members without occupations. The remaining third consisted of aristocrats, artisans, tradespeople, and civil servants. Among the artisans were Europe's finest manufacturers of keyboard and musical instruments, particularly string instruments. This artisan class also included the pioneers of what became a serious music publishing industry.[17]

Beethoven lived for the most part (except for the summers) among the 55,000 inside the city walls.[18] Despite the rapid growth of the outlying districts and the creation of theaters there, it is possible to speculate about what the majority of patrons and concertgoers in Vienna were like during Beethoven's day by extrapolating from the 55,000. Most of the public musical events took place inside the walls or close by (e.g.,

16. Karl Holz reported that, until 1816, Razumovsky played second violin when performances took place in his palace (Friedrich Kerst, *Die Erinnerungen an Beethoven*, 2 vols. [Stuttgart, 1913], 1:130–31; 2:184).

17. Alice M. Hanson, *Musical Life in Biedermeier Vienna* (Cambridge, 1985), 10, 20–22.

18. For a comprehensive account of Beethoven's many lodgings and a list of all concert locales, see Rudolf Klein, *Beethovenstätten in Österreich* (Vienna, 1970).

the Theater an der Wien). The expense, distance, and difficulty of transportation in and out of the city and the control of the limited number of city gates leading into the inner city made travel relatively difficult. Curfews required everyone to be off the streets by 10 P.M. (although each superintendent—der Hausmeister—might admit latecomers to their lodgings for a tip).

In 1780 in all of Vienna, including the outlying districts, there were only seventy-six schools and fewer than 9,000 pupils, less than a fifth of the school-age population. The most common type of school was the so-called Trivialschule, whose curriculum took only one or two years. Vienna had only four Gymnasien, schools that prepared students for university entrance. For the aristocracy, instruction at home—including music lessons—was common. In 1796 Beethoven agreed to give daily piano lessons for 20 florins a month, one of the highest fees charged by teachers of the day.

Given the economic realities and levels of education, it is not surprising that the musical circle of Vienna was small indeed. Counting musicians, instrument makers, music publishers, and the audiences of aristocrats, well-to-do civil servants, and merchant families (particularly members of the elite Jewish banking families), it probably consisted of only a few thousand persons.

Wages in Vienna were low and uneven in terms of their adequacy for participation in musical life. Novice clerks in service to Prince Liechtenstein earned 550 florins a year in 1821, rising to upwards of 2,000 after twenty years of service. A teacher could earn as much as 700, an actress in the Burgtheater as much as 5,000. Civil servants made between 400 (for postal workers) and 2,500 florins (for a nonaristocrat with the title of secretary). After years of service, the concertmaster of the opera orchestra earned a little over 1,000 florins a year, while an experienced Kapellmeister took home around 2,400. Inflation affected wages even then. Beethoven paid his female servants around 130 florins a year, almost six times as much as Haydn had paid only eleven years earlier.

The wealthy patrons of music in the nineteenth century lived in a world well removed from the one just described. A count had an income ranging anywhere from 30,000 to 100,000 florins a year. The estate of Prince Karl I, Schwarzenberg, worth 4 million florins in 1820, probably yielded each of his three sons about 50,000 florins a year, and the Archduke Karl is said to have had an annual income of over 100,000. Given this context, Beethoven's 1809 guaranteed annual subvention of 4,000 florins from his aristocratic patrons may seem modest, but it placed him near the top of the Viennese "middle class" of his day.[19]

Beethoven's income consisted of commissions, gifts from patrons, and moneys from publication, concerts, and teaching. The Op. 18 quartets resulted in a 600 florin annual subvention from Prince Lichnowsky. Prince Galitzin offered 675 florins for the composition of what became three of the late quartets. In 1801, Beethoven offered four works to a publisher for 315 florins, and three years later he asked 90 florins as a fee for publishing his quartets. In 1824 Beethoven offered the publisher Schott's Sons the Ninth Symphony for 1,000 florins and the Op. 127 Quartet for 225 florins.

The relationship between incomes and concert attendance can be inferred from the fact that a subscription to six Schuppanzigh performances of the Beethoven quartets in the 1820s cost 4 florins. In the years just after 1800, concert tickets cost about a florin. Assuming an average income for concert audience members of around 1,500 florins and an early nineteenth-century distribution of costs for basic needs, tickets were not inexpensive.

Sheet music, which was the only "recorded" form of music available, ranged from 11 florins for an entire opera score (a few hundred dollars in today's money) to a florin or so for a set of six songs. Schubert's *Erlkönig*, published by Diabelli in 1821, cost 1.8 florins. The first volume of a piano method published in 1828 in Vienna cost 3 florins. Renting sheet music was also possible. A Viennese lending library in the 1780s (10 florins a year for membership) charged as little as a tenth of a florin to rent the music for a string quartet.

One reason for sheet music's popularity was the comparative rarity of live concerts. A high percentage of the music written in Beethoven's day was directed at the musically literate player or would-be player as audience. Except for occasional large-audience events in the imperial palace, concerts were held either in one of the three theaters or in a few restaurants with second-floor rooms large enough to accommodate a concert or ball.[20] Chamber music concerts usually took place before audiences of 200 or less.

The rarity of public concerts was offset by musical gatherings in pri-

19. Hanson, *Musical Life*, 20–21; see also Hannes Stekl, *Österreichs Aristokratie im Vormärz* (Vienna, 1973), 217–22.

20. See Otto Biba, "Concert Life in Beethoven's Vienna," in Robert Winter and Bruce Carr, eds., *Beethoven, Performers, and Critics* (Detroit, 1980).

vate homes (some, though, open to the public). Outdoor events (weather permitting) in places such as the Augarten and the Prater also helped to bring music to a wider audience. A chronic housing shortage in Vienna contributed to the central role in the cultural life of the city played by restaurants and coffeehouses—gathering places for discussion, reading, entertainment, and music.

Between 1780 and 1830, most public concerts were played by amateurs or a combination of amateurs and professionals from the orchestras of Vienna's three main theaters. Concerts generally were sponsored by voluntary associations or by the composer/performers and attracted mixed audiences of other amateur players or friends of the sponsors. The results were uneven at best and the frequency low. Beethoven, as pianist or as composer, gave even fewer concerts in Vienna than Mozart.

These public events were not, however, where composers preferred to showcase their best new works. Instead, they tried to unveil them before select private groups, which included members of the aristocracy. As Beethoven wrote about Op. 95 to Sir George Smart: "NB. The Quartet is written for a small circle of connoisseurs and is never to be performed in public."[21] Musical literacy and taste were cultivated by amateurs in private spaces. The listener at the occasional public concert was either an amateur or someone who moved regularly in circles of those who had an interest in music making in private homes.

The Beethoven quartets were directed to three groups within the public for music: (1) the high aristocracy of Habsburgs, Schwarzenbergs, and so on; (2) the growing "second society" of banking families, manufacturers, and professionals; and (3) an emerging class of less affluent professionals, musicians, shop owners, artisan manufacturers, and lower-echelon civil servants. This last group would eventually come to dominate the musical scene in Vienna and would play a far greater role in shaping the career of Beethoven's younger contemporaries—Franz Schubert, for example.

But the crucial "second society" of Beethoven's day was probably the most influential. It was largely a product of Vienna's economic boom in the 1790s and early 1800s, and its leading figures included such stalwarts as Raphael Georg Kiesewetter, Joseph Sonnleithner (Beethoven's collaborator), and several prominent Jewish banking families (e.g., the

21. Ludwig van Beethoven to Sir George Smart, in *The Letters of Beethoven,* ed. Emily Anderson, 3 vols. (London, 1961), letter 664. Hereafter, citations to this work will appear in the form Anderson Letters 00.

Arnsteins, Eskeles, Rothschilds, and Wertheimsteins). Beethoven's friends from the Rhineland, Stephan von Breuning and Baron Ignaz von Gleichenstein, were also part of this group.[22]

The social demarcation between the second society and the high aristocracy was sharp, but the areas of music and theater provided a rare common ground. This common ground, upon which other areas of mutual interest—social and business—could be pursued, was a major motivation behind the second society's cultivation of the arts. It was the great leveler (for this stratum, at least) of Viennese society. The irony was that while Beethoven was alive the second society succeeded all too well, and the high aristocracy gradually ceded the high ground of music and the arts to the new monied aristocracy (Geldadel) and the bourgeois plutocracy (Grossbürgertum).

Part of this process was a response to the withering away of noble and aristocratic patronage. Grandiose subvention of musicians by the upper crust of Viennese society ended during the Napoleonic period, between 1809 and 1815 (Beethoven may have been the last composer in Vienna to get a large part of his income from individual aristocrats). However, the members of the elite aristocracy remained important players on the musical scene for some time. They were prominent, for example, in the Society of the Friends of Music, Vienna's leading concert-giving and amateur musical association. By 1815—beginning with the Congress of Vienna—most high aristocratic families were mixing more freely with the newer elite in private as well as public rituals.

Beethoven's aristocratic musical patrons were not typical of their class. High aristocrats like Archduke Rudolf or Count Razumovsky, who were accomplished musicians themselves, soon gave way to a new breed of scions of old aristocratic families with growing interests outside music and the arts—business and politics, for example. Over the course of the nineteenth century, the tradition of music making as part of a ritual of social intercourse in high aristocratic homes was all but extinguished.

Support of music by noble families in the late eighteenth century was in part a competitive social display, exemplified by the large presentation rooms of Vienna's baroque and neoclassical palaces. This interplay of architecture and culture left an indelible mark on the second society, particularly on the segment that did not receive patents of nobility, who

---

22. Elliot Forbes, ed., *Thayer's Life of Beethoven,* 2 vols. (Princeton, 1964), 1:335–36, and Anderson Letters 95.

emulated the eighteenth-century traditions of the high aristocracy in the opulent bourgeois apartments in the buildings of the 1850s and 1860s. Theophil von Hansen's 1870 design for the city's major public concert hall, the Musikverein, in its explicitly neoclassical mix of temple and palace design, also evoked this link to the large rooms of the aristocratic palaces of the eighteenth century.

What kinds of amateur musicians were the high aristocrats and avid musical enthusiasts of the second society? What was the character of their musical education and literacy? Around 1800, the primary vehicle of musical amateurism was stringed instruments. Eduard Hanslick, writing in the 1860s, noted about the late eighteenth century that "one let the musically talented sons gladly learn violin and cello, whereas today the domestic teaching of music has been absorbed entirely by piano instruction."[23] For the Viennese, Frances Trollope noted in the 1830s, "the piano is not, like the violin, an instrument to whose power of expression there is no limit."[24]

In Grillparzer's short story "Der arme Spielmann," begun in 1831, the violin is the vehicle of the protagonist Jakob, a beggar who creates an unconventional musical language that makes him stand out magically above all other musicians. Grillparzer's model for Jakob was Beethoven himself. In 1808 Johann Friedrich Reichardt noted that string quartet playing "essentially came from Vienna." Throughout the early 1800s the *Leipziger Musikzeitung* provided regular reports about the frequency and high level of quartet activity in Vienna. The violin was the primary instrument of musical activity.

The second significant instrument of musical amateurs was the voice, whether solo and small-group singing or choral activity. Before 1830, the Society of the Friends of Music was primarily a club that permitted singers and string players to perform together.

The third and most rapidly growing dimension of musical amateurism in Beethoven's lifetime involved the keyboard. Already indispensable for virtuosos such as Mozart and Beethoven (particularly for improvisation), the fortepiano became a favored instrument for women, who found the physical act of playing the piano more congruent with modesty. Its expressive potential seemed less dangerous. A Leipzig correspondent described a domestic Viennese musical evening in which "young girls ap-

23. Hanslick, *Geschichte des Concertwesens in Wien,* 202.
24. Frances Trollope, *Vienna and the Austrians,* 2 vols. (Paris, 1838), 2:75–76.

pear one after another, put their piano sonatas out and play on, [joined by] others who sing some arias from the latest operas."[25]

The essential basis of musicality among amateurs (string players and singers alike) in Beethoven's lifetime was the cultivation of pitch recognition and intonation (loosely speaking, the ability to perform in tune), which the amateur string player and singer had to master. Even amateur keyboardists of the time developed sensitive ears (e.g., for tuning instruments), more so than keyboardists later in the century. The remarkable spread, after 1830, of industrially produced pianos that could hold their tune for long periods facilitated the spread of a new kind of amateur— and a different musical literacy upon which music making and listening could be based.

Amateurs in Beethoven's time were required to anticipate pitch from a printed score or reproduce notes learned by rote (particularly with one's voice). The huge Viennese oratorio performances included, among the over 1,000 participants, many members of the second society, high aristocrats, and professionals, who performed with little rehearsal. This was possible only because so many amateurs and professionals could read music and accurately reproduce pitches vocally and on string instruments.[26]

By the 1820s, the decade of Beethoven's late quartets, the explosion in the piano's availability and the spread of published keyboard extracts from Italian opera had begun to diminish the popularity of the quartet form. Though the perception of string players as an elite among musical amateurs continued—an aura of association linked to the era of Mozart and Haydn—a shift from strings and pitch competence to mechanical facility on the keyboard was taking place. Ultimately the four-hand piano arrangements of the late quartets seemed easier and were more accessible than was the original string scoring.

But during Beethoven's life, the string and voice tradition persisted alongside the new developments. By 1827 the quartet form (the Beethoven quartets in particular) had gained augmented status as sophisticated and profoundly communicative pieces aimed at the truly educated. In contrast, the new genres of piano music available in the 1820s assumed the pejorative associations stemming from their more popular appeal.

25. Hanslick, *Geschichte des Concertwesens in Wien*, 202.
26. Hector Berlioz was impressed with the results of these events even in the 1840s. See Leon Botstein, "Music and Its Public: Habits of Listening and the Crisis of Modernism in Vienna, 1870–1914" (Ph.D. diss., Harvard University, 1985).

This aura of social and aesthetic exclusivity was already familiar to the young Beethoven when he arrived in Vienna in 1792. Haydn had elevated the quartet to a position of preeminence in instrumental music,[27] and Reichardt praised the quartet in 1773 for achieving the "full-voiced aspect of harmony" and true discourse through music.[28] In his *Volkommene Kapellmeister* of 1739 (a copy of which Beethoven owned) Johann Mattheson observed that quartet writing required "much more skill and development than usual" in order to permit "a single voice to speak in a conversational manner, with another in an equal manner." In another aesthetic tract owned by Beethoven, C. F. D. Schubart noted that the quartet expressed "the musical universe condensed into one work."[29]

Haydn, Mozart, and Beethoven in turn responded to these perceptions by enhancing the quartet with ever more elaborate and novel strategies of musical realization. For example, the use of counterpoint by both Haydn and Beethoven flattered the self-image of exclusivity and superior discernment among players and listeners by a self-conscious appeal to music history.[30] Beethoven also provided puzzles, jokes, and challenges to his listeners, deflating expectations of easy comprehension with respect to the parallels between music and the assignment of meaning in the imagination.[31] These sorts of complexities, mixed with moments of simplicity and surface clarity, were part of the peculiar intimacy between composer, musician, and listener in early nineteenth-century Vienna.

Through these devices, Beethoven constantly reasserted his own superiority and stature over patron and participant. Even though critical response to the Op. 59 Quartets was lukewarm, reviewers called these works "deeply thought through" and "finely worked out," revealing "a good opinion of the musical public." A flattering contemporary review of Op. 74 concluded that nothing so difficult had ever been written for a quartet. Perhaps the most perceptive comment came from Friedrich

27. See Ferdinand Ries's recollections in Albert Leitzmann, ed., *Ludwig van Beethoven: Berichte der Zeitgenosse,* 2 vols. (Leipzig, 1921), 1:61–63.

28. Johann Friedrich Reichardt, quoted in Ludwig Finscher, "Die Theorie des Streichquartetts," in *Studien zur Geschichte des Streichquartetts: Die Entstehung des klassischen Streichquartetts von den Vorformen zur Grundlegung durch Joseph Haydn* (Kassel, 1974), 287.

29. Finscher, "Theorie des Streichquartetts," 283 and 285. For a review of Beethoven's library see Leitzmann, *Ludwig van Beethoven,* 2:379–83.

30. See Richard Kramer, "Gradus ad Parnassum: Beethoven, Schubert, and the Romance of Counterpoint," *Nineteenth-Century Music* 11 (1987): 107–20.

31. See Maynard Solomon, "The Nobility Pretense," in *Beethoven Essays* (Cambridge, Mass., 1988), 43–55.

Rochlitz in his review of Op. 131, where he divided the public into two classes, one in search of entertainment and the other possessed of an "inner" drive to learn and devote all their spiritual and intellectual abilities to music.[32] In his new work, Beethoven addressed the latter group.

Contemporary critics also acknowledged that Beethoven's quartets could not be mastered by players or listeners upon a single hearing. Even for listeners who could read and "play along" with the written text (or convert sound into notation), the language of the Beethoven quartets was explicitly beyond facile comprehension. The quartets demanded repeated playings and rehearings and study to permit a deeper appreciation of their coherence and shape. This requirement was eased somewhat by the growing popularity of the piano, which encouraged a wider group of potential concertgoers to play the new repertoire on the keyboard at home. It also created a demand for public performances of the original string versions by professionals, which accelerated the shift of such music from domestic amateur to professional, often virtuosic, public display.[33] In part Beethoven sought to be not only strikingly memorable on first hearing but sufficiently intriguing to ensure a magnetic residue that would stimulate a return to a work, thereby defying the inherently ephemeral aspect of musical communication.

Even though Beethoven anticipated professional performances of the Op. 59, 74, and 95 quartets and certainly those after, there was no "mass" public for them before 1830.[34] In 1825 a Leipzig critic observed that Op. 132 lacked the impact of the earlier quartets because it had not been played for a "select" group in a "closed family circle." Instead, it had been performed in the quasi-public surroundings of a "low, oppressive, fully-packed room" (though fewer than 100 could squeeze in) at the inn Zum roten Igel.[35]

An increase in the number of professional performances of the quartets during this period helped the music publishing business to flourish and promoted new interest in music criticism. By the 1820s, connoisseurs and amateurs could subscribe to a variety of musical journals, and public interest in sheet music—particularly stimulated by the growing number of chamber concerts—also flowered. The dynamic between

32. Kunze, ed., *Ludwig van Beethoven*, 2:72; 72; 567.

33. See Hanslick, *Geschichte des Concertwesens in Wien*, 208–58; 324–52.

34. This is so despite Carl Dahlhaus's suggestion; see Carl Dahlhaus, *Ludwig van Beethoven und seine Zeit* (Laaber, 1987), 219–20.

35. Kunze, ed., *Ludwig van Beethoven*, 2:591.

performance and sheet music purchases emphasized the postperfor-
mance absorption by a reading public still intent on amateurism and
learning about music. By the end of Beethoven's life, public performance
in Vienna provided the occasional dramatic spectacle and experience
that supplemented more intimate enjoyment attained through published
arrangements digested in private settings.

Modern listeners are largely unaware of the profound reliance by listeners of the 1820s on their powers of memory. They possessed skills of
musical literacy and active amateurism that enabled them, with varying
success, to recall music once heard and to re-create music they heard in
public through the medium of sheet music. However, by mid-century
the Viennese audience was one whose listening habits had become more
dependent on the piano and written descriptions of music. Hearing had
become directed by reading about music and by simplified guidebooks.[36]
One consequence of these developments was the virtual disappearance
in Vienna of Beethoven's late quartets until the 1850s and 1860s. They
seemed incomprehensible and impenetrable.

Not surprisingly, then, in the later nineteenth-century process of re-
discovery the late quartets assumed special stature as secret, opaque, and
visionary objects requiring special extramusical commentary. After a
performance in Vienna in 1885, Hugo Wolf said that Op. 127 "spoke
to the assemblage and shared with them the wonders of [Beethoven's]
dreamworld."[37]

The Quartets, Politics, and Theater in Beethoven's Vienna

In 1792, the year Beethoven arrived from Bonn, Vienna was the social
and political center of the Habsburg Empire. The political culture of the
empire was shaped during the 1780s by the reforms instituted by Joseph
II, the relentlessly active son of Maria Theresa. These reforms, characterized by later generations as "Josephinism," framed the specific Austrian
outlook on the currents of the eighteenth-century Enlightenment. Beethoven's reading tastes in Bonn and Vienna reflected the influence of the
Enlightenment as well as the distinctive Josephinist appropriation of

36. See also Botstein, "Music and Its Public," vol. 4, and "Music in Vienna, 1848–
1898," in Linda Weintraub and Leon Botstein, eds., *Pre-Modern Art of Vienna, 1848–1898*
(Detroit, 1986).
37. Hugo Wolf, *Musikalische Kritiken* (Leipzig, 1911), 226.

ideas from Protestant German-speaking lands. Both the reaction against Josephinism after 1790 from conservative and liberal quarters and the cult of adulation that developed after Joseph's death defined the particular political world in which Beethoven lived.

The hallmarks of Joseph II's achievements were (1) the integration of tenets of freedom and tolerance into a traditional political framework in which the Catholic church retained a central role, but one subordinate to the state; (2) the systematic centralization of the realm, with Vienna as its economic and bureaucratic core; and (3) the Germanization of the Habsburg Empire with a view to establishing a cultural hegemony whose focal point was Vienna. In 1781 Joseph's Edict of Toleration proclaimed religious freedom for all, including Jews. Later Joseph II extended press freedoms, reformed the judicial and penal systems, and limited the autonomous secular power of the Church. He also founded hospitals, instituted greater protections to children, supported science, culture, and education, and encouraged economic entrepreneurship.

Under Joseph's rule, Vienna flourished. He improved the infrastructure and appearance of the city and its outer districts, which encouraged the aristocracy to spend more time in Vienna during the winter months. Although much of what Joseph attempted was an extension of his mother's initiatives, he pursued his goals with singular earnestness, even impatience. His intolerance of the slow pace of change helped strengthen the myth of his originality. The mix of achievement and myth left a lasting mark on the Habsburg Empire.

Joseph II's successors, Leopold II (1790–92) and Franz II (later Franz I, 1792–1835), who ruled during Beethoven's years of residence in Vienna, mounted a reaction against Joseph's reforms. As a result, Beethoven's Vienna lived self-consciously in the shadow of nostalgia for a great monarch and a progressive political past. Censorship returned to the city's cultural life, even though the economic growth set in motion by Joseph continued.

Fear of a spread of the French Revolution in the early 1790s helped fuel the sharp reaction against Josephinism under Franz II. In 1794, a small group of local Jacobins—pale imitations of their revolutionary brothers in Paris—were tried and sentenced to extreme punishments (in one case, death, which had been banned as a punishment for civilians by Joseph II) for advocating reformist policies. In Viennese politics, the term "Jacobin" would continue to refer to those who in other contexts would have been moderate liberals—men like Joseph Schreyvogel, an acquaintance of Beethoven's who later directed the Burgtheater. He remained abroad until 1796 to avoid prosecution as a Jacobin.[38] After 1794, Viennese political discourse was characterized by timid accommodation and fear of autocratic reprisal. Allusion and satire became the weapons of intellectual resistance and, together with the farce—laced with skepticism and cynicism while based overtly on current conditions—constituted indirect but safe vehicles of public social and political comment.

Two French occupations of Vienna during the Napoleonic Wars strengthened not only the cause of reaction but also the Josephinist tendency toward a German-centered national and cultural identity. French ceased to be the dominant language of Vienna's literate elite. Beethoven's legendary rejection of Napoleon was an example of a wider reaction against French influences among Viennese intellectuals. Beethoven, though essentially out of sympathy with the post-1815 Metternich repression, nevertheless harbored a traditional respect for Habsburg absolutism, Catholicism, and aristocratic privilege and authority.

The key quality of political life during Beethoven's lifetime, despite the tumultuous events, was the triumph of an essential coherence and continuity over the specter of radicalism. Austrian culture in the late eighteenth century had been imperial, aristocratic, and Catholic. Joseph II achieved even greater absolutism through his reforms. In exchange for greater secular political control located in the imperial bureaucracy, Joseph invested the Church with a strong educational role that sought to inculcate his subjects with loyalty and morality. Beethoven, swept up in this trend, displayed in the later years, after 1815, an anti-Enlightenment fascination with new expressions of Catholic religiosity.

Two art forms emblematic of baroque Vienna—music and theater—continued to dominate the city during Beethoven's lifetime. After 1792, however, that domination assumed a special significance. Despite a reactionary framework, new and liberal ideas from the outside kept appearing in a musical or theatrical context. They were camouflaged, of course, through devices of indirection, circumlocution, obscurity, satire, and seemingly innocent and illusionistic fantasy. But the subversive meanings lay evident below the surface.

Music, particularly instrumental music, offered a seemingly apolitical opportunity for people to gather freely. Public performances enabled

---

38. Maren Seliger and Karl Ucakar, *Wien. Politische Geschichte 1740–1934*, 2 vols. (Vienna, 1985), 1:165.

reflective Viennese citizens to engage in a form of significant shared discourse and conversation that might have been circumscribed in other settings. Music became a passionately practiced alternative to spoken or written language—in Wittgenstein's sense, one that could communicate logic and ideas. Music in opera could disguise and distract from the overt significance of an operatic text, making political intervention through censorship less likely than in the conventional theater.

From the 1790s through the mid-1860s, musical events and organizations were among the very few public events relatively immune from political control. The extended instrumental forms that flourished—sonata, symphony, and quartet among them—functioned as surrogate cultural narratives and modes of extramusical exchange and expressive communication. They required the audience to concentrate on, and respond to, meaning and narrative much as in the theater. The response to music also permitted subjective declaration among audiences and performers. Music triggered useful memories, stirred emotions, and more than occasionally evoked ideas. For the listener, the process of decoding out of the text and performance was, of course, difficult. The vitality of printed music criticism can be explained in part by the vacuum of political debate. Ideology inhabited the intense aesthetic discourse concerning musical events.

The true lasting and innovative formal musical achievements of the classical era, which evolved in Vienna in the works of Mozart, Haydn, and Beethoven, can be regarded as consonant with a local cultural tradition. The theatrical and the baroque spectacle of Catholic Habsburg Vienna's sacred ritual provided the seedbed for the dramatic gesture and narrative ambitions of the great classical instrumental repertoire. These, in turn, were later exploited in Vienna by an early nineteenth-century romanticism influenced by developments in northern Germany. In Beethoven's day, the legacy of expressive baroque theatricality permeated the life of the city, from its architecture to its sacred observances. Despite Beethoven's comparatively meager dramatic and operatic output, it would be an oversight not to consider the influence of the theatrical and dramatic conventions that flourished in Vienna on his instrumental music.

The connoisseurs to whom Beethoven addressed his quartets recognized the theatrical element. They took pains to learn the late quartets and to penetrate their quasi-theatrical devices. These consisted of indirect modes of representation concealing simple ideas, the crafting of subtexts beneath a disarming surface, and the use of recollection, remembrance, fragmentation, and resolution to engender emotional response from within a text marked by techniques of masking and circumvention.

In what musical formats were theatrical influences manifest? Certainly one of the most apparent was the effect of Mozart's operatic style and conventions on his own instrumental compositions. Gluck's operas made a deep impression on Beethoven. The concern for the theater can be seen in Beethoven's music for *Fidelio,* Goethe's *Egmont,* and Heinrich von Collin's *Coriolanus.* Beethoven's library was rich with the theatrical works of Schiller, Shakespeare, and Goethe as well as epic poets like Homer and Ossian. Schubert was driven by theatrical ambitions; his deepest hope was to succeed with stage works in Vienna. From the era of Pietro Metastasio (1698–1782) the engagement with the theatrical, as secular narrative experience or in the sacred Catholic ritual, created the dominant Viennese cultural tradition. Beethoven's patrons were, for example, enthusiasts of the theater.

Throughout the political and social ferment of Beethoven's years in Vienna, not only did theater flourish but so, too, did culture in terms of the size of the reading public, paralleling a similar expansion of interest in music. This development reflected the prominence of the second society and the ascent of a Viennese professional middle class, often civil servants, who fueled the enthusiasm for literary German classicism and early romanticism emanating from the north. The year 1809 was a watershed. The brief hiatus in censorship during the French occupation permitted the printing of cheap editions of authors such as Schiller, whose works until then had been hard to get. Beethoven, just three months into the French occupation, asked his publishers to send books as partial payment.[39] Censorship reappeared after 1815, and dissent was essentially banished to the camouflaged phraseologies of theatrical presentation.

Therefore, in the latter years of Beethoven's life, along with the evolution of dance music, the waltz, and the rage for Rossini and Italian opera, came new distinct Viennese outgrowths of the popular theatrical tradition of the later eighteenth century. Fairy tales, historical myths, and fantasy, with thinly veiled political allusions and social meanings, became popular. Satire, farce, and social criticism directed at local conditions eventually merged in the works of Ferdinand Raimund (1790–1836) and

39. Anderson Letters 224.

Johann Nestroy (1801–1862) (who made his theatrical debut as Sarastro).
A notorious habit of employing improvised deviations from censored
texts on stage to make a particular political point became dear to the
Viennese audience. At the same time, serious historical theater flourished (often impelled by the utility of classical themes in the critique of
contemporary politics and culture), exerting considerable influence on
Beethoven's musical strategies, which, after 1815, mirrored a turn to historical models.

The conception of tragedy in history that was celebrated by Viennese
dramatists such as von Collin and Franz Grillparzer was itself steeped in
Austrian Catholic ideology, in which the individual hero was an integral
reflection of part of a stable, fixed notion of God and the world. The
tragic predicament was real (e.g., for *Coriolanus*), but there was no cynicism or fatalism. Whatever the actual human historical outcome or
course of events, the hero remained triumphant in his spiritual com-
pleteness and inner freedom.

The world of the stage was, like life itself, an illusion and a spectacle,
a metaphor for the Church's concept of life's actual boundaries. In its
capture of the individual's spiritual victory over temporal defeat, the
stage became an arena for the "real" in its deepest sense. Given the
equation of stage and life, and life and illusion, the depiction of temporal
tragedy could assume an urgency and an exaggerated aspect without
challenging the axioms of a conservative religious and political world
view. The "real" in the sense of daily life, particularly the tragic predicament of the individual, could be given full voice since it was bounded
by a theology essentially redemptive and dismissive of temporal matters.
The Viennese embrace of the stage as secular analog to the ritual and
revelation of Catholicism enhanced the power of music as a nonreferen-
tial means to communicate essential, even extramusical, truths. Beethoven's Viennese patrons listened to his instrumental music with theatrical
expectations, seeking, through sound, analogs that linked music to
thought.[40] A quite individualistic surface coexisted with a dramatic strategy designed also to pierce temporal time and experience in order to
reveal universal spiritual truth.

40. This discussion is indebted to two seminal monographs on this era: Roger Bauer,
*La réalité royaume de Dieu: Etudes sur l'originalité du théâtre viennois dans la première moitié du
XIXe siècle* (Munich, 1965); and Herbert Seidler, *Österreichischer Vormärz und Goethezeit:
Geschichte einer literarischen Auseinandersetzung* (Vienna, 1982).

Beethoven's deafness kept him at a distance from much Viennese intellectual ferment, but his own reconciliation of classicism and the new romantic impulses can be seen as a musical parallel to the evolution of serious Viennese drama. He shared the enthusiasm for Schiller among contemporary intellectuals. He admired the tragedies of Goethe. Clearly Beethoven sought to emulate aspects of the theatrical in his music, not only in *Fidelio* but in the rhetoric of his instrumental compositions. This narrative dramatic impulse can be seen not only in Beethoven's well-documented later interest in Handel as dramatic master but also in the evolution of his middle-period works.

Owen Jander argues that Beethoven had particular stories and visual references in mind when he composed and that the logic of his instrumental structures become clearer if these underlying narratives are reconstructed.[41] In the Op. 59 no. 2 Quartet, for example, "the star-studded heavens" and "the harmony of the spheres" supposedly inspired the *Adagio*.[42] In theory, then, the mimetic link can be seen (albeit often with difficulty, even in middle-period Beethoven) in the illusionistic fabric of narrative in Beethoven's instrumental works, in a parallel to a descriptive tale. Although the concrete references in the late quartets often become more obscure, the surface theatrical impetus remains.

This link between the traditions of Viennese theater and Beethoven's quartets suggest that these works aimed at carrying the listener and player through a united dramatic experience analogous to opera, the comic theater, and historical or mythic tragedy. Contemporary critics of the quartets often fashioned analogies to painting—to Rubens and Raphael—in an effort to illustrate the link in narrative and formal terms between detail and the whole design in the late quartets. Yet by the early twentieth century Beethoven's achievement ultimately became celebrated as absolute, pure music, contrary to the Lisztian and Wagnerian models.

Nevertheless, understanding the seemingly "abstract" late quartets may depend on grasping Beethoven's use of musical time to evoke a dramatic experience, a sensibility in the listener comparable to the impact of the narrative frame of baroque spectacle and the tragic drama.

41. Jander's example was the Fourth Piano Concerto, particularly the second movement. See "Beethoven's 'Orpheus in Hades': The Andante con moto of the Fourth Piano Concerto," *Nineteenth-Century Music* 8 (1985): 195–212. See also Dahlhaus, *Ludwig van Beethoven*, 167–78.

42. Kerst, *Die Erinnerungen an Beethoven*, 1:52–53 and 62–63.

The quartets, in fact, may have been impelled explicitly by so-called extramusical narrative impulses.[43]

Beethoven's use of single instruments as leading voices (e.g., in Op. 132), the recitatives, interrogatives, and dialogic conventions (e.g., Op. 135), all harken back to models from the stage—something different from the painterly-poetic ambitions of Mendelssohn's instrumental works or the literary tone poems and program music of Franz Liszt and Richard Strauss. Direct imitative description or the elucidation of a poetic or epic program were not the issue. Beethoven's strategy was to adapt classical musical procedures to serve dramatic purposes. He created a family resemblance (in Wittgenstein's sense) to the theater.

The string quartet therefore offered an ideal format for an autonomous complex dramatic narration demanding a high degree of musical comprehension. The meanings, in the extramusical sense, were hidden by the fact of music and the complexity of Beethoven's elaborations. The quartet was, by tradition, a conversational/discursive, but not narrowly mimetic, form of exchange and response among four equal characters (players) directed at a literate public. Meaning in Beethoven's quartets from Op. 59 on can be constructed, therefore, in light of the vital additional influence that theatrical and dramatic practices—including indirection and allusion—exercised within the intellectual milieu of Beethoven's Vienna.[44]

The Quartets, Literature, and Philosophy in Vienna

During the last twenty years of Beethoven's life—and particularly the last twelve, from 1815 on—literary romanticism from the Germanic north rose to prominence in Vienna and throughout Austria. At the

---

43. See Robin Wallace, *Beethoven's Critics: Aesthetic Dilemmas and Resolutions during the Composer's Lifetime* (Cambridge, 1986), 2–3; 57–61.

44. In his treatise *Vom Musikalisch-Schönen* (1854), Eduard Hanslick argued against the use of parallels to language in music. He cited examples where the attempt to incorporate aspects of speech and linguistic narrative in instrumental works led to musical ugliness (*Unschönheit*). Hanslick, who later in the same work denigrated the Ninth Symphony, criticized "smaller" instrumental works that use contrasts, cadenzas, recitatives, mysterious moments, and interruptions of the melodic and the rhythmic flow, techniques that "disorient" the listener. Hanslick's attack, by its description of the culprit and the frequent discussion of Beethoven in the same portion of the text, seems directed at the late quartets.

same time, new local forms of dance, song, and poetry emerged, lending the period its distinctive character and name, *Biedermeier*. The protracted Congress of Vienna, with its stellar cast of characters, not only gave the city heightened political prestige but helped enlarge its economic and cultural stock as well. Private and public social events proliferated, establishing a practice of lavish parties and balls that persisted long after the congress had adjourned.

As Vienna grew into a center of diplomacy, entertainment, and gala social life, Beethoven's already not inconsiderable fame also increased steadily. By the time of his death he had long been a local legend. His funeral was one of the largest public gatherings since the Congress of Vienna. Its aura was enhanced by the fact that he was as famous as a mythic figure as he was as a familiar fellow citizen. He had been isolated from much of the city's mainstream by his deafness and the deaths of long-standing friends. This social distance mirrored the fact that his artistic roots in an eighteenth-century world harked back to an earlier age. The music he wrote between 1815 and 1827 was plainly out of step with contemporary fashion.

Beethoven flirted in his last years with the notion of moving to London, a reflection not only of his growing international fame but also his sense of loneliness and impatience with the Viennese public. The new rage for virtuosos (primarily Paganini), local dance music, and for Weber and Rossini annoyed and frustrated him.[45] Much of this early local Biedermeier culture was fueled by newcomers to Vienna from the less sophisticated hinterlands. Yet an elite interested in the musical traditions and conventions of the past persisted. It was made up of the members of the Society of the Friends of Music, Beethoven's musical colleagues, his remaining friends, and a cluster of younger admirers, including Schubert, to whom he was nearly a god.

It is within this context that Beethoven's relationship to romanticism in philosophy and art can be understood, particularly with respect to the character of his later music. Beethoven was intrigued with one crucial aesthetic controversy of the time, the clash of eighteenth-century Viennese religious and philosophical traditions with German romanticism and idealism. The literary by-products of this collision, among them a new taste for irony, humor, fantasy, and the jocular (*der Scherz*), helped shape the quartets of Beethoven.[46]

45. See Hanson, *Musical Life,* 102–8; and *Bürgersinn und Aufbegehren: Biedermeier und Vormärz in Wien, 1815–48* (Vienna, 1988), 80–91; 126–37.
46. See Dahlhaus, *Ludwig van Beethoven,* 94–99.

A by-product of the Viennese encounter with the romantic movement was a group of new local literary journals, including Schreyvogel's
Sonntagsblatt (1807–9), which was hostile to the new movement, and
the more sympathetic journal *Prometheus* (1808), of which Beethoven
possessed a complete set. These developments also lent Friedrich Schlegel's famous lecture series on art and drama in 1808 a historic significance. Schlegel's Viennese appearance helped to further delineate the
distinctions between the new romantics and the classical Weimar tradition associated with Lessing, Schiller, and Goethe. Despite bureaucratic
efforts at obstruction, the fifteen-lecture series finally began on 31
March. Many of Beethoven's friends and patrons—Lobkowitz and his
wife, Dietrichstein, Schwarzenberg, Kinsky, the two brothers Collin,
Palffy—were subscribers, along with the elite of Viennese aristocracy
and cultural leadership (including Prince Metternich himself).

Goethe, whom Beethoven admired, embodied a new classicism based
on the tension between reason and pure logic on the one hand and
emotion, visual perception, and love on the other—a tension that could
be resolved only in notions of beauty and organic unity. Goethe domi-
nated the literary scene because he carried forward the heritage of Lessing and Winckelmann while setting the stage for the romantic reaction.
But after 1800, Goethe's sympathies pulled him increasingly away from
romanticism toward the neoclassic model of poetic diction he exhibited
in *Faust,* Part Two.

But it was Schiller who exerted the strongest influence on Beethoven
and the romantic generation of early nineteenth-century Vienna. Schiller sought to understand the relation between poetry and nature and to
reconcile the sensual and the historical with the ideal. Schiller argued
that aesthetic education was necessary to induce human beings to act in
the rational, ethical manner suggested by Kant's moral philosophy.
Beauty, even in its highest form, was contingent, flawed, and capricious,
yet potentially ethically good—a response to the "play drive" (*Spieltrieb*)
in humans. Here lay the basis for the subsequent glorification, during
the nineteenth century, of the artist and art as central to the history,
politics, and morals of humanity, as a rational surrogate for religion.[47]

Against this background, Schlegel's lectures constituted a radical intervention. Aesthetics left the normative realm of Schiller's discourses.

47. See Friedrich Schiller, *On the Aesthetic Education of Man in a Series of Letters* (English and German texts), ed. E. M. Wilkinson and L. A. Willoughby (Oxford, 1967),
25–29 and 163–67.

Aesthetic meaning became measured not entirely against an ideal absolute conception but rather against the subjective intent of the individual and the historical context and function of art. Individuality—the particular self—became the starting point of art. The subjective experience is embraced as the means by which the ineffable is approached. At the same time the subjective culminates in the construction of historical progress. The new romantic artist had to transcend classicism and pursue the new and infinite, knowing that art and humankind would evolve. In place of aesthetic absolutes came a faith in the progressive development of art in history. The validity of historical objectivity in assessing the evolution of art was asserted. In his lectures, Schlegel also invoked the role of religion in art, a role that contrasted with the rationalists of the Enlightenment. Art and religion, he felt, could shape the connection between the mundane and the eternal. At the same time, Schlegel called for the rejection of rationalism and the restoration of religion—by which he meant Catholicism—in the education of humanity.

The reaction to Schlegel in Vienna was mixed. Schreyvogel (right after the lectures) and Grillparzer (who read them in 1817) attacked Schlegel in an effort to redeem classicism's emphasis on fixed norms and objective beauty. The vague notion of reconciling artistic and spiritual contradictions into a higher mystical unity was rejected by the Viennese conservatives. They favored a more traditional notion in which art celebrated history and nature as part of God's stage on which the individual struggled freely with authentic if not tragic constant limits. Through his reading of the journal *Prometheus,* Beethoven was aware of this struggle between the heritage of Schiller and Goethe and the claims of the early German romantics. Given the controversy surrounding Schlegel's lectures and his friendship with many who attended them—not to mention the importance of such discourse among the intellectuals of Vienna—he surely must have reflected on the central issues of the debates.

Schlegel's ideas and the reactions to the new romanticism influenced the late Beethoven quartets. Indeed, their structure and contents mirrored the philosophical tensions of the aesthetic debate, achieving a spiritual purity and authenticity through the use of highly personalized musical language drawn from personal reflections on the subjective historical moment. Contemporary observers noted that the surface of the late quartets was marked by breaks in continuity, moments of pure fantasy and irony, apparent inner dialogue, anger, and the rhetoric of spiritual struggle—hallmarks of the struggle by a romantic artist to break free of the formal canons of classicism. In 1825, reviewing Op. 132, one critic concluded that he was dealing with a true romantic, "our musical Jean Paul."[48]

For example, the quartets from Op. 59 encountered resistance (readily overcome) because of their technical demands and dramatic length. "Long and difficult," wrote the *Allgemeine musikalische Zeitung* in Leipzig in 1807, as it observed in a review that the three quartets were not *allgemeinfasslich*—"not generally accessible." Fourteen years later, the same journal still complained that these quartets were "significant" but "unpopular," utilizing "bizarre sounds."[49] Most contemporary critics viewed the quartets from 1809 to 1827 as innovative and challenging, if only for their striking sonorities and discontinuities. The later quartets were hailed as examples of the power of the subjective and the inspired flight of a unique imagination into the infinite. (Karl Holz reported that Beethoven regarded the C-sharp minor Quartet as his finest.)[50]

Fitting as transcendental an artist as Beethoven into a neat category has proved an exercise in frustration for more than one musical historian. Carl Dahlhaus suggested that although Beethoven's usages, even those as transparent on the surface as in the Op. 18 Quartets, were suggestive of the early romantics, he was not necessarily a romantic: "The shared characteristic is that the form does not emanate from the development of an original formulation, but out of pieces, that in retrospect, from the vantage point of the end itself, appear as an internally closed whole."[51]

The ambiguities, abstractions, and contrasts in the late works, however, may reflect Beethoven's explicit struggle to create a formal, classical whole from individualistic impulses derived from overtly subjective experience. In so doing he took part in the local contemporary conflict over the nature of drama and the concept of tragedy.[52] The late quartets were no longer designed to be comprehensible in terms of classical conventions. They required a romantic appreciation and a self-conscious

48. Kunze, ed., *Ludwig van Beethoven,* 2:208–9 and 591.

49. Reprinted in ibid., 2:72.

50. Kerst, *Die Erinnerungen an Beethoven,* 2:188.

51. Dahlhaus, *Ludwig van Beethoven,* 94–99; 217–21; 282–83.

52. The divisions between classical formal and "emotional" content analysis may be less striking or irreconcilable than some might think. Classicism and the romantic emphasis on extramusical significance—the philosophical and emotional centrality of music, or the debate between absolute and program music—may obscure coherences of so-called musical and extramusical impulses in Beethoven. See Wallace, *Beethoven's Critics,* 148–52.

probing of emotional memory by composer, player, and listener uncharacteristic of Beethoven's earlier music.

As one critic noted, one no longer "knew" in Op. 127 what one saw, heard, or felt as a result of following the music. Penetrating a work by grasping its formal structure epistemologically was no longer sufficient. A new kind of listening was being asked for. In 1828 A. B. Marx said the Op. 132 could be compared with the works of Heinrich von Kleist in its multileveled, almost "overstimulated" sources of meaning, feeling, and narrative. Like a tragic drama, these pieces contained monologues, soliloquies, dialogues, abrupt changes in scene and mood, moments of description, as well as gestures of response, inquiry, and deep meditation. Despite obscurities, musical action (so to speak) unfolded to reveal a "plot" whose end and subjective protagonist cast the entire work into a unified, meaningful whole.

A contemporary critic in 1826 observed that no "anatomical" analysis of the details would give a sense of the "totality" of Op. 127. In 1828, writing of Op. 131, the critic of *Cäcilia,* a journal published in Mainz, noted that Beethoven's work required careful study and compared Beethoven's intent to that of the *Dichter,* the poet: "Nowhere is it less permissible . . . to content oneself with the appreciation of individual details. For it is precisely through the realization of the total impression that the single idea [of] the poet is revealed."[53] The elements of the late quartets that at first taxed or baffled the hearers and critics by their nearly romantic originality of expression could ultimately be reconciled through careful study and rehearing, revealing an organic totality ironically related to and derived from criteria of classical unity. In this sense Beethoven and Goethe can be fruitfully compared in their respective struggles with classical and romantic impulses.

Finale: The Accumulated History of Listening to the Quartets

The relationship in Beethoven's last works between music and speech, and therefore between instrumental music and poetry/drama, was not lost on his contemporaries. His music was interpreted in terms of language and those art forms that used language. The issue of language as a metaphor of musical communication framed the aesthetic controversies

53. Kunze, ed., *Ludwig van Beethoven,* 2:575.

of the early nineteenth century. Ludwig Rellstab penetrated the romantic elements of Beethoven's art in 1825 when he identified the communicative dimensions of Op. 127:

> Thank heaven that there is still sufficient closeness between him and us for us to share a common language for our feelings, even if it is not completely comprehensible. . . . Beethoven has spoken with us in a way that is awe-inspiring and moves us to the depths. It is a somber message . . . the calm expression of suffering resisted by a soul that is deeply wounded but equally inspired by hope. It is the manly suffering of a Laocoon, which weaves its secret threads throughout the entire work, even in the profound scherzo where it seems to make fun of itself and in so doing only moves us to a deeper and more stirring response.[54]

Already with Op. 59, and certainly with the late quartets, there seemed something futuristic about the language and aesthetic of these pieces. This awareness that the work was not only difficult but novel in a way that future generations might better appreciate was indeed prescient. In the decades immediately after Beethoven's death, the sense that the late quartets possessed a unique, progressive, yet common communicative language was lost. By the turn of the century they experienced a renaissance. They were viewed as exemplars of the crisis of language and the failure of language to communicate and to enlighten. The quartets responded to those at the fin de siècle in search of a self-consciously modern sensibility.

Compare Rellstab's statement with Grillparzer's observation from 1834 that Beethoven's work exerted a negative as well as a positive influence. Grillparzer objected to the composer's use of excessive lyrical outbursts that "expanded the concept of order and connection of a musical work" beyond reasonable limits. But most of all—and here Grillparzer had the late quartets in mind—Beethoven encouraged the substitution of a classical emphasis on form with the notion of undisciplined personal expression. Beethoven fostered the illusion that music can be based merely on "the interesting, the strong . . . that which shatters and makes one drunk."[55]

Grillparzer's judgment of late Beethoven in terms of aesthetic norms was considered definitive for decades. A centenary festival was held in

---

54. Ibid., 2:550–51.

55. Franz Grillparzer, *Sämtliche Werke*, ed. Moritz Necker, 16 vols. (Leipzig, 1903), 15:199–200.

Vienna in 1870, when the cult of Beethoven was at a peak, particularly among the new and growing middle class. In this period of economic expansion and political liberalism—the so-called *Gründerzeit*—Beethoven (though not the late work) had become the cultural property of a new breed of listeners-concertgoers with limited musical literacy based usually on keyboard instruction, or philistines who engaged in public musical culture as means of social assertion and display.[56]

A superficial appreciation of Beethoven among these concertgoers was encouraged by Wagner's growing popularity and his evocation of Beethoven as a romantic rebel and as the inspiration for the music drama. Even the late works had a new programmatic meaning imposed on them. This mode of interpretation prevailed well into the early 1900s. An opposing element within the Viennese musical community, drawing on the traditions of Schumann, Mendelssohn, and Brahms, also considered Beethoven the central figure in music history but asserted, in defense of a new musical classicism, that the late music was entirely abstract. Both groups celebrated the romantic dimensions of Beethoven's late works—the subjective, extreme, and personal—about which Grillparzer was so dubious. And both regarded the late quartets as an esoteric and opaque treasure.

The prominent Viennese music critic Theodor Helm, an ardent supporter of Bruckner, summed up the later nineteenth-century view of Beethoven in an 1885 monograph: "Still today, among all the creations of Beethoven," he wrote of the late quartets, "they are the least understood and most in need of a psychological and musical commentary." Unlike their predecessors, they were "entirely individual, extremely personal, subjective, and wholly divorced from the outside world."[57]

It was not until the twentieth-century modernist attack on romanticism that the late quartets were seen again as formal achievements that redeemed the autonomous character of musical language and musical structure. It seemed necessary to rescue these precious gems from Wagnerians such as Helm. What remained hidden from Arnold Schoenberg and Heinrich Schenker—proponents of this modernist view—were the historically valid, dramatic, and narrative musical conventions that actually influenced Beethoven. They revived the notion that a true appreciation of late Beethoven required an elite audience

56. See Daniel Spitzer's satirical feuilleton, "Das Beethoven Jubiläum" in *Wiener Spaziergänge,* 6 vols. (Vienna, 1879), 2:163–67.

57. Theodor Helm, *Beethovens Streichquartette* (Leipzig, 1921), iv and 168.

with a new standard of appreciation of music as an autonomous art. Psychological, poetic, or descriptive aids were categorically rejected.

These polemical giants of the fin de siècle were blind to the importance for Beethoven himself of music as speech and language. They conceded that instrumental music could parallel linguistic art forms but could not concede that Beethoven's music actually could be understood with validity not only "autonomously" but as a vehicle of ordinary communication and expression for composer, player, and listener as an alternative mode of speech, poetic diction, and dramatic narration. As Rellstab recognized, part of Beethoven's achievement was his use of music as language in at once a comprehensible and yet ambiguous and secret manner, permitting the intimacy and profundity of genuine communication.

In retrospect, both Hofmannsthal and Wittgenstein (neither of them professional musicians but both steeped in musical tradition) provided the most subtle, historically grounded, and balanced reassessment of Beethoven's music in the twentieth century. Particularly for a modern listening audience with access to repeated flawless performances, the quartets represent a logical and powerful effort to speak with music of the deepest issues of meaning and life.

At issue for both Beethoven and his listeners, even 200 years afterwards, is the struggle to conceive and transmit the sense of beauty and goodness and the inner struggles with matters of existential meaning and truth in a way at once general and overarching and also individual and specific to the moment of hearing. In the cultural context of this century, in which ordinary language has become the object of distrust, music without words remains a refuge, a nearly logical but not mimetic mode of expression. In late Beethoven, the expression aspires to prophecy; to communicate across time and space, to connect the human community through a shared perception of art. Beethoven's musical and metaphysical achievement in the quartets is no less than the authentic attainment of aspirations that elude speech.

Beethoven's discourse in the quartets cannot be corrupted or invalidated by repetition and familiarity. Their inexhaustibility and uncompromised vitality have confronted past auditors and modern listeners alike. Wittgenstein, in a conversation with John King in the 1930s, captured best the paradox that the quartets communicate immediately yet at the same time elude a fixed description and precise reduction into comprehension. King recounted how "I once put on the second, third and fourth movements of Beethoven's Quartet in C-sharp minor, Op. 131. . . . [Wittgenstein] was rapt in his attention and most excited at the end of the playing. He jumped up as if something had suddenly struck him and said, 'How easy it is to think that you understand what Beethoven is saying' (and here he seized a pencil and a piece of paper) 'how you think you have understood the projection' (and he drew two thirds of a circle, thus): 'and then suddenly' (and here he added a bulge): 'you realize that you haven't understood anything at all.' "[58]

This daunting observation illuminates why the Beethoven of the quartets—perhaps the most complex and richest achievement of his musical output—can never, in Hofmannsthal's terms, be rendered mute.

58. Rush Rhees, ed., *Recollections of Wittgenstein* (New York, 1984), 69–70.

The Sequoia String Quartet was formed in Los Angeles in 1972. Pictured here, from left to right, are its members from 1975 to 1985: Robert Martin (cello), Miwako Watanabe (violin), Yoko Matsuda (violin), and James Dunham (viola).

The Quartets in Performance:
A Player's Perspective

ROBERT MARTIN

The decisions that shape performances of chamber music works are often supported by explicitly given reasons. This is so, in chamber music more than in other kinds of music making, perhaps because chamber music players must persuade their colleagues if they wish to realize their own musical ideas. Solo performers, except in teaching, have no need to verbalize their musical ideas, or the reasons behind particular decisions, if indeed these decisions are based on reasons. Conductors may choose to explain, but they need not persuade.

The Sequoia Quartet, of which I was a member, spent countless hours grappling with the decisions that needed to be made. We discussed, argued, and experimented in rehearsals; we even experimented in concerts and discussed these experiments in subsequent rehearsals (or immediately after the concert in a cab on the way back to the hotel). Besides the difficulties in arriving at the decisions themselves, there was the difficulty in understanding the decision-making process. This essay is the result of my attempt to answer the question, What principles, if any, guide decision making in chamber music? It represents only one player's perspective, obviously, and is only a first step in developing that

I received helpful comments on earlier drafts from A. Donald Anderson, Tyler Burge, Curt Cacioppo, James Dunham, Richard Goode, Robert Levin, Sylvia Martin, Robert Winter, and Kathleen Wright. A version of this paper was read at Haverford College in March 1989.

perspective into a general account. It is addressed to the general reader, not to professional musicians.

I start by describing bits of imagined rehearsals, mixed with my own observations and those I have collected from interviews with members of other string quartets. This first section can be thought of as providing data for the somewhat more theoretical discussion of the rest of the paper. In the second section I will attempt to classify the decisions that are in fact made. The last section concerns principles that govern those decisions.

Rehearsals

A young professional string quartet begins its first rehearsal of Beethoven's Quartet in B Flat, Op. 130. They are in awe of the work and filled with excitement at the prospect of learning it. How do they begin?

They start, characteristically, by reading the first movement through. The first violinist chooses a tempo and leads rather forcefully, especially after fermatas and at tempo changes. They listen, watch each other, and try to play their own parts well. They call out occasionally: "That was too much ritard." "Sorry, I was too loud." "Ouch!"

A great deal is accomplished in reading. Because the group has played together for several years, and has studied and performed several other Beethoven quartets, they have developed patterns and habits of interpretation. They have also learned to communicate effectively with very few words or with no words at all. As they read, they identify passages as examples of musical gestures with which they are familiar. For example, they carry the crescendo in the first measure of Example 1 to the very last moment, even stretching the pulse slightly, and then they "place" the following *subito piano* downbeat (i.e., delaying the downbeat slightly). This way of playing from a *crescendo* to *subito piano* is one that they have discussed and rehearsed in other contexts, and now it happens almost automatically. Similarly, the slight relaxation of tempo going into a fermata and the way in which a new tempo is established after the fermata are already part of the group's musical language and are communicated with subtle gestures or glances.

Many decisions are made without speaking. As similar phrases are tossed back and forth, one player may appreciate a phrasing, style of articulation, or particular kind of bowstroke "suggested" by another and adopt it. Sometimes there are reversals, in which two players silently

EXAMPLE 1.   Op. 130, first movement, mm. 1–2

resolve to imitate what the other has done; as they come to parallel passages later in the work, they discover with amusement that they have simply switched with each other. Often by the end of the first reading it is clear which bowings work best for characteristic, often-repeated motifs and how the main recurrent phrases are most naturally shaped. Extended discussion has been rendered unnecessary by musical "discussion."

The main purpose of the reading, however, is not to settle matters of detail but to get the feel of the piece: to activate the intuitions that become the raw data for the rehearsal process that follows. The movement's overall mood and color, its organization into sections, and those sections' general functions—transition, development, intensification, waning of energy, comic relief—these are what each player ponders. Ideas may not be grasped consciously at this point; they surface as opinions only later as the rehearsal progresses, pulled out of the experience of playing and listening.

After the reading, the first violinist, without comment, plays the running sixteenth-note passage that begins the first *Allegro* (shown in Ex. 2) and experiments with different articulations. The others comment: "Maybe a little shorter." "What would it sound like slightly off the string?" Everyone realizes that this is a crucial decision for all of them, since this figure runs throughout the piece in all voices—it is one of the two or three most important ideas of the piece. "What does Beethoven

EXAMPLE 2.   Op. 130, first movement, mm. 15–19

mean by *non ligato?*" (*Ligato* is Beethoven's spelling of *legato*.) In modern string terminology, *legato* means to play several notes smoothly under one bow; in that sense, the passage is obviously *non legato* because there are no slur marks. What more does Beethoven want? The first violinist experiments with a slightly stiff-armed, accented, detached stroke. The cellist worries that the sound is too loaded with musical connotations— "sounds too much like baroque style." Off the string sounds wrong to all of them—too light, capricious, not serious enough. A solution is found, for now at least: there should be a lot of energy in the bow changes, to give as much intensity as possible. Beethoven wrote *non legato* so it won't be like this: the violist illustrates with smooth bow changes. Now the second violinist joins with the countersubject in quarters and eighths. "How long should these quarter notes be?" Again, there are experiments and comments. "Which voice is more important?" "They're equally important." "The quarters have to be quite marked—long, but with accents—to come through clearly."

There is an interesting complexity beneath the surface of this discussion. The quartet members know how these passages sound in various recordings. Some may actually have listened to a favorite recording recently—others avoid this when they are studying a piece. But in all cases there are recollections of live and recorded performances that certainly influence the players. They try hard to ignore these influences, to make decisions with fresh ears and open minds; there is a natural striving for something that will distinguish their performance. But at the same time, the performance traditions surrounding the Beethoven quartets have an undeniable hold on most players. Their love of these works came in most cases from hearing certain recordings as children; their teachers are often the very artists who played those recorded performances. Further, the young players are acutely aware that audiences know the works not from scores but from recordings. Even when details of recorded interpretations are not remembered, there is a feeling of rightness that is associated with particular solutions to interpretive questions. Does this feeling of rightness—about a tempo, a texture, a sound, a bowstroke—come from personal musical convictions or from recollection of the performances that we happened to hear? Uncertainty about this complicates the rehearsal process. For example, when one player feels convinced of an unusual idea and meets with resistance, she may suspect that her colleagues resist simply because they are used to hearing the passage another way.

The players begin to work on a difficult passage in octaves, two measures before the second ending (Ex. 3). Intonation here is difficult; there is also disagreement about how much ritard to make while going into the fermata. None is indicated in the score, and so out of curiosity the players try the passage with the tempo strictly maintained. "It sounds awful." "The music unwinds at this point; we have to let it unwind." "It feels abrupt and mechanical." The players agree that some ritard is needed. But how much? The discussion proceeds by experimentation. One way of playing the second ending slows the pace into that of Tempo I; another way of playing it (with less ritard) makes Tempo I seem more of a surprise. What the players decide will be related to the way they treat similar seams throughout the piece.

EXAMPLE 3.   Op. 130, first movement, mm. 90–95

The Allegretto *(Third Movement) of the Quartet in
E Minor, Op. 59 No. 2*

The problem under consideration in this movement is that Beethoven's metronome marking is 69 to the measure (Ex. 4). The group begins by trying the movement at that tempo; it is very fast, much faster than they are used to hearing it. "It can work if we play very lightly," says one of the players. "It sounds downright silly," says another. They all agree that the fact that Beethoven did give a metronome indication merits serious consideration, but it is not at all clear that they will follow that indication.

The parts the players use do not have the Beethoven metronome

EXAMPLE 4. Op. 59 no. 2, third movement, mm. 1–9

markings—even most full scores do not have the metronome markings, even though there is no question as to Beethoven's seriousness in assigning the metronome marks. Only a few decades ago, as Rudolf Kolisch pointed out in a now famous article, most professional quartets were ignorant of, or dismissed, Beethoven's metronome markings.[1] The situation today is that, although the marks are not scrupulously followed, most groups at least take them seriously. "Beethoven's marking for the slow movement is perfect (60 to the quarter)—so why should we doubt his marking for the *Allegretto?*"

"Look, we play the slow movement around 60 because that feels right

1. Rudolf Kolisch, "Tempo and Character in Beethoven's Music," *Musical Quarterly* 29 (1943): 169–87 and 291–312; revised version in *Musical Quarterly* 77 (1993): 90–131 and 268–342.

EXAMPLE 5.   Op. 59 no. 2, third movement, mm. 129–35

to us—our reaction to the metronome marking is that he got it right! In the *Allegretto* he gives a tempo that feels wrong."

"It may feel wrong to you. I think we will get used to it, and anyway, it's what he wanted! You're not denying that, are you?"

A different tack: "This movement has a quality of sadness, wistfulness, that we must try to capture. Look at the closing figure in the cello, before the da capo [Ex. 5], and the falling intervals in the first violin part at the opening [Ex. 4]. I think that quality of sadness is lost if we play the movement as fast as 69 to the bar."[2]

Mischa Schneider told us (the Sequoia String Quartet) an interesting story about the tempo of this movement. The Budapest Quartet played the movement rather quickly, he said, until they were convinced otherwise by criticism of the conductor, George Szell. Szell sang the Russian folk tune of the trio (Ex. 6) as it appears in Mussorgsky's opera *Boris Godunov*, where it has a rather *pesante* flavor, quite restrained in tempo.

On the other hand, it would be just like Beethoven to enjoy the humor of drastically transforming the musical meaning of the simple folk tune. There is support for this toward the end of the trio, when the tune is subjected to a kind of whiplash treatment (Ex. 7). The fast tempo is

2. This was the point of view expressed to me by Paul Katz in explaining some of the considerations that led the Cleveland Quartet to their choice of tempo for this movement. Katz cited the expression "broken-winged gaiety," applied to this movement by J. W. N. Sullivan in his *Beethoven: His Spiritual Development* (New York, 1927), 108.

EXAMPLE 6.   Op. 59 no. 2, third movement, mm. 52–57

EXAMPLE 7.   Op. 59 no. 2, third movement, mm. 110–16

also supported by the good feeling of playing the opening of the trio at that tempo, where the rolling triplet figure "goes like the wind."[3]

What finally happens? The group realizes it has to make a decision— at least a preliminary decision, subject to change after trying it in a few performances—yet no considerations, so far, seem entirely decisive as to the tempo. So they decide to try to play the movement at the indicated metronome marking, and very lightly, with the hope that the fast tempo will not make the performance sound frantic.

The First Movement of the Quartet in F Minor, Op. 95

Again the issue is one of tempo since this movement contains another of the problematic metronome indications of Beethoven. (It should be mentioned that there are only a handful of notoriously problematic tempo marks in the Beethoven quartets. The ones that come to mind are the minuet of Op. 18 no. 5, movements 1 and 2 of Op. 18 no. 6, the *Adagio* of Op. 59 no. 1, the *Allegretto* of Op. 59 no. 2, the finale of Op. 59 no. 3, and the first movement of Op. 95. There are no metronome markings for the quartets after Op. 95.)[4]

The metronome marking is 92 to the half note. The opening of the movement (Ex. 8) as well as the closing sound wonderful to the players at this fast tempo. But the second theme of the movement, announced by the viola, presents a problem (Ex. 9): "It sounds terribly rushed and out of character at this tempo." "We can't really play the first and second themes at noticeably different tempos," says one member. On this basis, a somewhat slower tempo is chosen for the movement.

According to cellist Paul Katz, most modern quartets feel uncomfortable about changing tempos markedly within a movement when there

---

3. In a discussion of the tempo of this movement, Curt Cacioppo suggested that at 69 to the measure, but not at a substantially slower tempo, one can perceive an interesting rhythmic shift in the *Allegretto*: the F in the second measure of the first violin part (see Ex. 4) can be heard as an upbeat to a 6/8 pulse, beginning on the D sharp and lasting for eight measures.

4. There is evidence that Beethoven intended to supply metronome marks for the late quartets (letters of 28 January and the end of December 1826 to B. Schott's Sons); he wrote in the latter: "Do wait for them. In our century such indications are certainly needed" (*Letters of Beethoven*, ed. Emily Anderson, 3 vols. [London, 1961], letter 1545).

EXAMPLE 8.   Op. 95, first movement, mm. 1–5

EXAMPLE 9.   Op. 95, first movement, mm. 24–27

is no special marking to that effect.[5] It is felt that the unity of the move-ment requires a fairly high degree of constancy of pulse. Nowadays it seems objectionably self-indulgent to change tempos (except very sub-tly) to accommodate the second theme.

A closely related issue comes up in theme-and-variation movements such as the *Andante cantabile* of Op. 18 no. 5 and, particularly, the *Adagio ma non troppo* of Op. 127. It is important to capture the character of each variation, and there is consequently a natural tendency to indulge in slight, or not-so-slight, adjustments in tempo. There is the related ques-tion of connections between variations—should the pulse flow fairly steadily from one to the next (where no fermata or other special indica-tion is present), or should each variation be brought to a close with a small ritard and with a pause before the next?

These are very perplexing matters for performers, particularly because one feels that Beethoven might have offered a straightforward answer. Would you like all the variations in the same tempo? Or are you happy to have us alter the tempos of the variations to suit the material? Does your answer apply generally to variation movements or only to this set of variations? As we struggle with such questions, it is hard to resist the feeling that there is a right answer, if only we could find it. We need occasionally to be reminded that, as David Hamilton aptly comments, "most composers, far from thinking in terms of a single definitive perfor-mance, instead relish the variety of interpretations that result when different gifted individuals play their music."[6] There may, of course, be right answers to particular questions and not to others.

Classification: Kinds of Decisions to Be Made

The decisions we need to make seem to fall into seven interrelated areas: (1) overall character; (2) tempo; (3) tone color; (4) rhythmic contours; (5) dynamics and balance; (6) phrasing; and (7) intonation.

---

5. I encountered a contrary view in talking with László Mezo, cellist of the Bartók String Quartet. He took it as a matter of course that first and second themes in Beetho-ven first movements should have different tempos; he explained that Beethoven "wasn't allowed" to indicate these tempo differences within a movement or he certainly would have. In general, the Bartók Quartet, according to Mezo, does not give very great im-portance to Beethoven's metronome marks, finding that they are often not "best for the audience."

6. David Hamilton, *The Listener's Guide to Great Instrumentalists* (New York, 1982), 14.

I mean to use the word "decision" here in a rather broad way, to include not only decisions made consciously but also the intuitive, non-reflective doings that are common with gifted players. For example, a subtle adjustment of tone color in response to a change in harmony may constitute a musical decision, as I use the term, even if it is not performed consciously. That same adjustment might be a matter of conscious decision for another; even the same player may have worked consciously, on earlier occasions, to make such tonal adjustments so that now the response is automatic. It would be difficult in any particular case to say whether what appears to be intuitive and nonreflective is actually the result of earlier learned behavior that has become habitual or is genuinely instinctive (unlearned). The distinction is not important for my purposes; the mark of a musical decision is that it could be otherwise without constituting a clear-cut mistake. Playing the right pitches is not a matter of musical decision; nor does one have to decide not to add a beat to every measure. Decision making applies to areas of interpretive discretion.

1. *Overall character.*   What is the overall character and mood of each movement or section? Is there a texture or particular quality (for example, improvisatory, mechanical, controlled, or jagged) that is appropriate for a given section? The decision regarding overall character has wide-ranging effects. Tempo, rhythmic contour, and tone color, discussed below, are often determined by a decision about the mood of the movement. Influences often go in the other direction as well: decisions about tempo, for example, based perhaps on a metronome marking, can have a strong influence on a decision about the character of a section.

There is strikingly little explicit discussion of mood and characterization in most quartet rehearsals, given how important these matters are to listeners. Does the opening of Op. 131 express loneliness, tragedy, religious fervor, spiritual resignation, or something else? Are the opening measures of Op. 127 triumphant? What is the right mood for the opening of Op. 59 no. 1? Are the last measures of Op. 135 humorous? Many performers are uncomfortable with such questions, though they are not at all uncomfortable with emotionally expressive playing.[7] David Hamil-

---

7. Eugene Drucker of the Emerson String Quartet commented during an interview on 10 January 1987 that one of the aspects of the Emerson's rehearsal technique he liked best was that "we don't spend that much time discussing ideas in a general way." James Dunham tells me that in Cleveland Quartet rehearsals there is considerable discussion of mood and characterization.

ton is surely right in detecting an element of impatience with questions about mood and character: "Philosophers have debated the hows and whys of musical meaning for centuries, but in practice most musicians simply take that meaning for granted, and don't waste much time trying to find verbal equivalents for the expressive character of a piece; as Mendelssohn once argued, the meaning of music is actually more specific than that of words."[8]

Although I find Mendelssohn's idea more puzzling than illuminating, it does capture the prevalent feeling that "verbal equivalents" are somehow beside the point: if one has the music, why are words necessary? On the other hand, there are certainly situations in quartet rehearsals where it can become very important for the players to explain to each other what they understand to be the emotional content (mood, character, etc.) of a particular section. Sometimes, in Sequoia Quartet rehearsals, disagreements on details of phrasing and tone color, for example, could be traced to the fact that we had very different ideas as to the basic character of the section. Once we forced ourselves to say what we considered to be the overall mood of the section, we realized, with amazement, that we were working toward very different goals. This is another reflection of the fact that chamber music calls for a much higher degree of verbalization than other forms of music making.

2. Tempo.   There are actually a number of issues concerning tempo, calling for many interrelated decisions. First there is the matter of the basic tempo or pulse of a movement or section. Choice of a basic tempo still leaves undetermined a great number of details within the musical texture. One theme or motif can be played slightly faster or slower than another without destroying the basic tempo; also, "rubato" (literally, "robbing" bits of time from one part of a phrase and giving them to another part) is often desirable within a basic tempo. But a basic tempo must be settled on. To what extent is this to be done on the basis of internal evidence—the examination of particular figures, phrases, and passages within the movement? To what extent is this to be done on the basis of external indications such as metronome marks supplied by the composer? To what extent by intertextual considerations, such as comparisons with other movements for which Beethoven has given the same marking (e.g., *Allegro con brio*)? The question of basic tempo is further

8. Hamilton, *Listener's Guide to Great Instrumentalists*, 8–9.

complicated by the fact that very different characters can be conveyed within the same basic tempo; often, disagreements ostensibly about tempo are actually disagreements about character.

Aside from basic tempo, there are many tempo-related decisions to be made concerning the smaller events that make up the performance. Speeding up and slowing down are related to phrasing, to clarifying architectural features of the piece for the listeners, as well as to matters of character. Many decisions involve trade-offs between clarifying details, on the one hand, and achieving a sense of the large section, on the other.

3. Tone color.　Within a single dynamic, a passage can be played with a compressed, intense tone, with a loose, relaxed tone, and with countless variations in between. Tone color is determined by such factors as kind of bow attack, bow speed after the attack, bow pressure (floating, in the string, slow bow, fast bow), kind of vibrato (slow, fast, wide, narrow, none), and kind of bow pressure release. Changes in tone color are used to shape phrases, project moods, bring out interesting harmonies, and highlight structural divisions in a work.

4. Rhythmic contours.　Differences in the treatment of various rhythms can have a strong effect on characterization. Triplets can be played lazily or energetically; patterns of dotted eighths followed by sixteenths can be played so that they leap ahead or hold back (the effect of "pulling in the reins"). There are such choices to be made in the playing of almost every rhythmic pattern. For example, in the *Andante* of Op. 59 no. 2 (Ex. 10), Beethoven writes in four subtly different ways what might, incorrectly, be taken as the same rhythm: (1) dotted eighth note followed by sixteenth note, neither with dots; (2) dotted eighth note followed by sixteenth note, both with dots; (3) eighth note tied to a sixteenth note (with dot), followed by a sixteenth note (with dot); (4) eighth note, sixteenth rest, sixteenth note, with dot.[9]

5. Dynamics and balance.　How loud or soft should each passage be? Should printed dynamics be interpreted relatively or absolutely? With a relative interpretation of a passage marked *piano*, for example, it might be necessary for each member of the group to play even softer so that

9. Robert Levin has pointed out to me that the third of these is possibly to be played very differently so that one hears a slight articulation on the dotted note under the tie.

EXAMPLE 10. Op. 59 no. 2, second movement, mm. 82–92

EXAMPLE 11.   Op. 18 no. 1, second movement, m. 23

the group output is *piano*; if one voice then continues alone with the same marking, that voice would then have to come up to the level produced previously by the entire group. What "natural" or extra dynamics should be added, beyond those marked in the score? Which voice, in a given passage, is the main voice? Or should all be equal at that point? Is there also a main subsidiary voice? One of the clearest marks of a well-thought-out performance is that the important voices are always perceptible as such.

6. Phrasing.   What is the shape of each phrase? What is the high point of the phrase? How far does the phrase extend? Does part of the phrase have the manner of a question? Does part seem to be an answer? How should each phrase and phrase ending be paced (rhythmically) and shaped (dynamically)?

7. Intonation.   What are the possibilities in a particular phrase of so-called expressive intonation—the drawing up (or down) of semitones to enhance the sense of the melodic line or harmonic direction? An example, cited by Arnold Steinhardt, occurs in the slow movement of Op. 18 no. 1 (Ex. 11), where close semitones "increase the sense of expressive tension."[10]

Principles That Govern
the Decision-Making Process

From the examples in the first section I have tried to extract a rough categorization of performance decisions. The problem now is to find plausible conceptual apparatus to account for the way these decisions are made. More specifically, it is the underlying structure of musical reasons that I am interested in. There may be nonrational causes of musical deci-

10. *The Art of Quartet Playing: The Guarneri Quartet in Conversation with David Blum* (New York, 1986), 29.

sions, of the kind that a psychotherapist familiar with the members of the group might describe. There may be fully conscious though nonmusical reasons for musical decisions, such as the desire to keep a member from quitting! Neither of these cases falls within the scope of my investigation. I want to get at reasons and arguments that are based on musical considerations.

Clearly, musical considerations will rely heavily on the score. Therefore we shall need to sketch a general picture of the relationship between composer, score, performers, and performances. Within that general picture we can ask, more specifically, how particular decisions are made.

Literalism, the Buried Work, Textual Interpretation, and Collaboration

One possible account of the relation between composer, score, and performer, one that I take to be incorrect, is the literalist view, according to which the performers should simply play what is written and avoid what is not. The problem is that musical notation provides a very incomplete picture of what the composer intends—it functions effectively only because it functions within a rich framework of shared understanding between composer and performers. It is understood that all kinds of shadings, rhythmic flexibility, expressive gestures, phrasings, and nuances will be supplied by the performers. One may say that a score typically contains only those details that would not be obvious to an informed contemporary of the composer.[11] So the literalist view rests on a gross oversimplification.

Then there is the "buried work" account, according to which performers dig beneath what is superficial—the score—to get at the inner essence of the work. This view is sometimes vaguely associated with philosophical views such as Collingwood's, according to which the work of music exists in the mind of the composer and is communicated, through sounds, to those listeners who can reconstruct in their own minds what the composer created in his.[12] This view is one that gives the performers great license; it is as though they had adopted as a maxim, Determine the inner nature of the work, and let this determination

11. I owe this way of putting the matter to Robert Levin.
12. See R. G. Collingwood, *The Principles of Art* (Oxford, 1938), 139ff.

guide you in all matters of detail. The defect of this view is that there is no independent way of evaluating the results of the search for the essence of a work. Of course, there are many careful, responsible interpreters of music who speak the language of the "buried work" theory; it is not their interpretive practices but only the views suggested by their language that are to be criticized.

There is another view, which I will call the textual interpretation view, according to which the score of a Beethoven quartet is a text like that of a poem or a novel, standing apart from whatever may have been intended by whoever happened to have created it and subject to interpretation (i.e., performance), just as other texts. This is the view suggested by the harpsichordist Wanda Landowska's comment, "If Rameau himself would rise from his grave to demand of me some changes in my interpretation of his Dauphine, I would answer, 'You gave birth to it; it is beautiful. But now leave me alone with it. You have nothing more to say; go away!'"[13] The emphasis in Landowska's comment is on the independence of the text from the composer's intentions, and it is this view that is at the heart of what I call the textual interpretation view. Whatever musical texts and interpretation of them have in common with literary texts, there is one straightforward but crucially important difference between musical texts and at least one important class of literary texts. The difference is that a composer relies on performers to transmit the work, whereas a novelist, for example, does not. An interpretation of a literary text (one that does not also involve a performance) does not stand between a person and the text in the way in which a performance of a string quartet stands between a listener (who may not be able to read music) and a score. Accepted interpretations may color the way I understand and appreciate a novel, for example, but there is nothing, in the case of a novel, that quite corresponds to a performance in the case of a piece of music or a play. This simple fact places a special responsibility on the shoulders of the performer—a responsibility to convey the work accurately and sympathetically. The performer of music is the audible partner in the collaborative process of creating a performance and is morally obliged to represent the composer's intentions accurately, as far as possible. Even the most far-fetched interpretation of a nonper-

13. Wanda Landowska, *Landowska on Music,* ed. and trans. D. Restout (New York, 1981), 407, cited in R. Taruskin, "The Pastness of the Present and the Presence of the Past," in *Authenticity and Early Music,* ed. N. Kenyon (Oxford, 1988), 147.

formance literary work will be innocent of the kind of moral irresponsibility that is present in the case of careless performances, especially of new works.[14]

We come now to the collaborative account, some form of which I believe to be correct. It is the starting point of the collaborative account to recognize what was pointed out before—that the score underdetermines the performance. Performers bring a sense of style, the resources of individual talent, a feeling of personal involvement, and knowledge of performance conventions; these are used, all together, to fill in the gaps in Beethoven's instructions. The performers contribute, rather than submerge, their sense of how a performance could be made effective. Beethoven was a performer and had a keen sense of what would work in performance. The modern performer feels challenged to go beyond the indications in the score in a way that would please and excite Beethoven the performer.[15]

One starts by assuming that every *crescendo* and *diminuendo,* every dynamic marking, every articulation is there to be followed. Extra ritards, added "echo effects," unmarked *accelerandi,* and so on are generally to be avoided. It is a common pitfall for players to begin a *crescendo* before it is marked, and this can spoil the effect of a climax. It is also common to add dynamics. For example, the temptation to "shape" the mesmerizingly placid *pp meno mosso* section of the *Grosse Fuge* (Ex. 12) is to be resisted, as it is, in my opinion, a mistake to allow the relentless *forte* to subside in the loud sections of the same work. Fidelity to the score requires careful attention to the intricate, even fussy, shadings in the *Andante* movement (*Poco scherzoso*) of Op. 130 (Ex. 13). In the space of

14. This paragraph raises many more interesting issues than, at best, it resolves. What *is* the relationship between a musical text and the script of a play? What is there about this relationship that accounts for the fact that radical departures in productions of plays are more acceptable, or at least more common, than radical departures from the score in musical performances? What is the relationship between the sense in which we speak of a performer's interpretation of a musical work (i.e., a performance or group of performances) and the sense in which we speak of, for example, Susan McClary's interpretation of the slow movement of a Mozart Piano Concerto, K. 453, as a representation of the conflict between the individual (soloist) and the "overpowering requirements of social convention"? (See Richard Taruskin, "Why Mozart Has Become an Icon for Today," *New York Times,* 9 September 1990.) The only point I claim to have resolved is that any view about musical texts so extreme as to deny the relevance to interpretation (in the sense of performance) of the composer's intentions is simply wrong.

15. On Beethoven's enormous success as a pianist of "fire, animation and invention," see Elliot Forbes, ed., *Thayer's Life of Beethoven* (Princeton, 1967), 160ff.

EXAMPLE 12.   Op. 133, mm. 159–64

eight beats one finds a *crescendo* from *pp* to *poco forte*, followed by *mf*, then *subito piano*, a *crescendo* to *mf*, then one beat of *poco forte*, followed by another beat of *mf*. Considerable amounts of rehearsal time are spent simply in making sure that the players do what is marked and avoid interpretive additions that are thought to be incorrect.

One problem with this starting assumption is that there are many questionable markings and even outright mistakes in the printed parts from which performers play. It is certainly not surprising that this should be the case: Beethoven's manuscripts are difficult to decipher, the "fair copies" sent to the publishers were often done by someone other than Beethoven, and the engraving process introduced new errors, only some of which Beethoven caught in reviewing page proofs. (It is, however, surprising that there are no performance editions that include Beethoven's metronome marks.)

There are also markings whose interpretation is not clear. What does

EXAMPLE 13.   Op. 130, third movement, mm. 23–25

Beethoven mean by ties over repeated notes, as, for example, at the end
of the Cavatina of Op. 130 (Ex. 14), at the end of the first section of
Op. 131 (Ex. 15), and at the end of the slow movement of Op. 132 (Ex.
16)? Are the repeated notes sounded, despite the ties?[16] Similarly, what
of the tied eighths in the opening of the *Grosse Fuge* (Ex. 17)? It is less
common to rearticulate in this latter case. There are parallel cases in
other works—for example, the scherzo of the Cello Sonata, Op. 69, and
passages in the *Hammerklavier* Sonata, Op. 106, where tied repeated
notes are actually assigned different fingers by Beethoven.

    Looking for clues in similar passages in other works of Beethoven is
one way that such decisions are made. A more general kind of consider-

16. See Emil Platen, "Ein Notierungsproblem in Beethovens späten Streichquartet-
ten," in *Beethoven-Jahrbuch* 8 (1971–72): 147–56. This discussion is cited in Walter Levin's
review (in *Disso* [Zurich] 20 [May 1989]: 33–35) of the German-language translation of
The Art of Quartet Playing.

EXAMPLE 14. Op. 130, fifth movement, m. 66

EXAMPLE 15. Op. 131, first movement, mm. 118–21

ation can be called "stylistic"—performers rely on such historical knowledge as they can obtain of performance practices and conventions of Beethoven's time. There are of course great difficulties in obtaining accurate information on performance traditions of earlier periods, but there can be no doubt that this information is relevant to present-day performances. This is independent of whether or not we wish to copy, as fully as possible, the ways of earlier performers; historical information is relevant because Beethoven's decisions about what he needed to write would have been based in part on what he expected performers to do, given certain marks. It would be impossible to make use of the idea,

EXAMPLE 16.   Op. 132, third movement, mm. 210–11

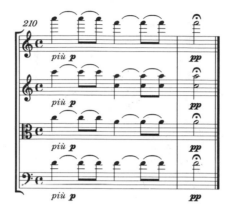

EXAMPLE 17.   Op. 133, mm. 26–31

EXAMPLE 18. Op. 18 no. 5, third movement, mm. 1–4

mentioned earlier, that a composer should be assumed to have marked only what he judged he could not take for granted, if we have no idea what performers would have taken for granted. For example, when we wonder what Beethoven meant by dotted notes under a slur, say in the opening of the *Andante cantabile* of Op. 18 no. 5 (Ex. 18), we need to know something about the specific execution that he would have expected to communicate by this.

The performer must do much that is not indicated in the score. For example, the score rarely tells us the length of a phrase, the high point of a phrase, or whether the phrase is to be sustained and handed on to the next voice or rounded off and brought to closure. The performers decide what are the musical questions and what are the answers; where is tension to be maintained and where is it to be released.

It seems to me that matters of phrasing are among the most immediate, least reasoned, kinds of considerations upon which performers base decisions. This is not to deny that performers think a great deal about phrasing, but the raw material for their deliberations is more like something "given" than something deduced. A performer's feelings that certain phrasings are simply not possible seems to be an example of musical instinct that is not learned and is beyond the range of inference or argument. Gifted players can apparently draw directly on a rich source of musical insight for their ideas and opinions about phrasing, texture, structure, nuance, expression, and other matters. These opinions may certainly change over time, and this source of musical knowledge can interact with more analytical, inferential knowledge of music, but there seems no denying the special, rather mysterious gift of musical instinct. All musicians can recognize the presence of innate "talent," which is another name for this source of musical insight.

There are in fact neurological data that suggest that it is not the part of the brain associated with analytic and linguistic capabilities (the left hemisphere) that is primarily responsible for musical understanding and creativity.[17] There are cases of people with extreme left hemisphere deficits, unable to function linguistically, who can still compose music and criticize performances with lucid musical understanding. This evidence helps explain the fairly common experience of finding that a performer who displays uncommon musical insight in performance may be completely unable to verbalize what he or she "knows" about the piece.

Decisions to Deviate from the Indications of the Score

We need to explain, within the framework of the collaborative account, performers' decisions not simply to add what is not indicated but actually to deviate from what is indicated in the score. I suggest that in every such case there is (1) pressure from considerations of performance effectiveness along with (2) the belief that the particular indications in the score are to be taken as providing performance options or advice rather than pointing to something integral to the work.

Decisions about repeats are a case in point. In one sense they are completely unambiguous: the repeat sign means to play the indicated passage again. But it is common among performers to treat repeats as essentially optional; they are certainly often ignored.[18] I suppose this would be justified by reference to the alleged fact that some repeat signs are the result of a compositional convention, not the result of a particular decision on the part of the composer. Perhaps composers of music for occasions (such as weddings, dinner parties, etc.) saw the practical advantage of optional repeats: to have an adjustable amount of music for the occasion. But very few if any repeats can be explained this way. In any

---

17. See A. R. Luria, L. S. Tsevetkova, and D. S. Futer, "Aphasia in a Composer," *Journal of Neurological Science* 2 (1965): 288–92, and T. Judd, H. Gardner and N. Geschwind, "Alexia with Agraphia in a Composer," *Brain* 106 (1983): 435–57, both discussed in J. Newmark, "Aphasia Without Amusia," *Classical Overtones* 1 (1988): 2–6. See also the title article in Oliver Sacks, *The Man Who Mistook His Wife for a Hat* (New York, 1970).

18. Joseph Kerman (in *The Beethoven Quartets* [New York, 1966], 74) comments in passing, of the Op. 18 no. 6 Quartet's first movement, "the second repeat is obligatory." This would come as news to most players.

case, it is unclear why performers almost always observe the conventional repeat structure of minuet and trio but often ignore first-movement exposition repeats. Why do performers often ignore clearly nonconventional repeats such as the second repeat of the first movement of Op. 59 no. 2? It is striking that performers will agonize over tiny, inaudible changes[19] and yet routinely skip repeats and thus drastically alter the length and proportions of movements. It surely means that the repeats are taken to be optional. Treating the repeats as options, the players respond pragmatically: decisions about repeats can be based on the length of the program, the familiarity of the work, the amount of time needed to get to the airport, as well as on aesthetic grounds.

On reflection one has to conclude, I believe, that the repeats in Beethoven's quartets should all be observed. The issue is not whether the repeats make aesthetic sense, though in fact they do; the repeats should be taken because there is no good reason (that I know of) to doubt that Beethoven intended them to be taken. In addition to the fact that the repeats affect the proportions of movements and works, there is another interesting aesthetic consideration in their favor. In much music in the decades before Beethoven wrote, repeats were the occasion for performers to add or alter ornamentation. Something of the flavor of this tradition is retained in repeats even when there are no literal changes; the performers can find subtle ways of playing the music differently, responding to the fact that the audience has heard it once. It is disheartening to hear a repeat performed with no feeling of freshness or change of perspective.

Beethoven's metronome marks are often not followed. One hears, over and over again, comments such as: "He added the metronome marks long after he wrote the pieces." "He was deaf." "How accurate was the metronome he was using?" "He seemed prone to extremes." "Composers are usually not the best interpreters of their works."[20] But the decisive consideration, most of the time, is how effective, in performers' minds, the music sounds at a given tempo. One of the members

19. See, for example, *The Art of Quartet Playing,* 74–75, where a probably imperceptible transfer of three notes from the first to the second violin is discussed. Arnold Steinhardt comments, "Although this is perfectly logical and sounds better, I do have a guilty conscience about the change."

20. The Guarneri Quartet members cite Arthur Rubinstein's amusing comment about Fauré's metronome mark for the G-minor Piano Quartet: "He turned the metronome on, checked the tempo, and said, 'Oh, yes, but that's only for the first bar.'" See *The Art of Quartet Playing,* 90.

of the Emerson String Quartet remarked, after a thoughtful discussion of Beethoven's metronome marks and tempo: "The piece still has to work."[21] It is more difficult to say what it means for a piece to "work" than to find other respected performers who say similar things. My point is that this practical view springs from the players' roles as performers and their consideration of the effectiveness of the performance.

The violinist Felix Galimir is a dedicated performer of twentieth-century music and a specialist in the music of Béla Bartók. Bartók was known to have been extremely concerned that performers follow his metronome marks exactly. An interviewer said to Galimir, "We know from listening to recordings of Bartók playing his own music that he did not always follow his own dynamic and tempo markings." Galimir responded, "No matter what he decided as a composer when he listened to the music in his head, as a performer his instincts were right. You have to feel the music first—its kinetic energy, its pathos, its connection to something very deep in the folk material from which it springs. You have to let your interpretive decisions flow from that feeling rather than from a too-literal fidelity to the score."[22]

The underlying question is, as Rudolf Kolish pointed out, whether tempo is integral to a piece of music.[23] When performers ignore a composer's tempo indication, are they failing to some degree to play the composer's piece, as though they had changed pitches and rhythms? Based on their practice, it is clear that most performers believe that the answer is No; they regard metronome marks as suggestions rather than directions.[24] They value the suggestion as coming from a particularly well-qualified source, but they are prepared to regard the suggestion as mistaken. There is of course a variety of attitudes here. Some thoughtful performers place greater importance on tempo relationships; if a metro-

21. Interview, 10 January 1987.

22. Eugene Drucker, "The Fourth 'B': Felix Galimir on Bartók," *Chamber Music* 5, no. 3 (Summer 1988): 25.

23. Kolisch, "Tempo and Character in Beethoven's Music," 174.

24. Cf. Virgil Thomson's comment in *The Art of Judging Music* (New York, 1948), 296: "The composer's specific indications are themselves not always a part of his original creation but rather one musician's message to another about it, a hint about how to secure in performance a convincing transmission of the work's feeling content." Cited in Alfred Schutz, "Making Music Together," in *Collected Papers 2: Studies in Social Theory* (The Hague, 1964), 166.

nome mark is departed from, it is departed from consistently whenever it reappears in a work.

Maxims

I wish to suggest a way of summarizing the considerations brought to bear during the decision-making process: perhaps the notion of a "maxim" will be a useful conceptual tool. By maxim I mean a consideration that an ensemble considers decisive unless it is countered by some other consideration. The maxims themselves are platitudinous—it is in their ranking and application to particular cases that musical judgment, or misjudgment, is exercised. Take, for example, this maxim:

1. Follow what is written in the score.

That maxim 1 is behind a remark such as "The third beat of measure 14 is *subito piano*" is shown by the fact that nothing further need be said— a marking that had been overlooked is now noted and is to be followed. If there is further discussion, it takes the form of either questioning whether the (unspoken) maxim really applies in this case ("Are you sure that's not an editor's marking?") or suggesting that some other maxim takes priority—"Isn't the *subito piano* really intended for the fourth beat, the way it is in the exposition?" The suggestion here is not that the marking is not Beethoven's but that it may not reflect his real intentions; a higher-ranking maxim is

2. Correct apparent errors in the score.

Another maxim is

3. Make sure that the most important voice or voices can be heard.

Thus, when I am asked to play softer in measure 10 so I don't cover the second violin, an appropriate (though possibly incorrect) response is that my part is more important—I am implicitly accepting the maxim but objecting to its application in this particular case. I may also say that I was not covering the second violin part—again, accepting the maxim but now denying on more subjective grounds that it applies in this case. Or I may point out that my part is marked *forte* while the second violin part is marked *mezzo forte*—in this case, I am appealing to the priority of maxim 1.

The response may be that the second violin part has to be heard because it continues the melodic line; if I yield at this point it is because
we have implicitly agreed to a higher ranking in this case for maxim 3.
On the other hand, a closer look at the score may indicate the possibility
of a miscalculation on Beethoven's part—it may appear that a *mezzo forte*
was left out of the cello part accidentally. In that case we have tacitly
applied maxim 2.

Here are some other maxims:

4. Phrase so as to maintain a sense of conversation.
5. Emphasize contrasts wherever possible.
6a. Similar passages should be treated similarly.
6b. Similar passages should be treated differently.
7. Maintain tension within a phrase.

It should be emphasized again that the maxims are self-evident; that
is exactly why they are decisive unless outranked by other equally self-
evident maxims. It is the application and ranking that matter. One could
go on listing maxims—it might even be possible to distinguish the approaches of various well-known string quartets by indicating particular
maxims that they appear to weight heavily. One might discern in some
cases the application of higher-order maxims (for example, When the
application of more than *n* maxims fails to resolve a dispute, it is time
for lunch). I will leave the matter for another occasion.

In general, the best performers have a strong sense of their roles as servants of the composer; when their instincts as performers lead them away
from faithful rendering of the score, they take pains to convince themselves that they are doing what the composer would have wished. This
is so even when, after years of studying and performing a work, performers feel they have made that work their own. Even then, their feeling is
one of having obtained some of the rights of joint ownership.

Two further concluding remarks: first, everything said so far assumes
that the players have the technical ability to carry out the decisions they
make. The fact is, however, that a great deal of rehearsal time is devoted
to trying to arrive at that level: there is endless work on intonation,
ensemble unity, rhythmic exactness, timing, and so forth, and this is
supported by a great deal of individual technical work. Ironically, much
of what an audience (and the critics) admire about a performance is just

the presence of this technical ability rather than the musical decisions it makes possible.

Finally, it should be noted that when it comes time for a performance, there is often a conscious attempt to cover up the hard work of decision making, to give the performance a feeling of spontaneity. A fine performance has a quality of inevitability about it, as though there had been no decisions to be made.

Notes on the Quartets

MICHAEL STEINBERG

Beethoven dedicated this early set of parts to his Quartet in F Major, Op. 18 no. 1, to his friend Karl Amenda: "Dear Amenda: Accept this quartet as a small token of our friendship, and whenever you play it recall the days we passed together and the sincere affection felt for you then, which will always be felt by: Your warm and true friend, Ludwig van Beethoven. Vienna, 25 June 1799." (Reproduced by permission of the Beethoven-Archiv, Bonn.)

The Early Quartets

STRING QUARTET IN F MAJOR,
AFTER THE PIANO SONATA IN E MAJOR, OP. 14 NO. 1

Allegro moderato
Allegretto
Allegro

This engaging work, not part of the canonical sixteen, may actually be Beethoven's earliest music for string quartet. In this form it probably dates from 1802; at any rate, Beethoven first mentions it in a letter of 13 July that year, and it was published in Vienna a month later. The work of which it is a transcription, the E-major Piano Sonata, Op. 14 no. 1, is rather earlier, though the chronology is not as clear as one might like. We know that the sonata was published at the end of 1799, but we don't know exactly when Beethoven wrote it. Likely enough, it is contemporary to the famous *Pathétique* Sonata, Op. 13, which comes from 1798–99, but the sketches suggest beginnings that go even further back into the 1790s. Some have speculated that Beethoven first intended it as a string quartet, that he changed his mind and made it into a piano piece instead, and that the transcription is thus a return to the original plan. In 1795, Count Anton Apponyi, godfather in 1793 to Haydn's Op. 71 and 74 quartets, asked Beethoven for a string quartet. For whatever reason, Beethoven never delivered—indeed, Apponyi disappears from the Beethoven biography at this point—but it could well be that Op. 14 no. 1 was a move in the direction of fulfilling that commission. As for Beethoven's first "real" quartets, the six of Op. 18, they were begun in 1798, probably also using material sketched earlier, but were not completed until late in 1800 or early in 1801.

In prephonographic times, transcriptions of all kinds—the absurd not excluded—were common, useful, and welcomed. Twelve of Beethoven's earlier piano sonatas exist, in whole or in part, in contemporary published transcriptions for string quartet. Most are anonymous. Good transcriptions are not easy to make. Like any sort of translator, the musical transcriber can be suspended in excessive literalism by reverence or sheer lack of imagination; on the other hand, carelessness, irrepressible creative impulses, irreverence, or an inclination always to know better can lead to risky departures from the original. (Not carelessness, of course, but the other qualities and their results we value highly when the name to the right of the hyphen is Bach, Mozart, Elgar, Rachmaninoff, Schoenberg, Ravel, Grainger, Casella, Webern, etc., but that is a story for another book.)

At any rate, on more than one occasion, the most famous being his dissatisfaction with Anton Halm's piano duet arrangement of the *Grosse Fuge,* Op. 133, Beethoven decided that it was worth his time and energy to make his own transcription. "The unnatural mania for transplanting piano stuff to string instruments, instruments so completely opposite in all ways, might well cease," he wrote to the Leipzig publishers Breitkopf & Härtel in 1802. "I firmly maintain that only Mozart, also Haydn, was capable of translating himself from the piano to other instruments, and without wanting to set myself up as the equal of those great men, I would maintain the same thing about my piano sonatas. It is not just a matter of totally leaving out and changing whole passages. One also has to add, and there is the stumbling block: to overcome it you either have to be the master yourself or to be at least his equal in cleverness and invention.—I have transformed only one of my sonatas into a string quartet, for which I had been urgently asked, and I know for certain that no one else is going to come along and do it equally well."[1] Something we do not know is who made that urgent request for a quartet transcription.

The quartet version of Op. 14 no. 1 was not included in the complete Beethoven edition that Breitkopf & Härtel published between 1864 and 1867, and the score was not published until 1910. As was customary

---

1. Ludwig van Beethoven to Breitkopf & Härtel, 13 July 1802, in Beethoven, *Quatuor pour deux violons alto et violoncelle d'après un sonate . . .* (London and Zurich, 1910), iv. Perhaps the worst thing string players know to say about what they are given to play—and one hears this only too frequently at orchestra and quartet rehearsals—is "It's piano music."

then, the 1802 publication provided only the parts for the individual players.

Making his transcription, Beethoven transposed the music from E major to F, in some ways a less convenient key for strings but in this instance offering the advantage of making the viola's and cello's low C available to sound the dominant of the home key. Beethoven also changed the tempo of the first movement from *Allegro* to *Allegro moderato*. It is a gentle piece whose opening theme climbs upward in a slow zigzag, and Beethoven enjoys demonstrating various ways at different speeds in which one can present this figuration that lies so comfortably under a pianist's hands (and almost as much so under a string player's). An interesting detail in the transcription is that while the piano version leaves the first beat of the first measure blank in the accompaniment, the lower strings provide a soft but firm "one."

Two further, contrasting themes follow—one chromatic and thus somewhat plaintive, the other vigorous. In the transcription, Beethoven sharpens the effect of the drumming upbeats by changing them from *forte* triplets to a *fz* (*forzando*) sixteenth with a pair of thirty-seconds. A bass variant of the opening zigzag closes the exposition, Beethoven adding a new, musing line for the first violin.

The development—or, rather, what we expect to be the development—starts with the zigzag, though the harmonies immediately veer into darker regions. But after this bow to the first theme, Beethoven devotes the next sixteen measures to an entirely new idea, a passionate melody for the first violin, and only in the ten measures of preparation for the recapitulation does he again allude to material from the exposition. This was Beethoven's plan from the beginning; in fact, he had even written a reminder to himself in the sketch: "ohne das Thema durchzuführen" (without developing the theme). Here, too, Beethoven deals skillfully with transcribing the accompaniment, changing the "steady-state" left-hand arpeggios to repeated notes punctuated by wide-ranging broken chords for cello and viola.

The recapitulation begins with a sonorous version of the opening theme, generously decorated with scales (up in the piano, up and down in the quartet). Where, in the energetic closing theme, Beethoven has to adjust the shape of the melody to the limited range of his 1799 piano, he can send the violin as high as he needs to. The coda is quiet and pensive.

The F-minor second movement—and this, by the way, is one of

those fairly rare classical works in which all the movements are based on the same keynote—is proto-Schubert, tinged with Danube valley melancholy. Beethoven's pupil Carl Czerny characterizes it as partaking of a certain mood of ill humor ("unmuthiger Laune") and says that its performance should be "serious, lively, but not humorous or playful." [2] It is a good prescription. The less-troubled trio is in a rich D-flat major. After the repeat of the first section, Beethoven brings back the end of the trio—plus a tag—to make a brief coda.

In the finale Beethoven again changes the tempo and character direction, this time from *Allegro comodo* to plain *Allegro*. Here, too, he is at his most clever and inventive in his transcribing. I cannot guess whether, if someone else had taken such productive liberties, he would have objected strenuously or would, with equal vigor, have cried "bravo." I hope the latter. The piano original is one of those gratifying pieces that come off as brilliant but without being notably difficult, and its translation cannot have been easy. In any event, Beethoven's changes are calculated to perfection; so much so that this movement is really more interesting in the quartet version.

The movement is a kind of rondo, but one whose episodes contain a good deal of development. The second of these episodes is quite thoroughly rewritten: the brilliant violin figuration with its forceful comments from second violin and viola is simple play with arpeggios in the piano original. To bold invention Beethoven adds bolder glosses. It seems as though the movement will end musingly, much as the first did, but at the last Beethoven gives us a forceful, almost epigrammatic close.

The Op. 18 Quartets

When Beethoven left Bonn in November 1792—for life, as it turned out—the object of his pilgrimage to Vienna was, in the words of his friend Count Waldstein, "through unremitting diligence [to] receive the spirit of Mozart at the hands of Haydn." But the lessons with Haydn were not a success. Through his whole life Beethoven learned profoundly from Haydn's scores, but when it came to formal instruction, he was better off with Johann Schenk, an experienced theater composer,

2. Carl Czerny, "Über den richtigen Vortrag der sämtlichen Beethoven'schen Werke für das Piano allein," in *Die Kunst des Vortrags der älteren und neueren Klavierkompositionen* (1842; rpt., Vienna, 1963), 38.

with the celebrated Antonio Salieri, and with that excellent pedagogue Johann Georg Albrechtsberger. All three were more attentive than Haydn and less inclined to be put off by the unconcerned religious views, the left-wing politics, and the rough manners of the young Rhinelander.

In 1795, the publishing firm of Artaria & Co. issued Beethoven's official Op. 1, three trios for piano, violin, and cello. Haydn advised withholding the third in the set, supposedly fearing that its probable shock would damage his pupil's budding career, a surprising attitude from a composer who was himself so bold. Perhaps he was nervous because jealous. Beethoven was also beginning to make a name for himself as an exciting pianist. In sum, he had quickly conquered the musical capital of Europe, he commanded good fees from publishers (these would be his chief source of income all his life), and he could live like a gentleman.

He had composed actively in Bonn and sometimes strikingly, but his earliest music now in normal circulation was written in Vienna (drawing occasionally on ideas that go back to Bonn)—the work, therefore, of a man in his middle and late twenties. If we hear his first Viennese works, the Piano Trios, Op. 1 (written 1794), the Piano Sonatas, Op. 2 (1795), the Cello Sonatas, Op. 5 (1796), the String Trios, Op. 9 (1798), and the String Quartets, Op. 18 (1798–1800 or 1801), from the vantage point of the "Archduke" Trio or the Razumovsky quartets—and this, to some extent, we cannot help doing—they will sound Haydnesque and Mozartean. Because of this, the young Beethoven is one of the most underrated of composers. In fact, though, you would have a hard time finding a dozen consecutive measures in any of these compositions that would fit plausibly into any piece by Haydn or Mozart. So famous a work as the *Pathétique* Sonata of 1799 is aggressively "new," but, even in the most demure and mannerly pieces of the 1790s, attentive listening reveals detail after detail, strategy after strategy, that attest to the presence of a personality not at all like Haydn's or Mozart's. The composer of Op. 18 was an assured young man, very much ready to set out on his own, and to give voice to his personality he quickly developed a correspondingly and constantly expanding musical vocabulary.

The Viennese house of T. Mollo et Comp. published Beethoven's first six string quartets as Op. 18 in two installments in June and October 1801. Almost certainly, Beethoven had planned the six pieces as a set from the beginning, presumably with Mozart's six quartets dedicated to Haydn and with several of Haydn's own six-headed opuses as his models. Like the symphony, the string quartet was recognized as an "important" genre, and a composer's first go at this medium was a consciously significant step.

Beethoven dedicated Op. 18 to Prince Franz Joseph von Lobkowitz, a Viennese nobleman slightly younger than himself, a generous and genuinely music-loving patron. Except for the Archduke Rudolph, Lobkowitz received the most remarkable list of Beethoven dedications of any of the composer's patrons and friends—the *Eroica*, the Triple Concerto, the String Quartet, Op. 74, the song cycle *An die ferne Geliebte* (*To the Distant Beloved*), and, sharing the honor with Count Razumovsky, the Fifth and Sixth symphonies.

STRING QUARTET IN F MAJOR, OP. 18 NO. I

Allegro con brio
Adagio affettuoso ed appassionato
Scherzo: Allegro molto
Allegro

Beethoven took pains over the sequence of Op. 18, which is not the same as the order of composition, and he put the most vigorously adventurous of the six quartets at the head of the collection. It was a good way to address a public that valued novelty. Scholars have inferred from the sketches that the D-major Quartet, Op. 18 no. 3, was the first to be composed and that the F-major, Op 18 no. 1, came next.

Beethoven thoroughly revised the latter work before sending it off to the publisher. Because he left copious sketches we know a lot about his work habits, how both the smallest motifs and the largest structural units took shape. With Op. 18 no. 1, however, we can examine two complete versions of an entire composition, a luxury otherwise afforded in Beethoven's work only in a few other instances. We can, for example, experience the "Waldstein" Sonata in its original form by playing the *Andante favori*, WoO 57, in place of the *Adagio molto*; we can restore the first version of the Fifth Symphony with its double trip around the scherzo-trio-scherzo cycle; all three versions of *Fidelio* are available; and we can hear the B-flat major Quartet, Op. 130, both as Beethoven first planned it, ending with the *Grosse Fuge*, and as he was obliged to revise it, with its new, spikily charming, Beethoven-posing-as-Haydn finale. (The piano and quartet presentations of Op. 14 no. 1 are, I think, not different enough to count as different versions in this sense.)

Most musicians would agree that Op. 130 is stronger in its original form. The earlier versions of the Fifth Symphony and *Fidelio* are interesting and flavorful enough, "special" enough, to be worth reviving from time to time. As for the "Waldstein," Beethoven was not less than 100 percent right in removing the leisurely *Andante* and replacing it with his inspired new introduzione, though he was in fact furious when the idea of revision was first put to him. Likewise, to listen to the original 1799 version of Op. 18 no. 1 is to understand the import of the letter Beethoven addressed on 1 July 1801 to his old and close Bonn friend Karl Amenda. He had sent Amenda a dedication copy of the first version one year before. Now he wrote: "Be sure not to hand on to anybody your quartet, in which I have made some drastic alterations. For only now have I learnt to write quartets; and this you will notice, I fancy, when you receive them."[3] He had learned—and learned mightily—both about composition (that is, how to get from one event to another) and even more about how to make the music sound, about those details of voicing and scoring for which he was to develop an ever more refined imagination to the end of his life.

The opening cost Beethoven a heap of trouble. He was certain that he wanted an F followed by a turn, but it took him nine tries in the sketches before he arrived at its present sharply profiled form (Ex. 1). Through all of its variety and breadth, this fiery movement is amazingly saturated with this idea. Literally or in close derivative, it is present in a bit more than one-third of the measures.

Forceful though they are, these first two measures are in fact *piano*. When Beethoven repeats them, as he does immediately, he ends on D rather than C. At the next repetition he moves on to a lyric phrase, and this takes us back to the beginning. The second time around, the start is *forte* and the lyric phrase is intensified harmonically and also heightened (literally) in pitch. In this form it leads to the first full and really settled cadence. Here we can note a characteristic example of one of Beetho-

3. Beethoven to Karl Amenda, in Emily Anderson, ed., *The Letters of Beethoven*, 3 vols. (London, 1961), letter 53.

EXAMPLE 1.   Op. 18 no. 1, first movement, mm. 1–2

EXAMPLE 2.   Op. 18 no. 1, first movement, mm. 5–8

ven's alterations between the 1799 and 1800 versions: in 1799 he had the first violin begin the lyric continuation by itself both times, but in the revision he harmonized it the first time and left the more vulnerable unharmonized version as a special effect for its reappearance (Exx. 2 and 3).

The two violins in dialogue use the motto phrase to propel the music forward. At first Beethoven is firm about staying in F major, but then the harmonies become quite adventurous—the *pianissimo* landing in A-flat major is especially lovely—and by the time he is ready to settle in a new key (the dominant, C major) and present a new theme, he has

EXAMPLE 3.   Op. 18 no. 1, first movement, mm. 13–20

covered a lot of ground.[4] Hearing it out of context, you could easily take much of this transitional passage as part of a development section. Even here the motto phrase is not forgotten, and we also get a taste of Beethoven's knack for using silence as a dramatic effect.

The exposition moves to a firm close in C major. The first time this leads by the most natural harmonic motion back to the beginning, from C to F. The second time it does not lead anywhere; rather, Beethoven throws us into A major, which is remote indeed from where we have been, and there he repeats in slightly varied form the flourish with which he ended the exposition. Haydn often begins development sections with such a leap, but the fire that fuels this gesture is all Beethoven.

Equally abruptly, the music moves on to B flat, and from there Beethoven plunges into a development that is harmonically wide-ranging, fiercely energetic, and from which the opening phrase is hardly ever absent until it is time for the leadback to the recapitulation. To heighten the effect of the return, Beethoven withholds the theme from this section, giving us instead a passage marked by brilliant scales and powerful offbeat accents. When the theme at last arrives, it is *fortissimo*. The transitional passage is even more developmental in character than it had been in the exposition, and the harmonic travels carry us all the way over to G-flat major. Finally there is the surprise of the coda, extraordinary

4. I cannot emphasize too much how important *pianissimo* is in Beethoven. It is never just a softer version of *piano*; rather, it is a request—command, more like it—for an entirely different, incorporeal sound. To go to *pianissimo* is to enter a new expressive world.

for its dramas in *fortissimo* and *pianissimo*, and not less so for its tautly muscled ending.

The *Adagio* is to be played tenderly and expressively—*affettuoso ed appassionato.* (This specific direction was one of Beethoven's afterthoughts: the 1799 version gives the simpler *Adagio molto.*) From Amenda we learn that Beethoven had the tomb scene in Shakespeare's *Romeo and Juliet* in mind. It is believable, for here Beethoven is at his most Italian and operatic. Here, too, he is preoccupied with turns, but of course with quite different affect than in the first movement. Over throbbing triplets the first violin sings a broad and intense melody that ends when poignant silences enclose a *pianissimo* sigh. The cello sets out to repeat what the violin has sung, but by the third measure it is clear that this will not be a repetition, nor even a variation, but expansion and development. A new and gently sweet idea closes this chapter.

The real development section begins *pianissimo* but almost at once becomes fiercely turbulent. Schubert, writing the slow movement of his great Cello Quintet, learned much from this page. In the recapitulation the accompaniment is more agitated; indeed, both this section and the coda remain scarred by the storms of the development. Neither Haydn nor the through-and-through Italian and operatic Mozart could have written any two consecutive measures of this amazing threnody.

The third movement is swift and witty, a one-in-a-measure scherzo much like those you find in Haydn's later quartets. The phrase structure is pleasingly odd—for example, 6 + 2 + 2 for the opening strain. Here also is one of Beethoven's exceedingly rare excursions beyond *pianissimo* into *pianississimo.* The trio, rambunctious, startling, and combining swift surface motion with a very slow rate of harmonic change, is utterly amazing. Both scherzo and trio revisit some of the harmonic strategies that had proved so effective in the first movement.

In the finale—originally *Allegretto,* now *Allegro*—Beethoven borrows from Mozart: at least I hear the device of a brilliant violin swirl in triplets followed by "tutti" punctuation as Beethoven's variant of the opening of the finale of Mozart's D-major Quartet, K. 499 (Exx. 4 and 5). The personality is of course quite different—earth and some fire as against Mozart's air. Later, Beethoven offers a more lyric theme and finds amusing ways of contrasting it against repeated chords, sometimes *pianissimo,* sometimes with biting offbeat accents. This movement has tremendous verve and surprisingly few rests. In the bright coda, counterpoint becomes the tool of wit.

EXAMPLE 4.   Mozart Quartet in D Major, K. 499, fourth movement, mm. 1–4

EXAMPLE 5.   Op. 18 no. 1, fourth movement, mm. 1–4

STRING QUARTET IN G MAJOR, OP. 18 NO. 2

Allegro
Adagio cantabile—Allegro—Tempo I
Scherzo: Allegro
Allegro molto quasi presto

This G-major quartet was probably the third in the set to be composed. Of the six, it is the one that looks most openly to the eighteenth century and to Beethoven's famous and daunting precursors for lessons in de-

EXAMPLE 6.   Op. 18 no. 2, first movement, mm. 1–2

EXAMPLE 7.   Op. 18 no. 2, first movement, mm. 1–8

meanor—not, however, without some sense of irony. In German-speaking countries, the graceful curve of the first violin's opening phrase (Ex. 6) has earned the work the nickname of Komplimentier-Quartett, which might be translated as "quartet of bows and curtseys." But like Haydn, Beethoven—even the young Beethoven—was a master at setting up something in the butter-won't-melt-in-its-mouth vein and then. . . .

For instance, he follows his little two-measure doffing of the hat with a completely different two-measure phrase, which in turn leads to a 2 + 2 couplet (Ex. 7). As the music continues from this point, drawing on the possibilities of these contrasted ideas, we quickly come to understand that, while the gestures themselves are ever so harmless, Beethoven works his two-measure units with wit and skill. Not least and once again, he has learned well from the intellectual brilliance and the humor of Haydn's late quartets. What is unlike Haydn, who liked to put a minimum amount of material through more paces than one would believe possible, is the irrepressible bubbling of Beethoven's invention, which gives us new idea after new idea. Often these are followed by instant and charming variations.

In the most orderly way, the exposition has gone to the dominant, D major. In Op. 18 no. 1, Beethoven began the development with a startling leap from C major to A major. Here, however, he does it a non-shocking way and begins by taking the exposition's last phrase, which is actually the 2 + 2 couplet from the beginning, and repeating it in D minor.

In this movement, Beethoven uses another favorite Haydn device, the false recapitulation. The first theme returns, *forte* and richly scored with a quadruple stop for the first violin. Something, however, feels wrong. Two things in fact are wrong. First of all, it is too soon: only nineteen measures of development have gone by, and the exposition was eighty-one measures long (162 if it was repeated, as it should be). Not that you were counting, but you can feel that disproportion. The other thing is that Beethoven has brought the theme back in the wrong key, in E flat. Obviously no composer expects you to have perfect pitch, but an attentive listener hears more than he or she can put a name to. The arrival at the recapitulation should feel like coming home, and a composer usually achieves this by returning both to the carefully established main key and to an equally well-established and well-remembered theme. Here the theme is all right, but part of the charm of this moment lies in the very thing that makes it not a true homecoming: like opening a window we hadn't noticed before, Beethoven takes us, not back to G, but into a harmonic world previously untouched (to be precise, touched only in the previous six measures by way of preparation for this grandly false arrival).

Four measures later, Beethoven admits that he fooled us, and the development continues in conspiratorial *pianissimo*. Some of the instruments are occupied with the skipping figure that made up measure 3, others with spinning long and connected lines. Eventually, and as though to make up to us for his previous naughtiness in the matter of the false recapitulation, Beethoven makes loud and ostentatious preparations for the real thing. This display is reduced to its simplest form, a series of accented reiterations of Ds and Cs, enough to suggest unmistakably the dominant chord that prepares the return to the home key. The only thing is that while these preparations are still being made and the announcements sounded, the cello plays the opening phrase. We are home and in the living room before mother has finished plumping up the pillows. This causes a bit of confusion, and it takes a few measures before everybody understands what is happening—or what has happened—and everybody can get organized for a proper homecoming and welcome, all together.

The return to G major and to the first theme has been a weighty business, and now, in his game of doing and undoing, Beethoven feels he has to compensate for that too. The highly organized and amusing chaos has subsided, but no sooner has he given us four admirably neat measures (the counterpart of measures 9–12 in the exposition) than he veers off—in *pianissimo,* always a sign we should pay special attention—into music that feels like more development and that sends us, in fact, into the delightfully remote world of E major. With this excursion Beethoven balances his earlier bold venture in the opposite direction, the E-flat major of the false recapitulation. (The sonorous *forte* of that earlier episode is now answered by the hushed *pianissimo* of the E-major passage.) From here on, the recapitulation proceeds normally, though the coda, three times coming to an unmeasured stop, reminds us that we might find shadows even in the cheerful world of this movement. The ending is cute.

The slow movement is grave in tone, formal in manner, and elegantly embellished. What is surprising, though, is the way it opens with a pair of three-measure phrases. A still more surprising departure from the expected comes up a little later, when it suddenly occurs to the first violin to pick up a fragment of a perfectly ordinary cadential figure and run with it. Not only are we suddenly embarked on an *Allegro,* we have also been moved from C major—an altogether normal key for the slow movement of a work in G major—over to F major.

Here I should guess that Beethoven had once again been looking at Haydn, specifically that most astonishing C-major Quartet, Op. 54 no. 2, in which, instead of the quick finale you expect, you get a slow movement. This, after a while, opens up into a *Presto,* so that you think, aha, the *Adagio* was just an introduction; however, you are soon disabused of that when the slow music comes back and turns out to be the main matter of this mind-boggling finale. Of course to do such a thing in a finale is far wilder than to put an *Allegro* episode into a slow movement as Beethoven does here; nonetheless, the effect here is witty and charming, and it certainly keeps us on our toes. When Beethoven's *Adagio* returns, it has acquired a touch of Mozartean darkening, and the ornamentation has become still more profuse.

The third movement is a scherzo in mood and by designation, but it is still almost a minuet in tempo—that is, one certainly feels three full beats per measure. The trio, in C major, begins sturdily but spends much of its second part in scurrying *pianissimo*.

With the finale, Beethoven returns to much of the mood and many of the shapes of the first movement. Rhymes and symmetries abound, but there is plenty of opportunity for humor and surprise. And who—until John Adams—could ring such delightful changes on a tonic chord. Altogether, this exuberant finale represents the young Beethoven at his most wittily inventive.

STRING QUARTET IN D MAJOR, OP. 18 NO. 3

Allegro
Andante con moto
Allegro
Presto

This appears to have been the first of the Op. 18 Quartets to be composed. Except for a sudden surge of energy in the finale, it is the gentlest, most consistently lyrical work in the set. It seems to begin in mid-thought and in a singularly enchanting way. The first violin, alone, soars from A to G, allowing a full measure for each of the two notes. The keynote, D, is at exactly the midpoint between A and G. The violin, in the elegant curve of its descent, lightly brushes that note seven times, but its real aim is to flutter past and come to rest on the F sharp below. Underpinning that sweet fall, the other instruments outline the simplest progression to confirm that, yes, the key is indeed D major. It is a moment of an ease and grace of a kind we don't always immediately associate with Beethoven, even though it is a trait we meet often in his music, late as well as early.

Both the soaring seventh and the downward flutter give Beethoven

EXAMPLE 8.   Op. 18 no. 3, first movement, mm. 1–4

rewarding material to work with, and the next paragraph offers a charming demonstration of this. After a breath of silence, the viola plays the soaring seventh and is immediately imitated by the second violin. Both instruments remind us briefly of how the descent goes, but it is the first violin, which compresses the seventh into a minor third, that makes something fanciful of the descent. By the time all the instruments have done with their thoughts on ascent and descent, the original ten-measure phrase has grown into a paragraph of twenty-five measures.

Subsequent developments bring some spice in the form of sharply accented offbeats, and then the quartet applies itself to the task of heading toward a new key. All signs point to its being the dominant, A, just as you would expect. But there is long hesitation on the doorstep, the first violin's repeated scales get derailed, and when things settle down and a new theme is presented, not without some air of triumph and self-satisfaction, it is, quite unsuitably, in C major. This gets easily turned into A minor, after which a delightful theatrical effect, a sudden turning on of bright lights, propels the music into A major. It settles there just as though nothing untoward had happened en route. Beethoven celebrates this belated but happy arrival by giving us witty variants of Example 8, one upside down (Ex. 9), the other right side up (Ex. 10).

A striking series of detached chords built upon a rising bass leads first to a repeat of the exposition, the second time into the development. This begins as though the players had lost track of what they were doing and are going to make a third trip through the exposition. We hear the opening idea at its original pitch, and only in the third measure, when

EXAMPLE 9.   Op. 18 no. 3, first movement, mm. 78–81

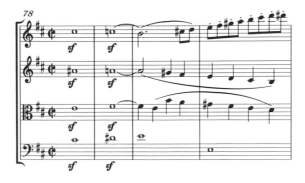

EXAMPLE 10.   Op. 18 no. 3, first movement, mm. 84–90

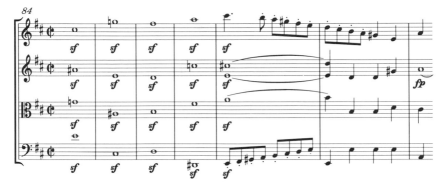

the three lower instruments enter, do we discover that this time Beethoven means to continue in D minor. During the development, which is neither elaborate nor long, he explores further possibilities in keys to the flat side of home (see "Circle of fifths" in the glossary).

The actual moment of recapitulation is deliciously imagined. The first *fortissimo* since the sudden landing in A major at the end of the exposition brings us to the doorstep of F sharp. This takes the form of two loud measures of emphatic chords of C-sharp major. Then only the C sharp itself remains in the cello and viola; the second violin decides to construe this as a possible bass to the soaring A/G seventh and so, in discreet *pianissimo,* offers to begin the recapitulation. This wakens the first violin, which takes on the task of recapitulation, but a bit more firmly, in *piano.*

We are home. Beethoven subtly adjusts the harmony: for instance, the first phrase ends, not on a D-major chord, as it did in the exposition, but in B minor, where it arrives by way of a deceptive cadence. The "wrong-key" joke is repeated, this time taking the music momentarily into F major. The coda revisits the opening phrase, the "wrong-key" theme, and the idea of traveling toward the flat side of the harmonic world (all the way to E flat this time!), and it is wonderfully poetic.

The idea of travel toward the flat side has taken hold, and the slow movement is, somewhat unconventionally, in B-flat major. "Slow movement" here means slow relative to the tempos of the other movements. This particular "slow movement" is an *Andante con moto,* which one might translate as "moving, but really moving"—in other words, anything but slow, though the division of beats into thirty-second notes does put the lid on the speed a bit. Not only is the key on the flat side of the quartet's home key of D major, but the whole tendency of the movement is to explore even further in that direction.

This is tenderly eloquent music, perhaps a first step in the direction that will lead, twenty-five years later, to the cavatina in Op. 130. The expressive range is wide. This becomes especially arresting toward the end of the movement, where an explosive *fortissimo* passage gives way to one of the earliest instances of those "broken" Beethoven codas, of which the most famous examples occur in the *Eroica*'s funeral march and the *Coriolan* Overture. With sighs and syncopations, the music comes to be ever more rhythmically afloat, fragmented, and hesitant, finally to disappear in scarcely audible *pianissimo* chords.

Now Beethoven returns to the bright world of D major with a vengeance. The third movement begins on F sharp, the one note that most specifically and emphatically defines D major and its distance from the *Andante*'s B-flat major. This is a quick, one-in-a-measure scherzo, full of sharp offbeat accents. The F sharp turns out to be more than an arresting first note in that F-sharp minor becomes the harmonic destination of the first eight-measure phrase. (Beethoven will do something similar but more elaborate with F sharps in the scherzo of the Second Symphony.) The harmonically flavorful trio, rapidly swirling scales for the two violins, is in D minor. Beethoven varies the return of the scherzo, first putting the repeat of the first eight measures up an octave, then omitting the repeat of the longer second section altogether.

As he does in Op. 18 no. 1, Beethoven begins the finale with the first violin alone, and here too the effect harks back to the finale of Mozart's

D-major Quartet, K. 499, while the shape of the theme makes it cousin to that in the D-major Quintet, K. 593. The music moves in a swift 6/8 meter. Having enjoyed administering in the first movement the shock of stopping in C major en route from D to A, Beethoven decides that, freshened up, the joke can be made to work again. This time he contrives a dramatic surprise landing on a chord of F major but compounds the surprise by veering off into A minor almost before we have had a chance to absorb what has happened. Then to get from A minor to A major is easy. But we also learn that that *sforzando* F-major chord was not just an aberration; before the exposition is over we hear some more quite emphatic remarks from that quarter.

The transitional passage back to the beginning is an amusing Ping-Pong of three-note phrases, and this same idea provides the material for the beginning of the development. Much of the development is energetically contrapuntal. This is a movement in which Beethoven first explores the idea of shifting the center of gravity toward the end of a multimovement work. This finale becomes more and more ambitious, adventurous, and humorous, developing an extraordinary forward-thrusting energy. The end, based on the three-note phrase from the exposition/development juncture, is a delightful joke. Haydn must have been pleased to be so skillfully emulated.

STRING QUARTET IN C MINOR, OP. 18 NO. 4

Allegro ma non tanto
Scherzo: Andante scherzo quasi allegretto
Menuetto: Allegretto
Allegro—Prestissimo

Number 4 actually is number four in order of composition. C minor, the key of the *Pathétique* Sonata, the Fifth Symphony, or the last piano sonata, is often thought of as *the* Beethoven key. Certainly it is the one we associate with the scowling portraits, with the gesture of defiantly seizing fate by the throat. Here is one of Beethoven's earliest C-minor essays, though it is preceded by three strong and interesting works, the Piano Trio, Op. 1 no. 3 (1794), the String Trio, Op. 9 no. 3 (1798), and the Piano Sonata, Op. 10 no. 1 (1796–98). In the quartet, Beethoven uses some material that he had brought to Vienna from Bonn in 1792, material older therefore than that in the works that were completed earlier.

In some ways Op. 18 no. 4 is the least typically C minor, the least stern, the least ferocious of the early pieces in that key; the first movement is, however, music of passion and urgency. The opening melody is forward-moving, but Beethoven applies a double set of brakes: the tempo is held back almost as though against the nature of the theme (the *Allegro*, he commands, must not be too *allegro*), and for the first six measures the cello, regardless of what is going on above, stays firmly glued to the keynote C. The scoring is grandly sonorous. The second violin is given the task of introducing a more lyric theme in a new key, the relative major, E flat. The development begins by reviewing the first theme in G minor, and the cello gets a turn at singing the second theme in its high register and in F major. This is the most straightforwardly presentational and least intricately worked of all the development sections in Op. 18. After a very direct recapitulation, Beethoven closes the movement with a powerful coda over a rising bass.

By contrast, the second movement presents itself as distinctly harmless. Beethoven calls it a scherzo, and it is important for the players to keep that designation in mind as they tiptoe through its *pianissimo* staccato tunes and administer the occasional *sforzando* pinprick; however, his use of the term here has nothing to do with the quick one-in-a-measure movements in the first and third quartets in this opus, nor with the movements that he labels scherzo in numbers 2 and 6. This piece, somewhere between *andante* and *allegretto*, surprisingly takes the place of a slow movement. In the matter of the types of movements and of their order, almost every quartet in Op. 18 offers some departure from tradition. With its naive 3/8 tune, this is clearly related to the second movement (marked *Andante cantabile e con moto*) of the First Symphony, though its fugal texture makes it a more ostentatiously learned cousin. The key is C major, but in the development section the music undertakes a considerable excursion toward the flat side that is the quartet's real harmonic home.

After the scherzo comes a minuet, made unruly by its offbeat accents. The trio is in A-flat major. It would be a sweet and lyric interlude but for the restlessness induced by the first violin's insistent triplets. Then Beethoven makes another departure from tradition by directing that the return of the minuet after the trio should be taken at a quicker tempo than the first time around.

The finale is a clean textbook rondo whose gypsy bounce is yet one more reminder of how much Beethoven had learned from his study of Haydn's music. The final return of the principal theme is made to charge forward at the fastest possible speed, and Beethoven contrives a witty, epigrammatic close.

STRING QUARTET IN A MAJOR, OP. 18 NO. 5

Allegro
Menuetto
Andante cantabile
Allegro

In this quartet, probably the fifth in order of composition as well as publication, Beethoven is very much engaged in receiving the spirit of Mozart, though by direct study of scores rather than "at the hands of Haydn." The model is the obvious and wonderful one, Mozart's quartet in the same key, K. 464.

A firm A-major chord sets everything in place metrically, though emphatic offbeat accents, a device we encounter constantly in Op. 18, express a need to contradict. On these offbeats, the first violin plays a three-note figure preceded by a turn, each time starting on successively higher notes of an A-major chord. By the third time, it has reached the right pitch and a sufficient amount of energy to start on an engagingly swinging theme (Ex. 11). As the music continues with an amusing cadential figure and moves swiftly toward the dominant, E, something that immediately strikes you as Mozartean is the abundance and variety of material. The landing on an E-major chord introduces, surprisingly, a new idea in E minor, the darker expressive implications of that choice being emphasized by the severe unharmonized octaves with which the new theme begins. For a moment this theme wants to go to G, its own relative major, but this maneuver is quickly headed off and we are back in E minor. In sudden *pianissimo*, minor turns to major. There is an awed silence. For a moment the exposition continues in *pianissimo*, further contemplating the new second theme. Then it drives toward its close, in high spirits now and with E major firmly established.

The development starts firmly, even dramatically, in F-sharp minor but soon settles into a more playful mood. Then the harmonies darken again, and Beethoven plans a beautifully gauged return to A major and

EXAMPLE 11.   Op. 18 no. 5, first movement, mm. 1–11

the opening theme. A recapitulation can start out exactly like the exposition, but where the exposition's task is to modulate to a new key as soon
as the home key is firmly established, the recapitulation must do precisely the opposite—in other words, not modulate but nail down the
home key more firmly than ever. This means that in the recapitulation
the composer soon comes to a fork in the road, the place where the first
time through he began his journey toward the new key but where now
he must rearrange matters so as not to find himself on that same path.
There are simple ways of doing that, but the greatest composers have
seen this moment of crisis as an opportunity to do something magical.

    Here is one of those moments. A harmonic sequence, so simple in
the exposition that we hardly feel challenged to pay special attention to
it, is now transformed into something to make us sit up. Example 12
shows what happens in the exposition. Example 13 is the corresponding

EXAMPLE 12. Op. 18 no. 5, first movement, mm. 16–24

place in the recapitulation. The astonishing thing is that both passages begin with the same jaunty A-major theme and both end with the same vigorous chord of E major. But the darker—and more elaborate—harmonic course of the second passage gives the E-major chord quite a different meaning when it arrives, and it feels like a completely natural consequence to have it now serve as an entrance into A minor. There Beethoven continues with the severe, initially unharmonized theme. The remainder of the recapitulation is straightforward, but Beethoven ends with a brief coda of witty play on the three notes with which the movement began.

Emulating Mozart's K. 464, Beethoven puts the minuet into second rather than third place.[5] He begins remarkably, with the melody in the

5. For Mozart this is a surprising choice inasmuch as his first movement is also in 3/4 time.

EXAMPLE 13. Op. 18 no. 5, first movement, mm. 151–64

first violin and an understated accompaniment in the second violin, while the two lower instruments remain silent. The next surprise is that the repeat of the first twelve measures is fully written out so as to give the viola an opportunity to play the tune. The second part begins sweetly, in the vein of the first, but takes a sudden turn into C-sharp minor and into a tone of voice reminiscent of the opening of the C-minor Quartet, Op. 18 no. 4. This *fortissimo* from an alien world produces a shocked silence, then the opening melody returns. At first it is as though nothing rude had occurred, but the change of a couple of G sharps to G naturals shows that the passionate C-sharp minor outburst did have its effect. The short trio is the kind of Beethoven I always think of as proto-Schubert: these are definitely country matters.

Next, like Mozart, Beethoven gives us a set of variations in D major. The theme, *Andante cantabile*, is warm and symmetrical—4+4 (repeated), then another 4+4 (also repeated, the last 4 being in effect the same as the first)—and its harmonic vocabulary is as simple as possible. There are five variations and a coda (Mozart has six and a coda). Variation 1 proceeds as a series of imitations that always build from the cello up. What is imitated is a staccato version of the theme, broken up into sixteenth notes, the cadences being enlivened by offbeat accents. By contrast, variation 2 tiptoes in *pianissimo*, the first violin moving in sixteenth-note triplets. In variation 3, the beats are broken down into still faster divisions as the second violin (and sometimes the first) accompanies phrases of the theme in thirty-second notes. In variation 4, Beethoven reverts to the simple quarters and eighths of the theme, but the harmonies are more highly colored, and, except for a single two-measure *crescendo*, the entire episode is held to *pianissimo*. Variation 5 bursts out of this hush with unbuttoned exuberance: second violin and viola play a jauntily decorated version of the theme, the first violin contributes jubilant trills and leaps, while the cello adds a terrifically energized bass, full of staccatos and offbeat accents.

This last variation is never completed. A deceptive cadence sends the music into distant B-flat major. For a moment the cello drums along by itself (in Mozart's final variation the cello's drum imitation is so explicit that the work is sometimes called the "Drum" Quartet), then various instruments musingly play fragments of the theme against a rich variety of accompaniments. This episode builds to a sonorous *forte*, after which, at a slightly slower tempo, the movement vanishes in *pianissimo*.

The finale moves like the wind, and its initial three-note upbeat is an extraordinary source of energy. Here, as in Op. 18 no. 3, is another movement where Beethoven begins to move the center of gravity toward the end of the work. Here he comes very close to the spirit of his model as well as to some of its technical details. By way of contrast to the swift first theme, with its chattering eighth notes, he gives us a theme that begins with four measures of whole notes and then continues in half notes. The development explores the possibilities of the minor mode. It is wide-ranging in its harmonies and full of busy, excited counterpoint. The coda is big and full of humor, and the last measures make a delicious send-off.

STRING QUARTET IN B-FLAT MAJOR, OP. 18 NO. 6

Allegro con brio
Adagio ma non troppo
Scherzo: Allegro
La Malinconia: Adagio—Allegretto quasi Allegro—Prestissimo

Just as he saw to it that Op. 18 opened with something especially strong, so did Beethoven take pains to place a particularly impressive and original work at the end of the collection. Opus 18 no. 6 begins with Beethoven's own version of crisp, Haydnesque good humor. Here he explores the pleasures of simplicity. As the music gets off to its cheery, relaxed start, everything is symmetrical, everything rhymes. Even the accents are *fp* rather than the sharper *sforzandi* of which there are so many throughout this opus.

The conversational exchange between first violin and cello, later first and second violins, are so simple that their very ease becomes amusing and draws a smile from the listener—and, like as not, from the players. In the first twenty-nine measures, there are not a half dozen beats where the harmony is something other than tonic or dominant. This—symmetries and super-simple harmonies—ought to be the unbeatable recipe for boring music, yet there is nothing more delightful in Beethoven than this inviting paragraph.

The modulation to the new key, F major, is quick, and, consistent with the simple manner he has established so far, Beethoven actually draws up to a formal halt before presenting a new theme. This, too, is as simple as possible. At least it starts that way, but already the second four-measure phrase sinks into F minor, and a very dark F minor at that.

With equal abruptness the major mode returns, and the exposition ends with dispatch, bringing a pleasant reminder of the opening theme.

Sometimes Beethoven begins his developments with a dramatic plunge into previously unexplored harmonic territory. Here—and this is comparable to his harmonic strategy at the outset of this movement— he stays for a surprisingly long time in F major, the key in which the exposition had ended. The material is the little turn that is so characteristic a feature of that theme. Then he begins to move out, first to D major, which he quickly interprets as the dominant of G minor. But at the point where we seem to be about to enter that key, everything stops. When, after an astonishingly long silence, the music resumes, it is indeed in G minor, but the opening theme is forgotten, and Beethoven's concern is now with the simple passage—a scale and some repeated notes— with which he had accomplished the modulation from B flat to F in the exposition. When the opening theme reappears once again in F, it turns out to be the beginning of the leadback to the recapitulation. Beethoven makes this process unusually long and suspenseful as well as amusing.

After enough times of "well? . . . well? . . ." Beethoven launches the recapitulation in a nice, orderly fashion. The second theme is, of course, in the home key this time, and Beethoven, with delightful wit, surprises us by making the passage toward it longer and much more complex than its counterpart in the exposition. In other words, he makes more of his nonmodulation than of the earlier journey from one key to another. And one more surprise: no coda. The last assertive measure of the recapitulation is also the last measure of the movement.

The slow movement is also a study in the possibilities of naiveté. So at least it begins, with a violin melody of beguiling simplicity. Soon, however, the atmosphere changes. Viola and cello punctuate the melody with a stalking figuration—"well marked," writes Beethoven—that prefigures the similar but even more powerful and disturbing gestures in the slow movement of the great D-major Cello Sonata, Op. 102 no. 2. Then it is not long before Beethoven darkens the scene further by going into minor, emphasizing the ominous implications of this change by leaving the music unharmonized and having it played in incorporeal *pianissimo*. Now the floodgates are open, and Beethoven uses unexpected accents, dissonance, and silence to create one of the most intensely expressive of his early slow movements.

With the scherzo, Beethoven makes an enormous leap into a totally original manner, one that must have struck many a player and listener in

EXAMPLE 14.   Op. 18 no. 6, third movement, mm. 1–4 (rhythmic outline)

1801 as rude indeed. The trouble—exhilarating trouble—is with the syncopations. Most of the time, viola and cello stand for law and order. The violins meanwhile play a tune that the ear can easily "read" as in three, but their "one" does not coincide with that of the lower instruments. Every so often their aberration is corrected, and those corrections carry their own delightful ambiguity. On the one hand they represent the necessary norm against which the violins rebel, and they do occur just often enough for the joke to work; on the other hand, each correction produces a new jolt. It is a wild ride (Ex. 14). The trio, with its gamboling violin figure, is tiny and capricious. Beethoven concocts a brief and startling mock-grim bridge back to the repeat of the scherzo.

What happens next is an even greater surprise—slow music, groping, full of harmonic mystery, strangely alternating between the hushed and the assertive. Beethoven calls it *La Malinconia*—melancholy—and he instructs the musicians that "this piece must be treated with the greatest possible delicacy." This is music for a quartet that really understands *pianissimo*. From time to time *malinconia* gives way to anguished *disperazione*. The harmonies move across the entire known universe, from B-flat major all the way to E major, than which there is no greater possible distance. Slowly, by half steps, the bass rises from D to A. At the same time, the bass notes and the chords that respond to them grow from *pianissimo* to *fortissimo*. A sudden hush, a pause, and the pensive broodings of this page—surely the most extraordinary in all of Op. 18—are dissolved in dance music.

Not that this German country dance is ordinary: the disruptive *sforzandi* on the second beats see to that. The tension grows and there is a crisis, a great *fortissimo* grinding into a diminished chord. *La Malinconia* returns. The dance music attempts to resume, strangely, in A minor, but after just three measures it breaks off. Another silence, and once more we hear *La Malinconia*, though only a fragment of it. Again the dance music resumes, this time in G major, but the shadows cast by melancholy are long. Quickly and easily the music works its way back to its proper key of B flat. Just once it slows down for a few measures, pensively. Then, leaping forward *prestissimo*, it makes its untroubled way to the end.

The opening page of the autograph to the breakneck finale of the Quartet in
C Major, Op. 59 no. 3. The direction *crescendo poco a poco* (growing louder little by
little) was added after the entire work had been notated. (Reproduced by permission of the Beethoven-Archiv, Bonn.)

The Middle Quartets

The Razumovsky Quartets

In 1801, Beethoven had published his first six string quartets, the set known as Op. 18. Four years later he returned to the writing of string quartets, the occasion being a commission for three such works from Count Andreas Kyrilovich Razumovsky, the Russian ambassador in Vienna since 1792 and characterized by a contemporary as an "enemy of the Revolution but a friend to the fair sex." Razumovsky was an art collector, an excellent amateur violinist, and serious enough about music to ask Beethoven for theory and composition lessons. (Beethoven sent him to his own former teacher, Emanuel Förster.)

From 1808 until 1814, when his town house burned down, Razumovsky maintained his own string quartet. Its leader was Ignaz Schuppanzigh, who had been a friend of Beethoven's since at least 1794, would be his concertmaster on more than one occasion (including the premiere of the Ninth Symphony), and be involved in the first performances of, among other works, the Septet, the Razumovsky quartets, the quartets opp. 95, 127, 130, 132, and 135, and the "Archduke" Trio. He also led the first performances of Schubert's Octet and A-minor Quartet, D. 804. Razumovsky usually played second violin; Louis Sina was his professional stand-in on those occasions when the count preferred to listen.

Since Op. 18 Beethoven had undertaken those immense voyages of discovery that had made it possible for him to compose such works as the *Eroica,* the "Tempest," "Waldstein," and "Appassionata" sonatas, the "Kreutzer" Sonata, *Fidelio,* and, in 1806, the year he finished the Razumovsky quartets, the Fourth Piano Concerto, the Fourth Symphony, and the Violin Concerto. Not surprisingly, then, the Razumovsky quartets are to their genre what the *Eroica* had been to the symphony and the "Waldstein" to the piano sonata. The Vienna correspondent of the Leipzig *Allgemeine musikalische Zeitung,* the most important musical magazine of its day, reported early in 1807 that "three new, very long, and difficult Beethoven quartets . . . are attracting the attention of all connoisseurs. They are profoundly thought through and admirably worked out, but not to be grasped by all."[1]

STRING QUARTET IN F MAJOR, OP. 59 NO. 1

> *Allegro*
> *Allegretto vivace e sempre scherzando*
> *Adagio molto e mesto*
> *Thème russe: Allegro*

As always, when assembling an opus consisting of several works, Beethoven took pains to achieve as much variety as possible. The F-major quartet is the one that the reporter for the Leipzig *Allgemeine musikalische Zeitung* must have had particularly in mind when he referred to Beethoven's new quartets as "very long." Only a couple of the late quartets surpass it in generosity of scale, and, unlike Op. 59 no. 1, they are in more than the standard four movements. What the writer for the Leipzig magazine could not have known is that Beethoven had originally envisioned a design still more ample than the one he actually filled in.

The opening—the slowly unfolding cello melody and its continuation by the first violin, with the harmony so skillfully set to convey a sense of suspended motion—at once suggests vast space and breadth (Ex. 1).[2] The harmony—six and a half measures of tonic, eleven and a half of dominant—moves by grand and leisurely strides. With the long dominant buildup, most of it poised on one of the less usual inversions of the chord (the fifth rather than the root of the chord is in the bass), goes a *crescendo,* and the arrival at *fortissimo* coincides with the first really firm-sounding tonic chord.[3]

---

1. Elliot Forbes, ed., *Thayer's Life of Beethoven,* 2 vols. (Princeton, 1964), 1:409.

2. The cellist for whom Beethoven wrote this glorious opening was Joseph Linke, who had come to Vienna from Breslau in Silesia. In 1815 Beethoven wrote the two Sonatas, Op. 102, for him, and he took part, with Schuppanzigh, in the first performances of most of Beethoven's late quartets.

3. Actually, root-position tonic chords, that is, F-major chords with F in the bass, have already occurred five times before this grand arrival in m. 19, but because of the way they are placed in the rhythmic flow, none sounds or feels stable. Four of them, in

EXAMPLE 1.   Op. 59 no. 1, first movement, mm. 1–8

With this arrival, the atmosphere changes, at least for the moment. From a smooth melody that moves mainly by step, Beethoven goes to an idea with leaps, staccatos, airspaces. Stretching out into very long notes, it gives way to a new theme in which first the two violins, then the viola and cello, play in so-called horn intervals (hearing them, you will immediately know why). This in turn leads to some recollection of the spacious opening melody, which is now given an extra charge of energy by decorative scales in triplets. The triplets take on a life of their own and lead, by way of yet another idea that proceeds staccato and by

---

mm. 1, 3, 5, and 7, are left quickly, and the first and last of these are also on weak beats. In m. 6, to be sure, the tonic chord is on the downbeat and lasts for three-quarters of the measure; what weighs more, however, is the function of that F in the cello melody, which is to press forward rather than to be an anchor. That sense is enhanced by the *crescendo* that Beethoven has marked for all the instruments. See Ex. 1. There is much to ponder here.

EXAMPLE 2.   Op. 59 no. 1, first movement, mm. 103–8

leaps, to a new key—C major, the dominant—and a new theme, conjunct and smooth like the movement's first melody. The triplets continue
to make their presence known, and so, in extremely heightened form,
does the idea of leaps. (The triplets, in arpeggios that cover nearly three
octaves, had prepared our ears for the notion of wide register changes.)
And so, with one more reminiscence of the opening melody, the exposition, extraordinarily rich in material and event, comes to an end.

Now, as is customary in the classical tradition, the exposition is repeated. So at least it seems. The cello begins its wonderful melody again,
and for four measures everything proceeds just as before. But the fifth
measure departs, and by the sixth measure the departure, harmonic and
melodic, is radical (Ex. 2). Beethoven must have thought that this deception, this "false repeat," was liable to engender confusion, because he
makes a point of adding a note to say that the exposition is to be played
only once. At one stage, however, he planned to have the development

and recapitulation repeated, which is what he had done the year before in the finale of the "Appassionata." He had also projected a large internal repeat in the scherzo and a short one in the coda of the finale. All these were dropped. Had he kept them, the quartet would have come out at least as long as the *Eroica*.

The development is half as long again as the exposition and deals by turns with lyricism (by way of reminiscences of the opening melody), triplets, arpeggios, and dramatic contrasts of register. In its first phase, Beethoven builds the tension by setting events over a steadily rising bass. He even introduces a new element in the form of some learned-sounding fugal music. The effect of this is doubly dramatized: the key is E-flat minor, the farthest departure from home in this movement, and the first sixteen measures are set in mysterious *pianissimo*. The music begins to edge toward the dominant, and it is clear that Beethoven is making preparations for a return, for the recapitulation. Eight measures of reiterated or sustained C, the dominant, confirm this.

And here Beethoven wittily deceives us. Everyone stops playing except the first violin, alone on a stratospheric B flat. From there it climbs another half step to B natural. It is obvious that C will be next, a C that can be underpinned with a dominant chord that would place us right on the doorstep of F major and home. C is indeed next, but under it Beethoven puts, not the C-major chord we expect, but a first-inversion chord of F major. It is as though we had leaped from the sidewalk across the doormat right into the house, though landing a little bit off balance.

Furthermore, the music we now hear—as distinct from the harmonic skeleton—is the theme with the staccatos and the leaps that came immediately after the broad opening melody. Has Beethoven decided to begin the recapitulation with the counterpart of the exposition's measure 19? Has he decided that in the course of the development we have heard enough of the opening melody, or that he should compensate for its "illegitimate" appearance at the beginning of the development by leaving it out now?

The theme with the staccatos and the leaps proceeds normally for a moment, then veers off into strange and transient harmonies. Was this then not the recapitulation after all? Swiftly Beethoven makes his way to a diminished seventh chord, that handy universal joint from which one can proceed in so many different directions, and in another two measures, the second of them filled with scales in vigorous contrary motion, he finds his way home.

There is a lovely subtlety to this because "home" means a less than perfectly stable tonic chord. After all, the first bar of the cello melody begins with a C in the bass, not an F (see Ex. 1), and in the exposition we had to wait till measure 19 for the first rocklike tonic downbeat. Always in the recapitulation there must occur a moment when the path diverges from the one taken in the exposition (see my account of the first movement of Op. 18 no. 5, pp. 165–67). Here Beethoven throws that switch surprisingly early, particularly for a piece laid out on so broad a scale: he changes direction only thirteen measures into the recapitulation. With an expressive darkening of which Mozart would have been proud, the harmony moves toward the flat side until the theme with the "horn" fifths comes, not in the tonic F, but all the way over in D-flat major. (Leaning toward the subdominant or flat side in the recapitulation is a way of balancing the drive toward the dominant or sharp side in the exposition.)

The harmony continues to move about without settling firmly anywhere. Meanwhile, Beethoven brings back material from the exposition, with the conspicuous absence of the theme with the staccatos and leaps that had made a premature return just before the real moment of recapitulation. The mood is ruminative and delicately shadowed. By the time the lyric second theme reappears the music is in F major, where it should be, but still Beethoven withholds what surely, even if unconsciously, we are waiting for: that firm downbeat on a root-position tonic chord. Indeed, the recapitulation is all but over before we are allowed that gratification.

Like the exposition, the recapitulation ends with a dreamy reminiscence of the opening melody. Now, however, what supports it is not merely the tonic F in the bass but an insistent drone on two-thirds of a tonic chord, F and C together. We have had to wait for eighty-six measures and through virtually the entire recapitulation, but now Beethoven gives us double security.[4] In the coda there is play, first, with triplets and arpeggios; then recollections of the opening melody send the first violin to an ecstatic high C. Beethoven makes for a poetic *pianissimo* close, but

---

4. Brahms learned deeply from this movement. In the first movement of his Fourth Symphony he emulates, worthily and poetically, the device of having the recapitulation begin as though it were a repeat of the exposition. More important, he became a past master at withholding the tonic (for an enchanting example, see his Intermezzo in B-Flat Major for Piano, Op. 76 no. 4).

EXAMPLE 3.   Op. 59 no. 1, second movement, mm. 1–4

at the last a sudden and quick *crescendo* leads the movement to an assertive final cadence in *fortissimo*.

Donald Francis Tovey points out how many of Beethoven's themes are instantly identifiable by their rhythm alone. The second movement of Op. 59 no. 1 is an example. I know a man who lives on a small island off the Maine coast, and to signal him that he is to row across the channel to the mainland and pick you up, you blow the pattern in Example 3 on your car horn. He could have picked nothing more distinctive or unlikely to be tapped out by chance.

The cello drums it on a monotone, *pianissimo*. Had Beethoven been writing 150 years later, he might have asked the cellist to tap it, unpitched, on the back of his instrument; as it is, he sets the signal on the movement's keynote, B flat. The second violin answers with a sharply profiled fragment of melody, also *pianissimo*. Viola and second violin, moving startlingly far afield harmonically, repeat the dialogue. Beethoven sees enormous possibilities in what these sixteen brief measures imply, the motto rhythm itself, the melody, the ideas of dialogue and of wide-ranging harmonic shifts. The quick tossing of the conversational ball from one instrument to another is delightful and becomes more and more important as the movement unfolds. To these devices Beethoven adds the contrast between swift progress and near stasis. It is enough to keep him—and us—amused for a long time.

A comic pratfall brings this phase to an abrupt end in C major. The movement is in B flat, which means that C is actually the dominant of the dominant, F. In other words, the music is now nicely poised to continue in F, just as we might expect. The surprise is that F turns out to be F minor. From here, Beethoven builds an expansive, witty, and ever more amusing and adventurous scherzo in sonata form. He reminds us as well that he is unparalleled as a master of silence. A huge first movement is no surprise, but a scherzo on this scale and so fully developed is astonishing indeed.

It is the second violin that begins the next movement, *sotto voce*. Its sustained middle C is a longitudinal reference point beneath which viola and cello lay out dark harmonies and above which the first violin sings a poignant melody. *Adagio molto e mesto* is what Beethoven directs—very slow and sad. *Mesto* is a rare word for him: this is his first use of it since the slow movement of his first absolutely great piano sonata, the D-major, Op. 10 no. 3, of 1798. The cello, up in its tenor register, repeats the melody, still in *piano,* but *espressivo* rather than *sotto voce.* A very brief passage that is continuation, development, and transition all in one leads to a new duet for cello and violin. This culminates in a most extraordinary keening passage, a music whose unabashed suggestion of weeping Beethoven will not attempt again until the great *dolente* aria in his Piano Sonata, Op. 110.

The movement continues to expand in Beethoven's most generous melodic style, exploring the rich soil of D-flat major. This wonderfully scored song dissolves at last into an ethereal cadenza for the first violin. Below that cadenza's closing trill, the cello introduces a robust tune that Beethoven marks *Thème russe.* Either at Razumovsky's request or possibly as a compliment volunteered by the composer, the first two quartets of Op. 59 include such a theme. A witty touch: the first notes of the *Thème russe* are a magnification of the two notes of the trill that introduces it (Ex. 4).

This Russian theme is the foundation of Beethoven's energetic and effective finale. In spirit this is a "relaxation finale" in Haydn's manner; it is, however, a considerable sonata form movement. The exposition is repeated. The development is long, though not notably complex; recapitulation and coda are full of invention. The coda falls to musing—slowing to *adagio* (but, Beethoven warns, *ma non troppo*) and sinking to *pianississimo*—but then a quick rally, *presto,* brings Op. 59 no. 1 to a vigorous conclusion.

EXAMPLE 4.   Op. 59 no. 1, fourth movement, mm. 1–3

STRING QUARTET IN E MINOR, OP. 59 NO. 2

Allegro
Molto Adagio
Allegretto
Finale: Presto

While the F-major quartet that stands at the head of Op. 59 is richly expansive in the new manner defined most strikingly by the *Eroica* Symphony of 1803–4, this work reflects Beethoven's parallel interest in the taut and terse statement. Especially its first movement is lean in sound, abrupt in gesture and sequence. No contrast could be more vivid than that between the cello melody that begins Op. 59 no. 1 and the two staccato chords that propel Op. 59 no. 2 into motion.

The two chords are those of the tonic and its dominant, E minor and B major. That is the most ordinary idea in the world; there is, however, nothing ordinary about these two chords. First of all, though their effect is of tremendous force, they are, like the two chords that begin the *Eroica*, not *fortissimo* but *forte*.[5] *Fortissimo* is held in reserve. Because of the use of the open E string in both violins, the sonority has a remarkable

5. One is quite likely to remember both the *Eroica* and the Razumovsky chords as *fortissimo*. In part, their rhetorical force accounts for this, but so, I am afraid, does the fact that many performers do actually whack them out as *fortissimo*.

EXAMPLE 5.   Op. 59 no. 2, first movement, mm. 1–8

bite, though this is of course more prominent on modern instruments
with their steel E strings than it would have been on Schuppanzigh's and
Razumovsky's (or Sina's) violins in 1807. Something else that makes this
pair of chords special is the positioning and voicing of the second chord.
The normal and obvious way to set such a chord would be with its root,
B, in the bass, but Beethoven chooses a more highly flavored solution
by making the D sharp the lowest note. As for voicing, no open strings
are available for this chord, but Beethoven compensates for this by including no third of the chord, no D sharp, other than the one in the
bass: everything else is ringing fifths and octaves (Ex. 5, m. 1).

   The dramatic effect of this summons to attention is heightened by the
silence that follows. The silence is in turn followed by a brief phrase in
pianissimo, a hushed sequence of tonic–dominant–tonic, couched as a
simple pair of arpeggios, ascending and descending. "Dominant" needs
to be qualified. The function of the descending arpeggio in measure 4
is that of a dominant, but the chord itself, with its "extra" seventh and
ninth, A and C, is spicier than just a straight dominant (Ex. 5, m. 4).

   This phrase, too, is followed by a silence. After the silence, the phrase
is repeated, in major, and half a step up. The chord based on the note
one half step up from the tonic is, for no very convincing reason, called
Neapolitan, and by extension we also speak of Neapolitan relationships.
It is a savory harmonic device that Beethoven and Schubert use especially effectively. Beethoven had just made powerful use of it in the first

movement of his F-minor Piano Sonata, Op. 57, the "Appassionata." In this quartet, Beethoven follows his momentary excursion to F major with another silence, then returns to his dominant ninth to move the music forward.

One characteristic of the opening theme is its tendency to dissolve into sixteenth notes. The music returns to the two-chord gesture and its consequent silence. The first violin proposes a new and urgent melodic fragment. Through storms and forceful accents, the music makes its way to a new key, G major, and a new theme. This theme, too, is brief and is soon transformed into sixteenth-note passages. An episode made mysterious by its harmonies, its syncopations, and the *pianissimo* in which it begins rises to brilliant and assertive arpeggios for the first violin and viola, and these nail down the modulation to G major.

The first time, this leads back naturally to the opening E-minor summons and so to the repeat of the exposition. The second time, a dramatic throwing of the switch turns G major into G minor. This opens the way to E-flat major, where Beethoven now repeats the opening pair of chords, *fortissimo*. After another silence the chords come again, but *piano*, and compressed in range. By way of a *pianissimo* harmonic pun that retains the top notes of the two chords but provides them with a different underpinning, Beethoven makes his way to B minor, where an expanded version of measures 3 and 4 (see Ex. 5) starts the development. Now he gives us a variant of his Neapolitan continuation, going from B minor to C minor. The harmonies move rapidly, especially in the early phase of the development, which is concerned with the pair of chords, the arpeggiated theme, and the mysterious episode with the syncopations.

The leadback to the recapitulation is managed with a rush of fierce energy: in a passage powerfully punctuated by trills and silences, all the instruments descend in octaves, *fortissimo*. This too spills into runs of sixteenth notes, but as these begin the cello forcefully recalls the two chords to our memory. The whole quartet reiterates them, but the swirl of sixteenth notes continues, filling what was previously the empty space between the chords and the first theme. The E-minor phrase is followed by a silence, as before, but its F-major Neapolitan echo is extended so as to fill what was previously a blank measure (Ex. 6).

F major gets one more brief but conspicuous play as the recapitulation gets under way. This time the destination is E major, and here Beethoven

EXAMPLE 6.   Op. 59 no. 2, first movement, mm. 141–48

went through with the idea he scrapped in the first movement of Op.
59 no. 1, that of asking for a second trip through the development and
recapitulation. To turn back to the E-flat major chords at the beginning
of the development makes for a dramatic wrench indeed. When you
come to the same junction the second time, the harmonic progression
echoes the one that took us from the exposition into the development: E major suddenly becomes E minor, and this opens the door to
C major.

The coda begins in parallel to the start of the development—the same
harmonic pun, the same sequences of the pairs of chords separated by
silences—except that this time it is set to begin from C rather than E
flat. The coda is big—about two-thirds the length of the recapitula-

tion—and adventurous. An amazing series of harmonic steps through C minor and G-sharp minor takes us back to the home key of E minor. The rate of harmonic change is slow, slower by far than anywhere else in the movement, and this heightens drama and suspense. After one last *fortissimo* outburst of the music from Example 5, the music moves quickly to a hushed close.

The hymnlike second movement offers greater breadth both of design and sentiment; it is not just slow but "very slow," to which Beethoven adds the instruction that "this piece is to be played with much feeling." The key is E major; in fact, all four movements are based on the same keynote. This quartet and the D-major Piano Sonata, Op. 10 no. 3, are among the few Beethoven four-movement works of which this is true. The inner rhythm of this movement changes little, but Beethoven is infinitely resourceful at varying degrees of nervousness in his accompaniments. The recapitulation, where the second violin soars in descant above the first violin's hymn, is a miracle. At the end, the hymn is grandly presented in slow chords by the whole quartet, and after this apotheosis, the coda, leaning slightly toward the subdominant side and anchored to a long pedal on the keynote, E, is of beatific serenity.[6] This is a vein Beethoven would explore again about nineteen years later in the Lydian-mode Song of Thanksgiving of the Quartet in A Minor, Op. 132.

As I noted in the essay on Op. 59 no. 1 (see p. 182), each of the first two Razumovsky quartets includes a Russian theme. In Op. 59 no. 2, this happens in the trio of the urgently forward-moving scherzo. The *Thème russe* is one also used by Mussorgsky and Rachmaninoff, and if Razumovsky was at ease with, to say nothing of delighted by, Beethoven's dissonant roughhousing with it and his mocking sweeping of its shards out of the door, he was an enlightened, forward-looking patron indeed. As for the scherzo itself, with its held-in energy, its arpeggio-based E-minor theme, and its emphasis on the Neapolitan F major, it suggests a ghostly visitation of the first movement. Beethoven asks for a double trip around the scherzo-trio-scherzo cycle.

Like the trio of the scherzo, the boisterous finale has something about it of country manners. It begins emphatically on a chord of C major, and both the cantering accompaniment and the first violin's country

6. Risking a generalization, I would say that movement toward the dominant or sharp side tends to produce excitement, while movement toward the subdominant or flat side tends to be calming.

EXAMPLE 7.   Op. 59 no. 2, fourth movement, m. 56

dance tune confirm this harmonic orientation, at least for the first six measures. In measure 7, the bass sinks a half step from C to B, and, two measures later, Beethoven contrives a firm cadence in E minor. No sooner is this accomplished than he bounces right back into C major to begin the process all over again. This time the stay in E minor is a little longer, but it is no more secure than before. Beethoven repeats this game twice more, and it is not until measure 52 that he gives us a firm arrival in E minor. Schumann enjoyed this game and imitated it in the last movement of his Piano Quintet. Beethoven's drawn-out and repeated indecision between an apparently irresistible C major and the "proper" E minor gives the movement an agreeable piquancy. I would guess that one reason for this heavily stressed off-key start—half of the fifty-two measures leading up to the first firm E-minor cadence are in C major— is to take the curse off his chosen homotonality (an ugly but useful word to denote the basing of all the movements of a multimovement work upon the same keynote).

This is music of roistering good humor. Beethoven has fun with a three-note figure with which, in his best Haydnesque manner, he can build suspense concerning where, if anywhere, he is going and when, if ever, he is going to get there (Ex. 7). On its next to last appearance, the C-major dance is enlivened by having the second violin imitate the first. Earlier flirtations with F major are not forgotten. After one last fling with the dance tune, *sempre fortissimo* this time, Beethoven turns the screw from *presto* to *più presto* as the quartet charges toward its final measures.

STRING QUARTET IN C MAJOR, OP. 59 NO. 3

Introduzione: Andante con moto—Allegro vivace
Andante con moto quasi allegretto
Menuetto: Grazioso
Allegro molto

If the A-major Quartet, Op. 18 no. 5, is a bow toward Mozart's quartet in the same key, K. 464, so does Op. 59 no. 3 owe something to Mozart's C-major Quartet, K. 465. It attests equally to Beethoven's apprenticeship with Haydn, not the Haydn of the indifferent lessons but the Haydn who composed the "Representation of Chaos" in *The Creation*. Mozart's C-major quartet is called the "Dissonant" in honor of the mysterious goings on in its slow introduction, and it is in Beethoven's no less strange and even more suspenseful introduction that we immediately sense the connection with his model. For all the distinctively Beethovenian caprices in demeanor and gait, there is much in this quartet and in this movement in particular that comes off as distinctly classical, particularly in the light of the other two first movements in Op. 59. (It is worth stopping a moment to reflect that when Beethoven worked on his Razumovsky quartets, K. 465 was relatively new music, only twenty-one years old, and it was only five years since the first performance of *The Creation*.)

The reviewer for the *Allgemeine musikalische Zeitung* whom I cited earlier (see page 176) characterized the "profoundly thought through and admirably worked out" Razumovsky quartets as "very long and difficult [and] not to be grasped by all except," he suggested, "the third one in C, which by virtue of its individuality, melodic invention, and harmonic power is bound to win every educated music lover." I wonder if the anonymous reviewer's picking this particular quartet as "most likely to succeed" also had something to do with Beethoven's occasional backward glances here, even though they are in part glances at some of the most "difficult" music of the recent and fairly recent past.

Here, at any rate, is yet another way of beginning. After the generous lyricism of the F-major quartet and the brusque rap to attention of the E-minor, Op. 59 no. 3 starts enigmatically. The simplest possible description would be to say that a quick movement firmly centered on C major is prepared by a suspenseful upbeat. Now what actually happens?

The first sound is a diminished chord built up over an F sharp in the cello. Now if Beethoven had scandalized theorists and shocked listeners

EXAMPLE 8.   Op. 59 no. 3, first movement, mm. 1–2

with his off-kilter beginnings in the First Symphony (1800) and *Prome-theus* Overture (1804), the opening chord of this quartet (Ex. 8) must really have stabbed the people who first heard it. Now, not even in 1807 was there anything intrinsically disturbing about the chord itself; it was a common enough component of harmonic vocabulary. The shock would have lain in its being the first sound to emerge from the silence. You could go fairly far in dissonance, meaning an unstable chord that needs to be resolved to a consonance, but the assumption was that dissonances would not only move on to consonance but would always emerge from consonance. To begin, as Beethoven does here, with an unprepared dis-sonance was to issue a challenge. The desire to shock is part of his design.

This is not the same as a desire to annoy. Beethoven was perfectly capable of that in life, but he did not waste his artistic energy on such games. No, what Beethoven wants to do here is to make you sit up, because he is going to do extraordinary things, things that ask your ut-most alertness. Let us now try to follow him.

That first chord is *forte*, though Beethoven marks a *diminuendo* across its four beats. (The tempo, *Andante con moto*, is neither slow nor fast.) After a brief silence there is another chord, *pianissimo*, and it is identical to the first except that the lowest note has dropped a half step, from F sharp to F natural. Those few vibrations make a staggering difference. Diminished chords such as the one in Example 8 are vague. They can be resolved in many directions. That is their technical advantage to the composer; that is their charm. The second chord unambiguously suggests a particular resolution or destination. That of course does not mean that Beethoven has to meet our very clear expectation, and in fact he does something quite different from what we expect. Still keeping the first violin on A as a connection and point of reference, he drops the bass another half step to E. At the same time he raises the second violin a half step, the two maneuvers together giving him a chord of A minor in its least stable position.

This, then, is how Beethoven proceeds. Over the course of twenty-nine measures the bass descends through an octave and a half from F sharp, through F, E, D, C, B, A, A flat, G, F, E, E flat, D, and C, to B. The chords erected upon these notes are never those we expect or foresee, yet each upon its arrival is totally convincing. As the cello descends, the first violin climbs from A above middle C to the D an octave and a half higher. Except for one chord whose *forte* and *diminuendo* repeat the dynamics of the first two measures, the entire introduction is held down to Beethoven's disembodied *pianissimo*. The phrases get longer (from twice two measures, to five measures, to fifteen) and the rate of harmonic change gets slower. These changes bring about a growing sense of mystery and suspense, a kind of inspired unclarity. At the same time we feel delight and faith that in the most purposeful way we are being taken somewhere, even though for the moment we may not have the slightest idea where.

When the first violin and the cello are separated as far as possible, the music has again landed on a diminished chord. (Hard technical reality compromises Beethoven's design: the cello cannot finally descend to B because the note is not on the instrument, and Beethoven has to settle for the B above.) After a long silence, that chord is repeated, but with the notes redistributed and everything returned to the fairly compressed registration of the opening chord. When the viola's A flat drops to G, we find ourselves on a dominant seventh chord that wants to go to C major. At this point all the cues, notably the long silence and the return to something like the original register, suggest that this at last is the destination, that the point of all this mystery, this probing, this exploratory touching of walls and boundaries, has been to lead us at last into the daylight of C major. This is exactly what happens.

Or does it? Yes, the dominant seventh does indeed go to a chord of C major, but it is *piano,* it is on a weak beat, it is just a short staccato

EXAMPLE 9.   Op. 59 no. 3, first movement, mm. 26–43 (outline)

eighth note in the new, very quick tempo. In sum, it is not nearly enough of a C-major chord to be a sufficient and convincing "answer" to that long and constantly amazing introduction. In other words, the mission is only half accomplished. We have arrived at the quick tempo that experience leads us to expect for the main part of a first movement, and we have heard enough to feel sure that C major will be home. We are not yet ready for a proper housewarming.

The first downbeat in the new tempo is another dominant seventh chord—in other words, one more chord of expectation rather than ful-fillment. The first violin uses it as a springboard from which to launch a leaping theme, quirky in character. The quartet applauds with a pair of chords rhyming with the previous pair but pointing in the direction of D minor. The first violin takes off on another solo flight, to which the quartet responds with a series of chords that takes care of two items of unfinished business. A chord of D minor resolves the dissonance left unresolved five measures before, and an expansive, emphatic, loud ca-dence at last settles us into C major on a good satisfying downbeat. Note, too, how unobtrusively yet how powerfully Beethoven has led to this moment of resolution by carrying the line steadily up from E to C (Ex. 9).

It is not surprising that, after all this, Beethoven affirms C major very assertively. Beginning with the great C-major downbeat, ten of the next fourteen measures are based on C-major chords, though Beethoven takes pains to inject much variety of spacing, rhythm, and figuration.

In what follows, the rhythm of the two chords at the beginning of Example 9 continues to be prominent. After his intensely characterized introduction, Beethoven now works, as on occasion he loves to do, with rather neutral material. One reason he likes it is that he is so good at it, another Haydnesque trait. The mood is generally playful. The inevitable sharpward trend of the exposition, whose destination has been G major, is countered in the development by an immediate tilt to the flat side. The first violin's quirky leaping theme is the first subject to be treated; later, the rhythm of the two chords comes in for extensive and varied attention.

The harmonies move over as far as D-flat major. After that extreme departure, Beethoven begins to make his way back to C major and the recapitulation. Again the journey is suspenseful, though briefer and far more extraverted than the one in the introduction. Beethoven takes witty advantage of the way the exposition began on the dominant. What he does now is to telescope leadback and arrival. The first violin plays a long trill on G (first minor, with A flat, then major, with A natural). Such a trill suggests leadback, waiting, suspense. But underneath, the rest of the quartet plays the two-chord figure, though it is greatly transformed—one instrument at a time, legato, and *pianissimo*. Then the first violin takes off on its solo flight, but this is now much gussied up. With some more delightful elaborations of detail, Beethoven again makes his way to an emphatic downbeat landing on C major. After this, the recapitulation proceeds regularly, surprise being reserved for the brief excited and accelerating coda.

While the first two Razumovsky quartets include something explicitly marked *Thème russe,* this one does not, but its strangely melancholic and obsessed second movement is perhaps the most fascinating and surely the most touching representation of the exotic in Op. 59. The first violin sings its distinctively east-of-Vienna A-minor song over a repeated plucked E on the cello, which is resolved to the tonic, A, only when the first phrase comes to an end. There are many such pedals in this movement—five and a half measures of A later on, six measures of G, nine and a half measures of C, and so on. The viola offers an even more pain-laden melody, but the theme played by the violin when Beethoven has modulated to C major is an attempt at consolation, a smile through tears. Beethoven marks it *dolce.*

This is an extensive sonata movement that modulates widely. In the recapitulation Beethoven redistributes the material interestingly among the instruments. The coda is a wonderfully expressive page—fourteen measures of A minor, asserted first by the cello's insistently repeated A, then by the motionless chord in the upper instruments, still pizzicato, wandering in search of . . . what? A, I suppose.

Next, Beethoven writes a minuet, and for the only time between the E-flat major Piano Sonata, Op. 31 no. 3, of 1802 and the Eighth Symphony of 1812.[7] How much of conscious backward glance can be inferred from his direction of *grazioso,* not the most characteristic Beethoven temper? (He asks for the same touch in the minuet that concludes the gigantic and wildly wonderful *Diabelli* Variations of 1819–23.) The music is smooth and lovely. The sixteenth-note scales that are passed from player to player are a severe if unobtrusive test of quartetmanship; that is, you notice how difficult they are only when the splices are bumpy. The trio, in F major, is part fanfares, part syncopated dance music. Here, too, there are scales in sixteenth notes, and they make an aural link with the minuet. The leap midway into A major is agreeably startling. Altogether, the impression of the trio is much more "modern" than that of the C-major minuet itself.

After the minuet is repeated, its sweetness turns to mystery in a coda that leans toward the flat side. Its function, it turns out, is to prepare what is not only the most vertiginously virtuosic of all of Beethoven's quartet finales but one that he would not equal in fierce energy for twenty years. Its brilliance is undoubtedly another reason for that early reviewer's optimism about the likely reception of Op. 59 no. 3.

The tempo is extremely rapid. Beethoven begins as though he were going to write a fugue: viola, second violin, cello, and first violin in turn enter with a subject in fluent eighth notes, though some of its energy resides in the little breaths, the silent punctuations at the beginning (Ex. 10). By the way, these eighth notes, if you follow Beethoven's metronome mark, go by at the rate of between ten and eleven per second. It soon turns out that Beethoven has no intention of writing a real fugue, and he abandons fugal texture almost as soon as the fourth voice, the first violin, has entered. At that point, the two violins take off with a figure of which he will make much later on (Ex. 11).

Just after that, Beethoven counters the extreme rapidity of events with six measures of an emphatic pedal on C, parallel to the C pedal early in

7. Opus 54 of 1804, that strangest of Beethoven's piano sonatas, begins with a movement marked *In tempo d'un menuetto,* but this is not "a minuet."

EXAMPLE 10.   Op. 59 no. 3, fourth movement, mm. 1–12

the first movement. Nonetheless, the rapid-fire rolling out of eighth notes does not stop; in fact, there are fewer than two dozen measures in the entire movement that lack the running eighths, and they, except for the final cadence, are always moments of calculated suspense. From time to time Beethoven returns to suggestions of fugue, and he makes something most beguiling of the shifts back and forth between the two textures, the learned and the sheerly kinetic.

He ranges widely through harmonic territory. Having gone early and normally enough to G major, he quickly and dramatically diverts the flow to E-flat major; later he reaches destinations as exotic for a C-major context as C-sharp minor and A-flat major. At one point, Beethoven offers the beginnings of something like a double fugue, adding to the original theme a subject in ticking staccato half notes. Example 11 is made to buzz furiously, like a bee caught in a jar. As a final resource of

EXAMPLE 11.   Op. 59 no. 3, fourth movement, mm. 38–43

extra energy, Beethoven injects syncopations and off-beat accents, also exploring the possibilities of jolting halts. The final charge to the finish line is managed with breath-taking élan and a master's impeccable timing.

––––––––––

STRING QUARTET IN E-FLAT MAJOR, OP. 74

Poco adagio—Allegro
Adagio ma non troppo
Presto—Più presto quasi prestissimo—Tempo I
Allegretto con variazioni

The three Razumovsky quartets, written in 1805–6, were followed a few years later by two single works in striking contrast to each other— Op. 74, written in the summer and fall of 1809, and Op. 95, composed a year later, in the summer and early fall of 1810. The terse Op. 95 is in every sense difficult Beethoven; by comparison, Op. 74 is genial and inviting of access, though at no sacrifice of the personal and original.

The year 1809 was horrendous. "Nothing but drums, cannons, human misery of every sort!" was Beethoven's description of life in Vienna that July. Since April, Austria had been at war with France for the fourth time in eighteen years. In May, Napoleon's armies were in the suburbs of Vienna. The empress left the capital with most of her family and household.[8] The French artillery began its terrifying assault. On the worst night of all, Beethoven picked his way through the broken glass, the collapsed masonry, the fires, the din, to find refuge in the cellar of his friend, the poet Castelli. There he covered his head with pillows in the hope of protecting the remaining shreds of his hearing. The Viennese garrison, unprepared to the point of having had to commandeer the muskets and halberds from the property rooms of the city's theaters and opera houses, surrendered the next afternoon. The war dragged on until mid-July. Peace brought punitive and ruinous taxes, levies, and tributes. The Burgtheater played to audiences of seven and nine. Vienna's principal newspaper, the *Wiener Zeitung,* carried the Napoleonic eagle on its masthead, and each citizen was required to have a lighted lamp in his window in celebration of the French emperor's birthday. Beethoven himself was shaken by the deaths of Haydn, with whom he had enjoyed such a complex relationship, and, before that, of Albrechtsberger, the teacher who used to find the mistakes Haydn had overlooked.

At the end of July, Beethoven told his Leipzig publisher, Gottfried Christoph Härtel, that he had not been able to summon a coherent musical thought since the beginning of May. But within a few days he regained his energy and ability to concentrate. In less than half a year he had completed three masterpieces, all in E-flat major, the so-called "Emperor" Concerto, the present string quartet, and the *Farewell* Sonata, as well as two smaller piano sonatas, the wonderfully lyric F-sharp major, Op. 78, and its snappy companion in G major, Op. 79. There is grief in the slow movement of the *Farewell* Sonata—it is titled "Absence"—but

8. Among those who accompanied the empress was her brother-in-law, the 21-year-old Archduke Rudolph, a student of Beethoven's since 1803 and, with the Princes Lobkowitz and Kinsky, one of the guarantors who undertook in 1808 to provide the composer with an income for life. Rudolph's departure and his return the following January are commemorated in one of Beethoven's most beautiful piano sonatas, the *Lebewohl* or *Farewell,* Op. 81a. Prince Franz Joseph von Lobkowitz was the dedicatee of the Quartet, Op. 74, as he had been of the Quartets, Op. 18.

EXAMPLE 12.   Op. 74, first movement, mm. 1–2

in the rest of this music is affirmation, triumphant in the concerto, serene in the quartet and the sonatas.

Beethoven begins Op. 74 with a slow introduction. True, he modifies *Adagio* with *poco;* nonetheless, this music is slow in a way that the *Andante con moto* that opens Op. 59 no. 3 is not. This spacious music leans at once and persistently toward veiled harmonies. The first sound, sonorous even though *sotto voce,* is a plain chord of E-flat major. Immediately, though, the cello descends a whole step to D flat, a note that is not part of the E-flat major scale. The resultant chord is one that points to outside of E flat to A flat, as does the chord that ends the phrase. Three things might be said about this. One: the second half of the first measure is startlingly soon for such a departure. Two: movement toward the flat side of the harmonic spectrum tends to generate a sense of calm. Three: note how the first violin traces and echoes a bit more broadly the cello's descent from E flat to D flat (Ex. 12).

This harmonic drift persists. There is a *crescendo,* only as far as *piano,* but enough to bring the music from *sotto voce* out into the open: Beethoven even writes *espressivo,* not a notably common direction for him. Twice the music is punctuated by a loud chord with double and triple stops, both chords still pointing toward A flat. The whole introduction is a kind of questioning, most so the final passage in which the first violin ascends by half steps through a whole octave. Then the sturdy and unambiguous start of the *Allegro* provides an answer.

The *Allegro*'s first measure brings the first root-position tonic chord

EXAMPLE 13. Op. 74, first movement, mm. 25–31

since measure 1. Beyond that, the next fifteen measures are firmly focused on the task of establishing E-flat major as the home key. What is striking, however, is that the first violin's lyric melody, soon echoed by the viola, though not at all subversive in its intentions toward the tonic, nonetheless includes an important and still alien D flat, the note that determined the strange harmonic drift of the introduction (Ex. 13).

Pizzicato is prominent early on, and Op. 74 is sometimes called the "Harp" Quartet. I know of no precedent for so much pizzicato that is not simply accompaniment. D flats continue to make themselves conspicuous before Beethoven diverts the harmonic stream in the opposite direction, toward B-flat major, the dominant. There the exposition closes quietly.

The reiterated cadence on B flat, eight measures' worth, leads smoothly and naturally back to the beginning of the exposition and that sturdy chord of E-flat major. The second time around, Beethoven makes a leap in the manner of Haydn and lands on a richly scored chord—ten notes—of G major. This feels far away and fresh; it is in fact the first G-major chord in the quartet. Here Beethoven plays with the lyric melody of Example 13, starting it at various angles and even managing to introduce for a moment the exact pitches of the beginning of Example 13. Then he seizes on the dotted rhythm in the third and fourth measures of that melody and gives over the rest of the development to putting that little feature through its paces in the first violin and cello while the inner voices supply an agitated accompaniment.

The turmoil subsides and the music settles expectantly on the dominant. On that chord Beethoven plots a series of arpeggios of ever greater range, first plucked, then bowed. A *crescendo* accompanies the expansion of range, and so the recapitulation is reached. This proceeds fairly regularly. There is some compression and some expansion, the most striking difference being that the pizzicato episode is now twice its previous length. The recapitulation comes to its *pianissimo* close. Then the music goes down even further, to *pianississimo*. Everything is extraordinarily still; at the same time there is something deeply disquieting about the sudden harmonic incertitude. Then the quartet wakes from its *pianississimo* dream, and Beethoven begins an amazing passage in which the "signature" pizzicato is dazzlingly combined with an excursion of concerto-like brilliance for the first violinist. Fragments of the opening of Example 13, back to bows now, inject further energy, and so this movement, such a fascinating mixture of the demure and the unpredictable, comes to its vigorous final measures.

The slow movement starts with a broad melody, marked *cantabile* for the first violin, with the accompaniment held to *mezza voce*. It is delicately varied on each of its returns, and each time the accompaniment is more active. Its serenity is soon darkened by Mozartean sighs and harmonies in minor, and these clouds will not be completely dispelled until the last measures of the poignant and beautifully settled coda. The retransitions, with their sighs and silences, to the various returns of the melody are no less remarkable than the returns themselves, and Beethoven always takes pains to mark them *espressivo*.

The C-minor scherzo is the most boisterously unmannerly sort of Beethoven. Its triple upbeat will inevitably recall the Fifth Symphony, completed in the spring of the previous year; looking ahead, we can tell how much this piece inspired Schubert's unfinished Quartet in C Minor

EXAMPLE 14.   Op. 74, third movement, trio, mm. 77–84, renotated in 6/8

EXAMPLE 15.   Op. 74, third movement, trio, mm. 77–84, in its real notation

of 1820, the so-called Quartettsatz, D. 703. The scherzo itself is *presto;* the trio has to go still faster, *più presto quasi prestissimo.* So fast in fact does this fierce C-major music go that Beethoven wants the players to imagine each pair of 3/4 measures as a single bar of 6/8. This raises the obvious question of why Beethoven did not simply notate this music in 6/8 (i.e., as in Example 14 rather than as in Example 15). The answer is twofold. Even where he changes the tempo, he prefers to leave the meter of a trio alone unless, as in the Ninth Symphony, he is also switching from triple to duple meter. The more interesting answer is that musical notation has a psychological as well as a practical value. To a player the 3/4 notation *looks* faster, more driving than the "easy" 6/8; the 3/4, therefore, is more likely to produce the wild result Beethoven is looking for.

The trio comes around twice, which is the sometimes rather arbitrary-sounding way Beethoven had at this time of making his scherzos match his expanding structures in scale. This, however, is an occasion when Beethoven makes special use of his double trip around the

EXAMPLE 16.   Op. 74, fourth movement, mm. 1–2

scherzo-trio-scherzo cycle. He changes the character of the scherzo by making it almost all *piano, pianissimo,* even *pianississimo* on its last appearance. Then, just as its mutterings seem about to subside completely, a deceptive cadence diverts the music onto a chord of A flat. This is the same cadence as the one that initiates the famous drumbeat bridge into the finale of the Fifth Symphony; here, however, there is neither a *crescendo* nor a triumphant C-major resolution. Rather, Beethoven calmly prepares E-flat major, the quartet's home key and the place where he will present six nicely uncomplicated variations of a clear-browed but also charmingly quirky theme. Its quirkiness resides chiefly in its rhythmic ambiguity, the "weak" upbeats being longer and thus more weighty in effect than the short and staccato "strong" downbeats (Ex. 16).

Variation 1 reduces the theme to staccato scales and stalking arpeggios. Variation 2, marked *sempre dolce e* [*piano*], gives the viola a tender version of the theme in triplets. In variation 3, the second violin and the cello play a variant of the theme in vigorous sixteenth notes, while the other two instruments add punctuations on the offbeats. After all this speeding up, variation 4 brings a simplified view of the theme, all in quarter notes. Here too Beethoven's request is for *sempre p*[*iano*] *e dolce.* In variation 5, the first violin becomes a bit showy, though this is sane indeed compared to its extravagance at the end of the first movement. Its upbeat accents make witty play with the metrical ambiguity of the theme (Ex. 17).

EXAMPLE 17. Op. 74, fourth movement, variation 5, mm. 101–3

Variation 6 offers to be a little rebellious. It is *pianissimo* throughout, breathless (literally), and the tempo is slightly speeded up. The cello won't move off E flat in the first part and is almost as stubborn about D flat in the second part. (Remember the E flat–D flat progression at the beginning of the quartet?) We are in a new phase of the movement. Beethoven is beginning to wind things up in a coda that begins by extending the last variation and that is full of surprises, right up to its last two chords.

STRING QUARTET IN F MINOR, OP. 95, *QUARTETT[O] SERIOSO*

Allegro con brio
Allegretto ma non troppo
Allegro assai vivace ma serioso—Più allegro
Larghetto espressivo—Allegretto agitato—Allegro

In the few years preceding the composition of Op. 95 (1810) and the four previous quartets (see my chronology of these on p. 196), Beethoven had composed the Fifth and *Pastoral* symphonies, the Fourth and Fifth piano concertos, the Violin Concerto, the "Waldstein" and "Appassionata" sonatas, and *Fidelio*. These, his most famous works of those years, are big and generally expansive pieces.

If, however, we examine Beethoven's work as a whole, we find that while he was driven to compose pieces bigger than their models in

Haydn and Mozart, and that in later years the *Hammerklavier* Sonata, the
Missa solemnis, the Ninth Symphony, and certainly several of the string
quartets from the 1820s would attest to his continuing interest in the
Massive Statement, there was also alive in him an appetite for compression, a desire to invent music whose tight packing was as unprecedented
as the breadth of his most roomy compositions. That side of him gives
us the wild first movement of the Fifth Symphony, the seraphic Piano
Sonata in F-Sharp Major, Op. 78, and the ebullient Eighth Symphony,
to cite three examples in which compression serves highly diverse expressive purposes. It also gives us the Op. 95 Quartet. Here, in the time
it takes him to get to the end of the first sentence of melody in Op. 59
no. 1—something like half a minute—Beethoven has twice brought the
music to a jarring halt; covered a wide range of dynamics, textures, and
modes of articulation; begun to transform and develop the idea he has
so violently flung out in the first two measures; and is already on the
verge of settling in a new key and presenting a new and contrasting
theme.

The mood of this explosive beginning is grim. This is one of the rare
occasions on which Beethoven gave a work a title (the *Pathétique* Sonata,
the *Eroica* Symphony, and the *Pastoral* Symphony are the most famous of
the others), his chosen heading here being *Quartett[o] serioso.* The mixture of languages is odd (Beethoven probably just forgot the "o" at the
end of "Quartett").

Beethoven begins with two measures, a fragment of an F-minor scale,
swirling from F down to C and back again, but sharply profiled by virtue
of the rhythm—the eruption of sixteenth notes to begin with, the continuation in staccato eighths, and the firm landing on a quarter note (Ex.
18). Silence. Then a three-measure response. In contrast to the first
phrase with its powerful assertion of tonic, these measures stress the
dominant, C; also, where the first phrase was scalar and for the most
part in steady eighths, this response is all leaps and dotted rhythms. After
another silence—this one slightly shorter, which contributes to the
sense of compression—the cello returns to the first idea but provocatively starts it on G flat, one half step up from F, and translates it
from minor to major. Beethoven had used the same harmonic strategy
to begin his "Appassionata" Sonata and the String Quartet in E Minor,
Op. 59 no. 2 (regarding this "Neapolitan" harmonic relationship, see
p. 184).

EXAMPLE 18.   Op. 95, first movement, mm. 1–5

The melodic contour and much of the rhythm are as they were, but everything else is changed. I have mentioned the higher pitch and the change from minor to major. The dynamic markings are different. The first time the phrase was plain *forte*. Now it has acquired a sharp accent on the second beat, and by the next measure it has quieted down to *piano*. And here is a still more striking difference: the first time, all four instruments played the phrase in octaves, unharmonized, while this time, on the *sforzando* second beat, the violins and the viola highlight the cello's switch from F minor to G-flat major by joining in with a G-flat chord. Furthermore, instead of crashing into silence as before, the music continues without break and proceeds to the dominant, which is stated both in the steady chords of the higher instruments and the dramatic arpeggios of the cello (Ex. 19).

In other words, measures 6–7 (Ex. 19) are a Neapolitan translation of

EXAMPLE 19. Op. 95, first movement, mm. 6–10

measures 1–2 (Ex. 18), and measures 9–10 (Ex. 19) are the counterpart of measures 3–5 (Ex. 18). This is an extremely high density of variation and development for Beethoven to throw at us so early in the game.

Again in sharp contrast to his play with silences in measures 2 and 5, Beethoven now continues seamlessly. Quickly he makes his way back to the opening phrase, this time finding a way dramatically to telescope statement on the tonic and repetition on the Neapolitan. Going up one half step more to G natural opens the door that allows for a modulation to a new key (Ex. 20).

The scales in measure 20 outline a chord that leads to A flat. A flat is the relative major of F minor, which would be the most natural and obvious secondary key. Beethoven, however, does not treat A flat as a new key. Barely touching it, he treats it as yet another dominant and uses it to move on to D-flat major. There the viola and cello offer a new theme, more lyrical in character than the turbulent first theme, but no less compressed.

Having been in a tremendous hurry to get away from his principal key, Beethoven is astonishingly expansive when it comes to settling in the new one. By measure 20 he was already on his way out of F minor; now he lavishes nearly twice that amount of time on D-flat major. With some fierce references to the flurry of sixteenth notes at the head of the first theme, he heads for a strong, confirming cadence; however, just when we expect this closure, he contrives a brutal interruption, a two-

EXAMPLE 20.   Op. 95, first movement, mm. 18–21

octave scale in A major, *fortissimo,* another dramatic introduction of a Neapolitan relationship.

Having subjected us to this shock, Beethoven, with wonderfully perverse humor, calmly, in sweet *piano,* gives us the D flat whose expected arrival he had frustrated a moment before with that *fortissimo* A-major scale. Not only does he give us D flat, he stays there for most of the next twenty measures, which, given the pace of procedures here, is a long time. His one departure is brief and violent, and it too takes us to Naples—another *fortissimo* scale, D major this time, and followed by a silence. I can see Beethoven's self-pleased smile in that silence. This Neapolitan explosion is not, by now, surprising to read about, but it is of an exhilarating rudeness when the music hits us.

Properly enough, for a movement so obsessed with compression and pushing forward, there is no repeat. With another of his nonmodulations, Beethoven suddenly pounces onto a loud, brightly scored chord of F major, the cello growling the first measure of the first theme. This is the way the development begins. Brief, it is chiefly concerned with the sixteenth-note flurry and the dotted rhythms. Then Beethoven prepares the return to the recapitulation with a powerfully suspenseful and long buildup. Again, "long" means long in the context of this amazingly terse movement.

Now Beethoven shows how tight tight can be. The first four measures of the recapitulation are the counterparts of measures 1–2 and 19–20 of the exposition. This means that by the fifth measure of the recapitulation

Beethoven is ready to launch the transition to the second theme. First he pretends to have forgotten that this is the recapitulation, that he is not supposed to be going to a new key, for the next passage is identical to its counterpart in the exposition, and before we know it the viola reintroduces the second theme—in D flat! Only when the cello starts to repeat this melody does Beethoven throw the switch that will point everything in the direction of F, where the second violin duly repeats the second theme.

F major is where the music now stays, though one more *fortissimo* scale rudely interrupts the quiet settling into that key. But Beethoven is not done yet. The *pianissimo* quasi-calm is broken by another *fortissimo* outburst. This time it is a D-flat major chord with F on top and with the cello again playing the beginning of the first theme. This is a neat and witty elision, the F in the first violin suggesting the principal key, the D-flat harmony taking us back to the secondary one. And the cello, playing the theme associated with F minor, but playing it in D flat, straddles both worlds. The coda continues ferociously, with pounding *sforzandi* and the persistent grumbling presence of those four sixteenth notes. It sinks finally into *pianissimo*. There is no room for rhetorical flourishes or purely formal reiteration of tonic chords.

After the violent abruptions of this *Allegro con brio* comes music that is virtually devoid of physical energy. Like the first movement, the *Allegretto* is far-ranging in harmonic exploration, but, instead of conquering new territories by ferocious thrusts, it wanders into them like Keats's knight-at-arms, "alone and palely loitering . . . so haggard, and so woebegone." The tempo is neither slow nor fast, and Op. 95 is in fact one of those Beethoven works without a real slow movement. The Seventh and Eighth symphonies and the E-minor Piano Sonata, Op. 90, are among its immediate neighbors of which this is also true.

The cello, *mezza voce,* begins by itself, outlining part of a D-major scale in detached notes. D major is far away from F minor, but to some extent a few of the crazy harmonic explosions in the first movement have prepared the ground for this departure. With the harmonic context thus established, the first violin begins a melancholy song. Both melody and accompaniment are repeatedly darkened by B flats that suggest the world of D minor.

The first time this paragraph seems about to arrive at a full cadence, the D-major chord played by the first violin and the cello is disturbed by the alien notes added by the second violin. The viola breaks the

EXAMPLE 21.   Op. 95, second movement, mm. 22–24

EXAMPLE 22.   Op. 95, second movement, mm. 35–38

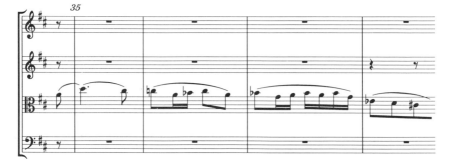

ensuing silence with a steadying D (Ex. 21), whereupon this dialogue is repeated with an even more poignant dissonance. Only then does the music move to full though dark-hued closure in D major. This could well be Schubert's model for that magical passage for horn and strings in the *Andante* of the "Great" C-major Symphony, the measures so famously described by Schumann: "a horn, as though calling from afar, seems to come from another world. The instruments stop to listen, a heavenly spirit is passing through the orchestra."[9]

Now the viola starts a fugue on a highly chromatic, descending subject (Ex. 22). Second violin, cello, and first violin respond, but the fugal

9. Robert Schumann, *Gesammelte Schriften über Musik und Musiker,* 5th ed., 2 vols. (Leipzig, 1914), 2:459.

project does not get far. The harmonies move far afield toward the flat side, the voyage being marked by weighty accents. Before long, the cello is back with the forlorn scale with which it began the movement. One difference is that this time it begins *pianissimo* in A flat, the farthest possible distance from D major; another, that the violins and viola add poignant commentary in the harmonic style of the proto-Schubert passage (Ex. 21); a third, that this A-flat beginning is but the start of a descending sequence that allows Beethoven to make his way to a dominant seventh chord with A natural in the bass.

That chord is the doorstep to D major, but Beethoven, in a manner characteristic for this work so full of subtleties and surprises, has something less obvious in mind. He starts the fugue again, and indeed on D major; this time, however, he begins with a long preludial B flat, which both refers to the persistent theme of darkening and is a way of doing something beyond just a plain dominant-to-tonic cadence. Furthermore, the fugue is now a double fugue, with the first violin adding a subject in staccato sixteenth notes (Ex. 23).

After a time the cello becomes extremely insistent on D and so persuades the other instruments that it is time to begin a recapitulation. That is a special Beethoven touch, too—to prepare something, not by a preparatory note, but by its own self; in other words, to prepare D by asserting D rather than its dominant, A.[10] Toward the end, in a movement notable for ideas whose gamut tends to be narrow, the first violin goes off in passages of remarkably wide range. The movement makes its exit in a series of sighs. After two D-major chords, the first violin and the cello play an unharmonized *pianissimo* D. Next comes a chord, still with D on top, that destabilizes everything and in fact is a bridge into the next movement.

For this scherzo, Beethoven returns to his invented Italian adjective and directs that the music should be *Allegro assai vivace ma serioso,* a very alive *Allegro* but serious. It begins, unmistakably, as a movement in C minor. That is to say, everything about the beginning points that way, and Beethoven arrives at a cadence in that key in measures 8 and 9. This double arrival is tricky, amusing, and full of serious consequence. In measure 8 the cello does not join the other instruments on C, landing

10. For a marvelous example of thus preparing an arrival by anticipating it—in this instance preparing the return of B flat by actually being there already—listen to the leadback to the recapitulation in the first movement of the Fourth Symphony.

EXAMPLE 23.   Op. 95, second movement, mm. 65–82

EXAMPLE 24.   Op. 95, third movement, mm. 7–9

instead on B flat so as to echo what the first violin just played. The cello duly arrives on C in the next measure, but at that point Beethoven interprets the note for us, not as a tonic (or pseudo-tonic), but as the dominant of F. With the upward leap of cello and viola in that measure, Beethoven is finally ready to establish the movement's real key of F minor (Ex. 24).

The mood is stormy, rather in the manner of the first movement, and the trio is too restless in its harmonies to give repose. The restlessness is of course planned in the most purposeful way, from the start in G-flat major (that Neapolitan relationship again) to the extensive revisiting of D major. (G flat and D are as far apart as it is possible to get.) The close is in a totally unexpected and previously unvisited key, B minor, the relative minor of D major. B is the bass note of the diminished chord that took us from the second movement into the third; now that same chord serves for the transition from the trio into the repeat of the scherzo. After this repeat, Beethoven goes into the trio once more, though starting in D major this time and cutting it down to half its previous size. The third and final trip through the scherzo is not only drastically abbreviated to one-third of its original length but has to be played faster than before. These compressions are very much in the spirit of the first movement.

After all this compaction, Beethoven now takes time—not many seconds by the clock, but much psychological time—for a pathos-filled slow introduction to the finale. As in the first three movements, the music is, at the beginning, broken by silences. The main part of the movement is *agitato,* and the music touches both the stormy world and the ghostly. Unexpectedly, it sinks to a halt on an F–major chord, whose effect is more wan than cheerful. This turns out to be the herald to a swift coda, mostly in *piano* and *pianissimo,* and even in the final rush rising to no more than *forte.*

One of the more than six hundred pages of sketches for the Quartet in C-sharp Minor, Op. 131. This page shows an early draft for the close of the dancelike fifth movement and the opening of the slow sixth movement. Its last measure contains, in the first violin, a recall of the opening fugue subject, subsequently incorporated into the fast finale. (Reproduced by permission of the Stiftung Preussischer Kulturbesitz, Berlin.)

The Late Quartets

When, early in 1822, Beethoven again turned his mind to the writing of string quartets, he had done nothing in that genre for twelve years. Troubled years they had been, many of them. The "Emperor" Concerto of 1809 represents the summit and, in a way, the termination of what Alan Tyson has called "the heroic decade," of the big manner defined so unmistakably by the *Eroica* in 1803. The works of 1810 to 1812—the *Egmont* music, the Op. 95 Quartet, the "Archduke" Trio, the Seventh and Eighth symphonies, the G-major Violin Sonata, Op. 96—are postscripts of extraordinary potency.

Then comes a time of exploration, also one of near silence. The major works between 1813 and 1819 are the piano sonatas, Opp. 90, 101, and 106, and the two Cello Sonatas, Op. 102. That, in the decade before, would have amounted to about one year's work. This is, as well, a period of massive personal crisis. The year 1812 is the year of Beethoven's encounter with Antonie Brentano, the "Immortal Beloved," the year of his last long journey, the year in which his hearing began its final, sharp decline. In 1815 came the death of Beethoven's brother Karl and the start of that ravaging litigation over the guardianship of Karl's son, then nine years old. But, although Beethoven completed few large compositions in those years, it was a useful fallow period in which his mind sought new things to say and new ways of saying them.

With the great *Hammerklavier* Sonata, Op. 106, of 1818, Beethoven once again set out on a new path. Or on many. His work of the next eight years includes his most rhetorical music and his most inward, his most public and his most esoteric, bigger pieces than any he had written before and ones more compressed, works at the summit of the virtuoso tradition and others that seem to ignore the physical limitations of fingers and lips and vocal chords, compositions that proclaim the inexhaustible possibilities of the sonata style and some that propose utterly new ways of articulating material, music reaching extremes of the centered and the bizarre.

These are the years of the last three piano sonatas and the *Diabelli Variations*, of the Ninth Symphony and the *Missa solemnis,* of the last string quartets. One by one the genres drop away. Though he still harbored plans for a second opera and had begun to sketch a Tenth Symphony, Beethoven, save for the occasional canon tucked into a letter to a friend, in those last years concentrated exclusively on string quartets. He had not ceased to learn or to explore. "A pity, a pity—too late," he whispered when a gift of Rhine wine arrived two days before his death.[1]

Here is the order of composition of the last quartets: Op. 127 (completed February 1825), Op. 132 (July 1825), Op. 130 in the first version, with the *Grosse Fuge* as finale (November 1825), Op. 131 (May 1826 or possibly a month or two later), Op. 135 (late September or early October 1826), the new finale for Op. 130 (November 1826). Beethoven died on 26 March 1827.

STRING QUARTET IN E-FLAT MAJOR, OP. 127

Maestoso—Allegro
Adagio, ma non troppo e molto cantabile
Scherzando vivace—Presto—Tempo I
Finale—Allegro con moto

Twice in the summer of 1822, Beethoven offered the Leipzig publisher C. F. Peters a string quartet together with the *Missa solemnis* on which he had been working off and on for more than three years. Having just completed the piano sonatas, Opp. 110 and 111, he had begun to sketch a quartet in May; the Mass was complete in outline, though it would be another year before Beethoven put the final touches on the score. Peters provisionally accepted the Mass, unaware that Beethoven was also offering it to several other publishers, but turned him down on the quartet. Laying aside those sketches, Beethoven returned to the Mass, of which

---

1. Elliot Forbes, ed., *Thayer's Life of Beethoven,* 2 vols. (Princeton, 1964), 1050. Hereafter, references to this work will appear in the form Thayer-Forbes 1964.

his biographer Alexander Wheelock Thayer wrote that it was "several times completed but never complete so long as it was within reach."[2] He also continued to add to the *Diabelli* Variations (this, too, work in progress since 1819), began to give serious thought to a ninth symphony, and composed several shorter works, among them the overture and chorus *For the Consecration of the House.*

In November 1822, the quartet project came to life again when Beethoven was approached by a St. Petersburg amateur, Prince Nicholas Galitzin, with a request for one, two, or three such works. Galitzin, then 27, had lived in Vienna for a while and was well versed in the music of Haydn, Mozart, and Beethoven. An excellent cellist and married to an accomplished pianist, he was both skilled and enthusiastic enough to have made quartet and quintet transcriptions of all of Beethoven's piano sonatas. It is also because of him that the first performance of the *Missa solemnis* took place in St. Petersburg. Much excited by *Der Freischütz,* new in June 1821 and wildly successful, he had first thought to offer a commission to Weber, but Karl Zeuner, the violist in his private quartet and a composer himself, persuaded him to turn to Beethoven instead.

In the summer of 1823, Beethoven once more dug out his quartet sketches but again put them away when he decided to focus first on completing the Ninth Symphony. So it was not until a year later that Beethoven began serious work on his Galitzin commission; over the next seventeen months, however, he completed three quartets for his new Russian patron—Op. 127 in February 1825, Op. 132 in July of that year, and Op. 130 four months later in November.

The Schuppanzigh Quartet gave the first public performance of Op. 127 on 6 March 1825. It was a failure, and when Joseph Böhm, playing with the same three partners as Schuppanzigh, led two performances in one evening later that month, he met with only slightly more success. A reviewer reported that the work was well received only by that minority of unconditional enthusiasts who approved everything of Beethoven's on principle. For the writer—and most of the audience—the work was an "incomprehensible, incoherent, vague, over-extended series of fantasias—chaos, from which flashes of genius emerged from time to time like lightning bolts from a black thunder cloud."[3] Much of the early commentary on the late quartets reads like this; on the other hand, it is

2. Ibid., 813.
3. To Burg, liner notes to Beethoven, *String Quartet in A Minor, Op. 132,* EMI (Unvergänglich Unvergessen 209).

not strikingly different from what had been written twenty years before about the first performance of the *Eroica*. Schott's Sons, in Mainz, published the work in 1826 and gave it the opus number 127.

For Beethoven, E-flat major is often a key of grand rhetoric and emphatic gestures, and the majestic declamation of the first measures of Op. 127 is one of his typical E-flat openings in the tradition of the *Eroica* (which combines breadth of design with fiery temperament and speed) and the "Emperor" Concerto. The call to attention in a spacious tempo and the neutrality of the material suggest the traditional slow introduction; the passage, however, dissolves into the *Allegro* much too quickly for that.

If this *Maestoso* (majestic) is too short for a real introduction, what is it? It is also not a question of a theme or a thematic group in two tempos such as we find, for example, in the first movements of the Piano Sonata, Op. 109, and the other two Galitzin quartets. Perhaps one can think of it as something like an illuminated initial at the head of a chapter. It elides into what comes next much the way such an initial is continued in the rest of the word; it is also, as we shall see, something that can be dispensed with once the theme—that is, the *Allegro* theme that follows—has become so familiar that it no longer needs such a grand exordium. (In some respects, the slow one-measure arpeggio at the beginning of the D-minor Piano Sonata, Op. 31 no. 2, is a parallel instance.)

Simple as they seem, these six measures are cannily written (Ex. 1). Like the *Eroica* chords, they are *forte* rather than *fortissimo,* but they are voiced for effortlessly rich sound. As Tovey and many others have pointed out, Beethoven had a knack at making ordinary chords extraordinary. The ones that begin the *Eroica,* the Fourth and Fifth piano concertos, the Seventh Symphony, and the *Missa solemnis* are all more or less ordinary statements of the tonic, yet each is instantly recognizable as belonging to that particular work. It is equally true of the opening of Op. 127.

Few composers, told to write alternating tonic and dominant chords for five measures, would come up with something so arresting, yet so unfussy, as what Beethoven gives us here. Neither of the dominants (mm. 2 and 4) is in root position; not only, therefore, are these two chords especially flavorful, but because Beethoven presents them in two different inversions, the first with the fifth (F) and the other with the seventh (A flat) in the bass, they are differently flavorful. Beethoven is

EXAMPLE 1. Op. 127, first movement, mm. 1–6

T = tonic
D = dominant
S = subdominant

equally inventive with his three tonic chords (mm. 1, 3, and 5). The second (m. 3) is a heightened variant of the first (m. 1): the ringing fifths in the viola and cello remain the same, but the second violin now has a double stop and the top of the chord in the first violin is raised by a third from E flat to G. The third tonic chord (m. 5) is built up on G rather than E flat and so takes on a special flavor comparable to that of the two dominant chords.

The six measures of this pseudo-introduction convey a powerful sense of direction and intention because in the outer voices, as the arrows in Ex. 1 show, Beethoven has the music climb the E-flat major scale from the keynote up to C, the note that becomes the point of takeoff for the *Allegro*. (Clearly, C can only be a way station in E-flat major, but Beethoven makes us wait another quarter minute or so before resolving that issue: more of that in a moment.) Finally there is the rhythm, which is a war of the *sforzandi*. The dominant chords start on offbeats (mm. 2 and 4), and their forceful accents lend the passage a bit of exotic east-of-Vienna charm; both these measures, however, are followed by tonic chords that are given the extra wallop of a *sforzando* even though they occur on downbeats. For some reason these four measures seem totally to confound most quartet players rhythmically. I have heard the rhythms

EXAMPLE 2.   Op. 127, first movement, mm. 1–2

a. as dotted quarter plus eighth

b. as 3/8

c. as 5/8 2/4

shown in Example 2 and other variants, but almost never a performance from which, if I did not know it already, I could infer what Beethoven actually wrote.

The last of the three tonic chords leads to the subdominant, and there a measured and accelerating trill forms the transition into the *Allegro*. In the trill measure, the dynamic level also drops away from the *fortes* and *sforzandi,* and the *Allegro* begins with the directions *sempre p[iano] e dolce* and *teneramente* (tenderly). The wistful mood of this music is perhaps illuminated by the knowledge that some of the early sketches were headed "la gaieté."

The first violin's melody is of touching sweetness (see Ex. 3). Four statements of that phrase make up the first paragraph of the *Allegro*. Each is more elaborate than the previous one in the way it is scored and set into the texture, and each moves to a slightly different close. The fourth statement goes to the keynote, E flat, and with that we come to the end of the paragraph and also to the first firm tonic cadence. Not least, this arrival also at last completes the ascent begun in the *Maestoso* (Ex. 1).

Now the music moves forward with captivating verve, resembling in spirit the first movement of the great Piano Trio in the same key, Op. 70 no. 2. As Beethoven moves away from the home key, the texture becomes more polyphonic and knotty. His destination is not, however,

EXAMPLE 3.   Op. 127, first movement, mm. 7–10

the one we expect. At least it is not the conventional one, for instead of going to the dominant, B-flat major, he heads for its relative minor, and so it is there, in G minor, with no relaxation of energy and no forgetting of the opening melody, that he carries the exposition to its close.

The *Maestoso* returns. This time it is in G major, and, taking advantage of all the open strings that both the tonic and dominant chords offer in that key, Beethoven gives us a bigger, more sonorous scoring than the first time, though still only *forte*. As before, six measures of *Maestoso* lead into the gentle *Allegro* melody, also of course in G major. This time, though, the paragraph gets no further than the second statement before Beethoven sends the music off into new directions. The development has begun. The subject under discussion is the opening melody, particularly its first three notes. The viola is the first to darken the harmonic palette by suggesting the possibility of G minor as an alternative to G major. Once that first E flat has entered the picture, the temper of the music changes quickly. A stormy climax—and the first *fortissimo*—is reached in B-flat minor, which, even though it is part of the E-flat family, is far away from the sunny G major where the development began.

Abruptly, Beethoven shoves us into C major, where the *Maestoso* makes its third appearance, finally in *fortissimo*. Beethoven also telescopes proceedings by omitting the final subdominant measure and picking up the *Allegro* violin melody in mid-flight. Again the music is quickly diverted into a passage of great density and almost violent energy until, without feeling prepared for it at all, we realize that we are already in

EXAMPLE 4.   Op. 127, first movement, mm. 135–43

the recapitulation. One reason we are taken by surprise is that this new chapter has begun, not with the *Maestoso,* which we will not in fact hear again, but with the soft violin melody (Ex. 4).

The recapitulation resembles the exposition in character and shape, though Beethoven takes pains to balance the development's excursions toward G and C by emphasizing the flat side of the harmonic spectrum. The transition from recapitulation to coda neatly corresponds to the earlier move from exposition in the development. Again Beethoven leaves out the *Maestoso,* and this time the violin theme is heard in A flat, the subdominant. There has been enough of storms, and the mood of the coda is gentle. Beethoven achieves this not only by staying within the piano range but also by a more leisurely rate of harmonic change and a greater prevalence of long notes than we have previously experienced in this rich and astonishing movement.

The bent toward the subdominant at the end of the first movement is also a preparation for what comes next, a set of variations in A flat. The movement itself begins with an act of preparation. In a rhythm carefully kept vague, the cello, *pianissimo,* sounds its lowest E flat, and to this, one by one, viola, second violin, and first violin add D flat, B flat, and another D flat, all at the low end of their respective ranges. In this way Beethoven builds an idiosyncratically distributed dominant seventh chord, one with no third (G) at all but with the seventh represented twice. (Beethoven would again use the same device of building up a first chord note by note at the beginning of the variation movement of his last quartet, Op. 135.) An upbeat with a slight *crescendo* into *piano* leads into the theme itself.[4] What Beethoven does with this upbeat subsequently provides some of the most beautiful and subtle detail in this movement.

Late in life, Beethoven turned to variation form more and more frequently, often using it, as he does here, in contemplative breadth as a contrast to the terseness and drive of his sonata forms. His theme in Op. 127 is a rapt and expansive melody. The tempo is *adagio* "but," Beethoven adds, "not too much so, and very songful." The first violin plays four broad measures, which the cello repeats with a different ending. Then come another four measures for the violin, now *pianissimo,* though this time what we assume will be the cello repetition moves into a different direction. Not only that, the second violin sings in duet with the cello while the first violin adds comments made from fragments of the melody. Beethoven has started varying even before he has finished stating the theme. And more—the theme has its own poignant two-measure codetta.

Then come the variations proper, and there are six of these. In the first, the music is elaborated in rhythm and texture. G flats and B double-flats darken the harmony; swells, quick successions of *crescendo* and *decrescendo,* abound. The serenity of the theme is no more.

Variation 2 brings a sense of greater speed. Beethoven actually calls for a quicker tempo, *Andante con moto,* but he also changes the meter from 12/8 to 4/4, which makes for a tighter pattern. Over a perky staccato accompaniment in the lower instruments, the two violins carry on a playful dialogue.

The suddenness with which this breaks off stops our breath. In midphrase, Beethoven moves into a new key, not by modulating, but with an imperious gesture of godlike ease. Simply lifting C natural to C sharp, he transports us in one second to the mysteriously remote key of E major. The notation, with its change of key signature from four flats to four sharps, makes the new key look even more remote than it is, but it is in any event quite distant enough. What the ear makes no mistake

4. Here is another controversial point of interpretation. Does the sequence *pianissimo–crescendo–piano* mean a considerable *crescendo* after which one falls back into *piano,* or is it just a *crescendo* from *pianissimo* to *piano*? Common sense as well as a taste for unfussy solutions suggest the latter; however, quartet players and conductors seem fond of the effect of the sudden hush, and one hears the former version more often than not.

about is that Beethoven means to make the most of that distance. The pace, too, is different. Beethoven writes *Adagio molto espressivo,* but he also indicates that he wants the players and listeners to feel two big beats per measure rather than four. The quarter notes are actually a little faster than those in the preceding *Andante,* but the music "feels" slower, not only because of the broader pulse (two beats rather than four) but also because this variation has very few quick notes. We have entered a new expressive world: this is the first time that the direction *espressivo* appears in this quartet, likewise the first *cantabile.* The manner of this variation lies somewhere between opera and hymn and is a sublime heightening of both styles. Here is the expressive climax of this extraordinary movement.

When this variation comes to an end and the first violin has reached the keynote, E—and it does so alone—the other instruments begin a soft pulsation, also on E, that gently returns the music back to the 12/8 meter of the theme and the first variation. Beethoven leaves E major just as he entered it: he simply drops all the Es down to E flat, almost inconspicuously, on a weak beat. E flat is the dominant of A flat, and so we are back on the doorstep of the home key. The variation that now emerges is an ecstatic, high-flying song for the first violin and cello in alternation. Each accompanies the other, the cello with wide-ranging arpeggios, the violin with a combination of similar arpeggios, leaps, and trills. In the last phrase, the second violin and viola join the cello in its song. In disembodied *pianissimo,* the second measure of the codetta leads the music into a new key, D flat, for the next variation (Beethoven does not, however, change the key signature to the five flats of D-flat major).

Beethoven writes *sotto voce* at the beginning of variation 5, and this sets the tone for the whole of this mysterious episode. It is as unpredictable—tentative, almost—as the previous variation was direct. The second half is in minor. For easier reading, Beethoven writes it in C-sharp rather than D-flat minor (which would entail a horrendous key signature of six flats and one double-flat), but the sudden appearance of four sharps after the four flats of the prevailing signature effectively heightens the sense of remoteness for the players.

In variation 6, the first violin takes off on a fanciful flight in which the theme becomes a stream of running sixteenth notes. The accompaniment consists of simple, slow notes for the other instruments; Beethoven, however, distributes them so that each instrument plays on a different beat of the 12/8 measure (second violin on 2, 5, 8, and 11,

EXAMPLE 5. Op. 127, second movement, mm. 122–23

viola on 1, 4, 7, 10, and cello on 3, 6, 9, and 12) so that, even though the individual notes are calm, the pulse is continuous. After the first four measures, the first violin's sixteenth notes leak into the other instruments.

This variation ends but does not finish, stopping abruptly, in mid-phrase, on the dominant. There is a long silence. The *pianissimo* pulsation on E flat begins again in the second violin and viola. The first violin enters, strangely, on G flat, nudging the music toward the subdominant and tranquility; at the same time, the cello, pizzicato, contributes to the darkening by touching briefly on B double-flat. The codetta is strangely suspended in the region of D-flat or C-sharp minor. The second violin holds on to its A flat/G sharp, and under that note the viola and cello slip a cadence in E major. It is as though, in the midst of all these silences and soft pizzicatos, we had, for a fleeting and shattering moment, revisited the wondrous world of the great E-major variation (Ex. 5).

The first violin, calmly and surely, returns us to A-flat major, and there the movement ends. Even the final cadence is mysterious and special, for Beethoven achieves a wonderful effect of weightlessness by setting the penultimate chord, the dominant, not on its root, E flat, but on its fifth, B flat (Ex. 6). Schubert learned well from this movement when, the year after Beethoven's death (and just two months before his own), he came to write his C-major Cello Quintet, D. 956.

The sound of plucked strings, so prominent in the *Adagio,* but not hereafter heard in this quartet, starts the scherzo with four chords that in the neatest possible way define rhythm, key, character, and speed. The

EXAMPLE 6.   Op. 127, second movement, m. 126

hopping figure that follows in the cello is heard many times, but overall the large rhythmic picture is fascinatingly varied by cross-rhythms, silences, and the occasional intrusions of measures in a different meter (2/4) and tempo (*allegro*). The trio is in E-flat minor, and it moves like the wind. There are extended visits to D-flat major and G-flat major. In the scherzo of Op. 135, Beethoven would again play with the idea of thus juxtaposing big blocks of harmony. The da capo is fully written out, but the internal repeats are omitted, and Beethoven contrives some witty variation of detail for the reentry. It seems for a moment as though this will be one of those Beethoven pieces that make a double trip through the scherzo/trio cycle, but the impending expansion is choked off. Like the first movement, the third ends epigrammatically.

In the finale, the robust rhythms, almost gypsylike, are offset by a generally subdued level of dynamics and, as so often in Beethoven's late music, by choices of chords or chord spacings that are not the most emphatic (cf. the final cadence of the slow movement). Beethoven gives no tempo indication, just the word "Finale," but the character is unmistakably *allegro*. The movement starts from an odd harmonic slant: the first two and a half measures sound like C minor, though by the fifth measure, when the real theme arrives, the music is clearly settled in E-flat major. As at the beginning of the *Allegro* in the first movement, the mood is gentle; here too, the music thrives on repetition. Things then become more energetic, and as Beethoven first approaches a new key, B-flat major, and then settles in it, the atmosphere becomes decidedly rustic. The spicily dissonant thigh-slapping climax (and its recapitulation later on) brings the only (and very brief) *fortissimo*. The development begins by pretending to be a repeat of the exposition.

Until the end of the recapitulation, this movement, for all its high spirits and warmth, suggests a reversion to an older, lighter type of finale, but the amazing coda dispels that idea. As the recapitulation seems to be drawing to its close, the climate changes. The forward drive relaxes. E flat and G are heard together, sounding first like E-flat major, then like C minor. E flat turns into E natural, and the music dissolves into a long trill on a C-major chord. When we emerge from that trill, there is a new sense of motion: the meter is 6/8 and the measures are broader than before, though filled with very fast notes. Garlands of scales move mysteriously about an altogether unearthly transformation of the main theme, first in C major, next in A flat, then back to the *Adagio*'s heavenly region of E major, and at last home to E flat. An emphatic tonic pedal in the cello celebrates that return. With easy and assured breadth, wholly purified of rhetorical gestures, the quartet moves to its conclusion, a miracle to the last of rhythmic and harmonic delicacy.

STRING QUARTET IN B-FLAT MAJOR, OP. 130

Original version:

Adagio ma non troppo—Allegro
Presto
Andante con moto ma non troppo
Alla danza tedesca: Allegro assai
Cavatina: Adagio molto espressivo
Grosse Fuge:
    Overtura: Allegro—Meno mosso e moderato—Allegro
    Fuga: [Allegro]—Meno mosso e moderato—Allegro molto e con brio

Revised version:

Adagio ma non troppo—Allegro
Presto
Andante con moto ma non troppo
Alla danza tedesca: Allegro assai
Cavatina: Adagio molto espressivo
Finale: Allegro

Opus 130, begun in August 1825 and completed in its original form in November of that year, is the third in order of composition of the three quartets that Beethoven composed for Prince Nicholas Galitzin. (For more information about this commission, see page 217.) What can Ignaz Schuppanzigh and the colleagues with whom he gave the first performance have thought when they received the music? What, for that matter, must Galitzin's reaction have been? Whatever their individual peculiarities of detail, the E-flat quartet and the A-minor would have looked familiar from the point of view of overall design, even with the "extra" march movement in the latter piece. But the B-flat? Here is a first movement of, generally, the sort and scale one would expect. But then the quartet seems to go off into the world of divertimentos or suites, for what follows is an altogether strange miscellany of movements. And, to conclude, a fugue of outsize dimensions and outlandish difficulty.

In this quartet Beethoven continues the formal adventures of his last two piano sonatas, Opp. 110 and 111, written in 1821–22. In Op. 110, after a sonata-form first movement and a scherzo, he gives us an operatic slow movement (the aria preceded, quite properly, by a recitative) and a fugal finale. Well and good, except that he follows that with a second version of the aria and finale, so that he ends up with a six-movement work whose fifth and sixth movements are variations on the third and fourth. Then in Op. 111, as though to compensate for that extravagance, he offers a two-movement design, a sonata movement followed by a hugely expansive set of variations. It is a perfect example of his use of contemplative and broad variations as contrast to a terse and driving sonata form. The six-movement Op. 130 is inspired eccentricity *in excelsis*.

The first movement seems at first to conform to the familiar pattern of a slow introduction leading to a movement in a quicker tempo. Still, the beginning itself, calm though it is, is strange. It is common enough for slow introductions to begin unharmonized, in unisons or octaves, though this is a less frequent practice with Beethoven than with Haydn. Here Beethoven does begin that way, modestly (just two octaves deep), with a four-note chromatic descent from B flat, the keynote, through A and A flat down to G. The B flat and A are fairly long, the A flat and the G move more swiftly. This implied division of the four into 2 + 2 will be of some consequence later on. The G is not, however, the end of the phrase, for the flow continues unbroken into a half cadence, the second half being fully harmonized. Now it is also common enough for slow introductions to begin with full harmony, but the switch in mid-

EXAMPLE 7.   Op. 130, first movement, mm. 1–2

Adagio, ma non troppo

phrase from austere octaves to rich chords is surprising and also somehow very touching (Ex. 7).

Then, demurely, Beethoven answers the first phrase with another—
fully harmonized from the beginning—that rounds off the sentence
with a full cadence on the tonic. The second phrase begins with the
same four melody notes—B flat, A, A flat, G—as the first. With some
rhythmic foreshortening and a surprising offbeat accent, Beethoven
moves forward to another half cadence, and here, taking the F that is
the basis of the last chord as its point of departure, the cello begins a
new thought. This has something of an "antique" flavor, though the
phrasing and dynamics are distinctly 1820s modern (Ex. 8). One by one
the other instruments join in, all remembering something of the four-
note chromatic motion with which the music began, and move into
another half cadence. Two things distinguish the second section of this
Adagio from the first—the more contrapuntal texture and the darkening
of the harmony as G flats begin to appear here and there. The music
has begun to draw some conclusions from the chromaticism of the first
four notes.

Suddenly the first violin bursts out in a flurry of sixteenth notes. The
Allegro has begun. Under the first violin's runs, the second violin plays a
fanfare in which there is a curious contradiction: the upbeat is loud but
the downbeat to which it leads is soft. Beethoven always likes to unsettle

EXAMPLE 8.   Op. 130, first movement, mm. 7–9

our expected ideas about rhythm and accent. All the instruments take up the running sixteenths, but when the *Allegro* has gone no more than five measures the *Adagio* interrupts it again. This too lasts five measures, just enough for a rich variant of the opening pair of cadences. The *Allegro,* with its combination of fanfares and running sixteenths, resumes as though nothing had happened. The next new idea is not in fact new but a revival of Example 8 in the *Allegro* tempo.

Emphatically, the music goes to F, the dominant. There, not surprisingly, the unexpected occurs. In Beethoven, as in Haydn, you must always expect the unexpected. The landing on F produces, not a new theme in the dominant, but a chromatic scale for all four instruments—twice four notes plus one, F, G flat, G, A flat; A, B flat, C flat, C; and then D flat. The first eight notes are staccato, the D flat is long. With the first eight notes goes a diminuendo from *forte* to *piano*. This D flat turns out to be the dominant of where Beethoven really means to go. The cello, *sotto voce,* describes a graceful descent to G flat, and there Beethoven offers a new theme. Its outer reaches are defined by pairs of semitones so that the idea of four semitones is still present but in a different form (Ex. 9). This comes with a pendant of groups of staccato sixteenth notes, and these very naturally lead to a variant—now *pianissimo* and legato as against the previous *forte* and "non ligato"—of the running sixteenths. The music builds up to a proud new version of the fanfare in ringing *fortissimo* (the first one in the piece), and there the exposition comes to a close.

Quiet eighth notes lead to a broad cadence on B flat, A. Those were the notes with which the movement began, and they take us now into

EXAMPLE 9.   Op. 130, first movement, mm. 55–57

the repeat of the exposition. When the exposition has been played for the second time, the quiet eighths go instead to a similar cadence on G flat, F, and there the development begins. Most strangely. Just as the B flat, A of the first ending lead to a return of the opening *Adagio* B flat, A, so does the G flat, F of the second ending lead to a return of the opening music but beginning—in the cello—on G flat, F. This gets as far as the first half cadence and there it stops, uncertainly. The two violins, *pianissimo,* suggest taking up the *Allegro,* one playing the fanfare, the other the running sixteenths. This, too, peters out almost at once. The three lower instruments resume the *Adagio,* this time carrying it to a full cadence, but in D major, which is far indeed from the half cadence on G flat four measures earlier. The violins, willing, agree to that key and take up the *Allegro* there. The *Adagio* returns once more, and in two measures, whose gestures bring recitative to mind—they also bring the first instruction to play *espressivo*—the instruments seem to signal pleasure at the violins' agreement to the idea of D major. Now, with a return to *Allegro,* the development at last gets under way.

After so much preparation it is strangely brief. Its topics are the fanfare and a fragment of the graceful line with which the cello made the transition into G-flat major in the exposition. New are a sighing accompaniment of pairs of slurred notes (many of them semitones) and a rapturous phrase given three times to the cello and twice to the first violin. The latter is a heightened version of Example 9. As the violin is playing this phrase for the second time, the other instruments suddenly cut in with the vigorous running sixteenths. The first violin catches the cue and hastily switches to the fanfare. We are in the recapitulation. This of course brings plenty of rich variation of detail, but its general plan is straightforward enough. There is an amusing impudence to the way the transition to the second theme (Ex. 9) is handled, and, in a nice touch of telling surprise, Example 9 itself appears first in D flat and only then in the home key of B flat.

The transition from recapitulation to coda is broader than the corresponding bridge from exposition to development. The difference is slight, just one measure, but it is a sign of Beethoven's exquisite sense of rhythm and overall energy: enough has happened since the beginning of the development, enough new energy has been built up, for him to feel the need for that extra measure for the "grounding" process before the coda makes final confirmation of the tonic. Once more we hear the first four measures of the *Adagio,* though this time they go to a deceptive cadence on G minor. Again there is uncertainty—both playful and genuinely hesitant—between *Adagio* and *Allegro.* Then, confidently, easily, quietly until the last couple of beats, the music moves toward the final cadence, which is as simple and as unrhetorical as possible. This first movement is expansive; at the same time it strikes us as extremely taut, being densely saturated by a very few ideas. In a way that is characteristic for his late style, Beethoven confronts us constantly with extremes—unisons and densely polyphonic textures, the odd and the straight, the propulsive and the hesitant.

After this rich essay in sonata style, Beethoven gives us four shorter character pieces. The first of these is like one of his late bagatelles for piano—drastically brief, a rushing *presto,* most of which, except for a stomping interlude for the first violin, passes in a mad whisper. The key is B-flat minor, but the stomping trio of this mini-scherzo is in B-flat major. The semitone idea is not forgotten: the first violin's first breathless word moves from F to G flat while the second violin begins its accompaniment by descending from D flat to C.

Beethoven fits an incredible amount of delightful detail into these not quite two minutes. Throughout the trio, we do not know—and are meant not to know—which are the upbeats and which the down. The skidding scales that form the transition back to the beginning come near to slapstick. The reprise itself is deliciously varied in texture and details of scoring. There is a tiny, almost whimsical coda; then, unceremoniously, Beethoven kicks this little piece off the stage.

The next movement, in a tempo neither slow nor fast, moves with a luxurious sense of time limitlessly available. The heading of *Andante con moto ma non troppo* is one of those bet-hedging instructions of which Beethoven was fond, and he backs it up with a character direction, *poco scherzoso:* moving along, but not too much, and just a little bit jocular. The first violin begins alone on B flat, the keynote of the two previous movements, but what the second violin and viola slip under that note— E flat and C—signals that this time B flat is not the key. Sighing, the first violin drops a semitone from B flat to B double-flat. (Next, it will go down one more chromatic step to A flat.) The second violin and viola are no less melancholy, though their sighs carry them upward. It is a witty inversion of the way the second movement began, with rising first violin and falling accompaniment. The score reader who has seen the word *scherzoso* knows that something is up; the innocent listener could well take this pathos at face value, as Beethoven probably hoped he or she would. (That's the trouble with program notes.) In any case, in the third measure the viola begins an insouciant tune to which the cello supplies a jaunty accompaniment, and with that the climate changes. It is also clear that the key is D-flat major, the relative major of the second movement's B-flat minor.

It is a marvel of gentle humor, this movement: *poco scherzoso* is exactly right, and in its moments of tenderness Beethoven pleads for *cantabile* and *dolce.* It is exceptionally rich in texture as well. Its exquisite, beautifully "heard" sounds—heard by a composer who in the literal, physical sense had heard nothing for ten years—are a feature that is exceptionally lovely and almost unbearably moving. One's first and, if you like, naive reaction to the idea of a deaf composer is to marvel that he or she (I do not forget poor, tormented Ethel Smyth) can do it at all. The more experienced and knowledgeable person knows that the essential part of composing happens in the imagination, in the inner ear, as it were, and that many composers write at their desks, not their pianos; in that knowledge you can almost underestimate the frustration, the agony, of deafness. But then you are confronted with the near-incomprehensible miracle of the deaf Beethoven. Not only did his musical thought become steadily, incredibly richer with the years, so did his fantasy for the physical details of sound. Not only did he compose more beautiful music for the string quartet and the piano the older he got; the more beautifully, imaginatively, and effectively he composed string quartet and (*pace* the late Vladimir Horowitz) piano music. The end, with its sudden rush of energy, is more than *poco scherzoso.*

Now comes another drastic change of scene. The key, G major, is at the furthest possible remove from the D-flat major of the previous movement. To an ear attuned to classical harmony, that first G-major chord—D natural on top as the melody note—sounds as though your CD player had skipped to the wrong band. *Alla danza tedesca*—in the manner of a German dance—is the sort of piece Mozart called a "teutsche." It is quick, very quick—*Allegro assai*. It is also amiable, up to a point; at the same time it is not quite uncrazy either, a kind of proto-Mahler. In humorous emulation of a wheezing hurdy-gurdy, but also to keep us on our toes, to make sure we do not get lulled into thinking that just because it is a string quartet it has to be all housebroken and dressed up and nice, Beethoven constantly breaks the flow with hairpins, rapid *crescendo/decrescendo* sequences. Especially when this dance goes fast enough—and quartets often play it too slowly for an *Allegro assai* in 3/8—these hairpins can produce something close to seasickness, the kind you induce with delicious deliberateness on a merry-go-round at the fair.

The movement covers a lot of harmonic territory, and I would guess that a model, a very much larger one, that Beethoven might have had in mind, both for harmonic motion and for unbuttoned rustic good humor, was that astounding drinking chorus at the end of "Autumn" in Haydn's *The Seasons*. Toward the end, Beethoven plays with the broken-work textures that so amused him in the scherzo of the F-major Quartet, Op. 59 no. 1. Here he is even bolder, because not only does he parcel out the tune (Ex. 10a) at the rate of one measure per instrument, he delivers the measures in the wrong order (Ex. 10b).

From this dance emerges one of Beethoven's most inward and wonderful slow movements. He calls it a cavatina, an operatic aria. Writers often comment on its simplicity. It is indeed simple in design, in its brevity (it takes about half as long as the slow movements of Opp. 127 and 132), and, not least, in its direct emotional force. On the other hand, it is extraordinarily complex in texture; neither is there anything obvious about the melody. The first violin is the principal singer, and at no point, were the song to break off, could we foretell its continuation, for all that whatever does come always sounds like the inevitable way. What the other instruments play is active and organic, always closely related to the song itself. Never before was an "accompaniment" so little inclined to be "accompanimental." Not until Brahms do you again encounter the like (and the way Brahms writes a song for solo oboe and wind ensemble

EXAMPLE 10.   Op. 130, fourth movement

a. mm. 1–8

b. mm. 129–36 (original measures indicated in parentheses above music)

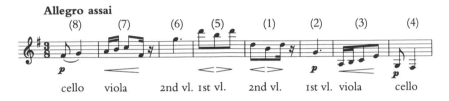

at the beginning of the slow movement of his Violin Concerto is remarkably like).

The three lower instruments begin. None is neutral: the cello line has
a striking profile, the viola has a strong melody in the middle of the
texture, and the second violin part is something we could easily take for
a theme in its own right (Ex. 11). The two violin lines serve as an example of how tight and organic the relationships among the parts are.
The top and therefore most prominent line in the accompaniment, that
of the second violin, begins by going from G to B flat and continues to
dwell on what is in effect a long, embellished B flat. When the first
violin begins the principal melody, it reverses that procedure by beginning with a powerful leap from B flat to G, then staying on what is
similarly a long and embellished G. Example 12 shows the two lines
reduced to skeleton form.

I described the cavatina as "emerging" from the German dance. The
harmonic connections—or jolting nonconnections—from movement
to movement are exceptionally beautifully judged in this quartet. Recall,
at one extreme, the way Beethoven softens the transition from the second movement to the third by beginning the latter with an unaccompa-
nied B flat, the keynote of the former. At the other pole he does every-

EXAMPLE 11.   Op. 130, fifth movement, mm. 1–2

EXAMPLE 12.   Op. 130, fifth movement, mm. 1–2 in skeletal form

thing he can to make the entrance of the less than perfectly housebroken German dance as shocking as possible from the outside.

At this point he wants to be softly conciliatory again. The German dance has ended on an eccentrically scored G-major chord, three of whose four notes are Gs. (The fourth note is a B, but the normal thing would be for one note to be a D so as to complete the G-major triad.) The cavatina begins on an equally eccentrically scored E-flat chord, two of whose three notes are also Gs. (The normal thing would be to have a B flat to complete the triad and, if any note is to be doubled, for that to be the keynote, E flat.) From G major to E-flat major is a fair distance, but with this extra and unusual emphasis on G, Beethoven emphasizes the common ground of the two keys. G obviously matters. We may remember that it was important at the very beginning of the quartet, being the last note of the unison descent by semitones in the first measure and also the note that gets the prime emphasis in the next new idea (Ex. 8). And we are far from having heard the last of it.

The first violin sings its cavatina, and each time it pauses for breath, the other instruments, led by the second violin, jump in to continue the melodic flow. It is a long, thirty-nine-measure paragraph of inspired melody whose vocal gestures cry out for an opera-loving violinist. Beethoven heads the movement *sotto voce,* and the song, intensely expressive though it is, stays within *piano* almost the entire time.

Suddenly the level drops down to the completely different world of *pianissimo.* The three lower instruments play agitated triplets, all on E flat. Then the cello shifts to D flat and thus moves the harmony away by a great distance. Over these triplets—*sempre pianissimo,* Beethoven warns—the first violin begins a music, stammering and hesitant, that is unlike anything else he ever composed. We know from the recitative and aria in the Piano Sonata, Op. 110, from the recitative for cellos and basses in the finale of the Ninth Symphony, not to forget the song we have just heard, how close Beethoven could take instruments to human utterance. This, however, goes beyond. To guide the violinist, Beethoven writes *beklemmt.* The word carries meanings and associations in the range of oppressed, weighed upon, suffocated, straitened, anxious. You can be *beklemmt* by the air just before a thunderstorm, by a nightmare, by an agonizing wait. It helps to have a sense of the word, but what you really have to understand is Beethoven. This episode lasts scarcely more than half a dozen measures, but it is a look into the abyss.

As though drawing back quickly from the edge, the music returns to the cavatina. Beethoven powerfully telescopes this transition. The first violin part of the *beklemmt* speech ends on B flat, and if we had it before us by itself we would expect it to be harmonized with a half cadence on a chord of B flat. In other words, we would now be on the dominant, poised to return to E-flat major and a reprise of the cavatina melody. In actuality, though, Beethoven arranges the harmony so that, by the time the violin reaches its B flat, the other instruments have already arrived on an E-flat chord. We are not expectant, we are there. To arrive at an expected harmonic destination but to arrive at it unexpectedly soon is a device Beethoven used ingeniously and with dramatic power all his life.

The reprise of the cavatina is compressed from thirty-nine measures to eighteen, to which the first violin adds a one-measure gesture of elegiac farewell. In Thayer's Beethoven biography we read that Karl Holz, the young second violinist in Schuppanzigh's Quartet, a good

EXAMPLE 13.   Op. 130, fifth movement, m. 66

friend to Beethoven in his last years, and a truthful witness, recalled that the cavatina "cost the composer tears in the writing and brought out the confession that nothing that he had written had so moved him; in fact, that merely to revive it afterwards in his thoughts and feelings brought forth renewed tributes of tears."[5]

The last chord of the accompaniment is special. Beethoven writes four eighth notes—*crescendo* from *piano* and *diminuendo* to *pianissimo*—but ties them together. The result, neither a single, sustained chord nor four distinct chords, is a poignant throb (Ex. 13). (Beethoven confounds pianists by giving them long sequences of single notes tied in this fashion in the Sonata, Op. 110—a piece, as I have noted, of great vocal ambition.)

The cavatina has floated to silence on an E-flat major chord whose top note is G. This G is now picked up in a grand unison and the work is capped by an uncompromisingly difficult fugue finale that accounts for a little over one-third of the length of the entire quartet. It was on 21 March 1826 that the Schuppanzigh Quartet gave the first performance. Beethoven had learned about fugues when he played *The Well-Tempered Clavier* as a boy in Bonn. Was he aware it was Bach's birthday? Surely not—neither he nor anyone else at that gathering.

Beethoven himself did not attend the first performance but waited in a nearby tavern for reports. That the audience demanded encores of the second and fourth movements, the "bagatelle" and the German dance, did not impress him. Why not the fugue, he wanted to know. "Cattle!" he roared. "Asses!"

Some listeners had been exalted and excited by the fugue; rather more

5. Thayer-Forbes 1964, 975.

EXAMPLE 14.   Op. 133, mm. 1–10

were bewildered. The players had great difficulties with it. Professionals pronounced it incomprehensible. Beethoven had never been easily pushed around by publishers, performers, and friends, but this time he was persuaded to take the fugue out of the quartet and to write a new finale in his most noncontroversial vein. We will come to that later.

Beethoven of course never doubted the intrinsic quality of his fugue, only its function in the context. It was much discussed in Viennese musical circles, and in May 1827, two months after Beethoven's death, Mathias Artaria published it by itself, both in its original form, as Op. 133, and, as Op. 134, in a piano duet arrangement by the composer himself. The duet version is all but impossibly difficult, but it is also marvelously illuminating in the ways it sorts out strands of polyphony and the dynamics. Opuses 133 and 134 were both dedicated to Beethoven's friend, patron, and pupil, the Imperial Archduke Rudolph, recipient of a long and impressive list of Beethoven dedications including the "Emperor" Concerto, the "Archduke" Trio, the *Farewell, Hammerklavier,* and Op. 111 piano sonatas, and the *Missa solemnis.* The fugue seems not to have had another public performance until 1853, when the Maurin Quartet played it in Paris, and it was not until the 1920s that quartets again began to play Op. 130 with its original finale. Current taste is decisively in favor of the fugue finale.

The title page of Opp. 133 and 134 described the piece as "Grande fugue, tantôt libre, tantôt recherchée"—in part free, in part studied or worked. (Stravinsky liked to call it "die sehr grosse Fuge.") The beginning, which Beethoven titles *Overtura,* is as *libre* as can be. In its thirty measures it changes tempo twice and character more often than that. In music of extreme disjunction, its gestures separated by unmeasured pauses, Beethoven hurls scraps of material about. Pairs of semitones are prominent, as in Example 14. Beethoven gives us the figure marked "A"

EXAMPLE 15.   Op. 133, mm. 31–35

in four versions—powerfully declamatory (Ex. 14), wild, lyrical, and in almost tentative *pianissimo*. From here on it is the task of the composition to demonstrate the coherence of what is presented in so aggressively and violently dissociated a manner.

After five beginnings, each a little less assertive than its predecessor and each broken off in mid-flight, the fugue proper, the *recherchée* part of the composition, gets under way. It is a double fugue, with the theme of the *Overtura* played by the viola while the first violin adds a leaping figure of ungainly and totally captivating energy (Ex. 15). The viola has tied eighth notes, similar to those in the final cadence of the cavatina. The second violin joins in with the leaping theme, followed by the cello with the one with the semitones. These ideas are explored over 128 measures as though in a series of variations of growing rhythmic and textural complexity, unrelieved in ferocious vigor, limitlessly bold in

EXAMPLE 16. Op. 133

a. upbeat to m. 31

b. m. 58

c. m. 111

EXAMPLE 17. Op. 133, mm. 161–65

harmony. The semitone theme retains its identity, which is not surprising, given the role of semitones throughout this quartet, its predecessor,
Op. 132, and the following one, Op. 131 (on the order of composition,
see page 216). At the same time, the rhythm of the music that surrounds
the semitone theme becomes ever more energetic (Ex. 16a–c).

The tempo slows—*Meno mosso e moderato* is Beethoven's instruction—
and a more conjunct and lyrical idea in sixteenth notes, first proposed
in the *Overtura* by the viola, is now explored (Ex. 17). It is also in a softer
key, and this surprise appearance of G-flat major is a reference back to
the comparable key change in the first movement (Ex. 9). The main

EXAMPLE 18.   Op. 133

a. mm. 237–39

b. mm. 416–18

fugue theme is still present but tamed. Essentially this is an interlude, more *libre* than *recherchée,* and all but ten of its seventy-four measures are *pianissimo.*

Motion almost comes to a halt on a slow, measured trill, which during its course changes from minor to major—and characteristically, not on a beat where we expect a change. From this there leaps forth a new movement in a new meter, 6/8, and at a new tempo, *Allegro molto e con brio,* faster than any we have heard in the *Grosse Fuge* so far. The disjunctions, the violence of the leaps, also surpass anything we have heard up to now. The main subject is the jagged theme with the semitones, but to this Beethoven also adds a new, simple, and almost jaunty transformation of the semitone idea (Ex. 18a). Example 18b, on the other hand, is an example of the opposite extreme. The semitone is pried open to stretch into a minor ninth, and at both beginning and end the metrical dislocation is extreme. There are many interruptions as well as reappearances of earlier passages. These are at times so startling that you could almost think you were dealing with a copyist's error or a badly spliced tape. The interference of the *libre* with the *recherchée* is fierce and outrageous.

Without preparation the slower music (Ex. 16c) returns, but in a new key, A-flat major. It is completely transformed in character. So reticent before, it is loud (just to make sure, Beethoven marks *forte* on every

EXAMPLE 19. Op. 133, mm. 493–95

single beat!), assertive, with the jagged semitone theme appearing simultaneously right-side up (first violin) as well as upside down (viola), and with a new, churning accompaniment in the cello (Ex. 19).

This breaks off suddenly, on an expectant chord, a tonic six-four. The normal sequence of events after such a chord is to go to the dominant and then to a firm, root-position tonic. Beethoven gives us the dominant but in an eccentric form, oddly placed as to meter, and with a trill on the bass note. Then a long silence. Then, instead of the expected tonic, another chord, also with a trill in the bass, moving the harmony into quite a different direction, possibly toward the relative minor, F minor. Then more alternations of silence with strangely restless chords (all with trills in the bass). The while, the dynamics go down from *forte* to *pianissimo,* and the tempo accelerates steadily. It looks clear on the page, but the combination of the rhythmic placement of the chords and of the speeding up is a canny way of creating the effect of something improvised and totally puzzling to the listener. These changes of course and those that follow all look back to the similar disruptions in the first movement.

In fact, though, this series of unpredictable chords returns us to the home key, B-flat major; thus, in delightful paradox, the purpose of this extremely puzzling passage was something very purposeful indeed. We are also back in the 6/8 *Allegro molto e con brio.* The crazed anger that

EXAMPLE 20.   Op. 130, sixth movement, mm. 133–36

possessed this music before is now diffused. It moves now with easy, good-humored grace, even taking the time to slow down for a rapt contemplation of the theme in very long notes and of course in the most hushed *pianissimo.*

But Beethoven is not yet done with shocks. The music loses momentum, then stops, uncertainly, on a dissonance. Silence. The two violins offer to start the fugue over from the beginning (Ex. 15). This is a bad idea. Silence again. Then what about the gentler *Meno mosso e moderato* (Ex. 17)? Also not the right thing. The four instruments then unite in strong octaves like those at the beginning of the *Overtura,* and from there, Beethoven moves swiftly to the end. The resolution of these extraordinary, unprecedented conflicts that the *Grosse Fuge* has posed is surprising and touching—a mixture of the exalted and the humorous that only Beethoven could have invented.

In September 1826, six months after the first performance, Beethoven sketched a new finale, which he then composed in October and November. It turns Op. 130 into a completely different piece. In the original version everything leads up to the fugue, while in the revised edition, the much lighter finale places the center of gravity on the cavatina. Not surprisingly, Beethoven retains the idea of using the cavatina's closing G as the point of departure for the finale; this time, however, it is a charming vamp-till-ready that gets the movement going on a piquant, rather Haydnesque harmonic slant. (Schubert liked the effect and emulated it, not without some of Beethoven's sense of drama, in his last piano sonata.) Beethoven also makes casual reference to the theme of the exiled *Grosse Fuge,* readily recognizable even though he has shuffled the intervals around (Ex. 20). This movement was the last piece Beethoven completed, and it is music of consummate grace, robust humor, warmth, and, in all its modesty, fullness of invention.

STRING QUARTET IN C-SHARP MINOR, OP. 131

Adagio ma non troppo e molto espressivo
Allegro molto vivace
Allegro moderato
Andante ma non troppo e molto cantabile—Più mosso—
  Andante moderato e lusinghiero—Adagio—Allegretto—
  Adagio ma non troppo e semplice—Allegretto—
Presto
Adagio quasi un poco andante
Allegro

Between 1822, when he returned to quartet writing after a long interval, and November 1825, Beethoven composed three such works on commission from Prince Nicholas Galitzin (see p. 217). But even with the Galitzin commission fulfilled, he kept right on going, and on 20 May 1826 he wrote to the publisher Schott's Sons in Mainz that he had finished another quartet. "Finished" was probably an exaggeration; at any rate, it was not until mid-August that Beethoven delivered the score. This is the present work, announced by Schott for February 1827 but not actually in print until June of that year, three months after the composer's death.

It does not seem that there was a public performance of Op. 131 until 1835, when the Leopold Jansa Quartet played it in Vienna; there had, however, been private auditions by Joseph Böhm's quartet before that. Franz Schubert's last musical wish was to hear Op. 131, and this was fulfilled on 14 November 1828, five days before his death. "The King of Harmony had sent the King of Song a friendly bidding to the crossing," said Karl Holz, the second violinist of the Schuppanzigh Quartet, who was present at that gathering.[6]

Beethoven had intended to dedicate Op. 131 to Johann Nepomuk Wolfmayer, a wealthy textile merchant, keen musical amateur, and a good friend, but at the last moment he changed his mind, writing to Schott that the work "must" be dedicated to Lieutenant-Marshal Baron von Stutterheim. Beethoven felt profoundly indebted to von Stutterheim, who had secured a place in his regiment for Beethoven's nephew Karl after the young man's suicide attempt in January 1827. At Holz's suggestion, Wolfmayer was compensated by the dedication of Op. 135.

6. Otto Erich Deutsch, *Schubert: Memoirs by His Friends* (London, 1959), 300.

I have mentioned before that one of the phenomena we can observe in Beethoven's later years is his growing tendency to question the primacy of the standard three- and four-movement designs. This issue had in fact interested Beethoven for a long time: think of the two Piano Sonatas, Op. 27 (1801), each of which he designated as *Sonata quasi una fantasia;* of the various two-movement sonatas, which go all the way back to Op. 54 in 1804; also of the "Waldstein" Sonata and the Triple Concerto (both 1804), perhaps even the Fourth Piano Concerto (1806), in which the slow movements, though of great expressive *gravitas,* are strikingly smaller in scale than those that precede and follow them and in which they function almost as transitions or introductions to the finales. (The *Adagio molto* of the "Waldstein" is headed *Introduzione.*)[7] The last two piano sonatas, Op. 110 and 111, composed between 1820 and 1822, are extraordinary instances of unusual design in Beethoven's later piano music.

Then, in the last quartets, we see Beethoven go from the four-movement Op. 127 to Op. 132, in which the four-movement design is interrupted by the "extra" march and recitative that come between the great Song of Thanksgiving and the finale. The next work, Op. 130, is totally wild—a six-movement work beginning with a highly unusual sort of sonata movement, ending with the maddest fugue in Western music, and including movements that range from the wispiest of bagatelles to the most expressive of slow movements. Now, in Op. 131, he takes the next step and gives us a seven-movement work.

For Beethoven to begin with a slow movement is rare: for the last precedent you have to go back twenty-five years to the Piano Sonata in C-Sharp Minor, the so-called "Moonlight." For him to begin with a fugue is without precedent, though there is plenty of fugal music to be found in Beethoven, especially in his later works. The piano sonatas, Opp. 101, 106, and 110, the *Diabelli* Variations, and the *Missa solemnis* all include fully worked-out fugues; above all one cannot forget the quartet immediately preceding this one, Op. 130, whose finale is the famous *Grosse Fuge.*

The title page of that finale describes it as "tantôt libre, tantôt recherchée"—in part free, in part studied or worked. Its daring *libertés* and its *recherches* are by no means necessarily discrete sections; indeed, what

---

7. Beethoven always tended to use his piano sonatas as proving grounds.

EXAMPLE 21. Op. 131, first movement, mm. 1–4

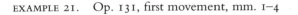

is most astonishing about this music is the way in which Beethoven combines these seemingly opposite categories.

By contrast, the fugue that opens Op. 131 seems to be all *recherchée* and to show the possibilities of that manner at its most serenely and richly beautiful. It is as though Beethoven, after the inspired and magisterial audacities of the *Grosse Fuge,* were rendering a peace offering to the fugue gods. The Op. 131 fugue reminds us that as a boy of twelve in Bonn he had played all of *The Well-Tempered Clavier,* put into his hands by his teacher, Christian Gottlob Neefe. Forty-two years later, Beethoven revisits—and transports us into—the world of the sublime C-sharp minor, F-sharp minor, and B-flat minor fugues in book one and the E major in book two. But it is more the manner—and the manners—than the substance of this fugue that creates an air of Apollonian calm in contrast to the Dionysian abandon of Op. 133; that and, of course, the fact that it is a single movement in a consistent tempo. But as we listen, we shall encounter much that is *libre* in the Op. 131 fugue as well.[8]

Like Opp. 132 and 130, Op. 131 takes pairs of semitones as its point of departure (see pp. 265 and 228). Here, to begin with, Beethoven brackets one pair (B sharp/C sharp) inside the other (G sharp/A), and it is in part to make sure that we hear this connection, which means hearing the connection between G sharp and A, the two outer notes, that he prescribes a *crescendo* across the four notes and puts an accent on the fourth (Ex. 21, mm. 1–2).

The tempo is slow, but two things indicate that it must not be too slow: the alla breve time signature (¢), which tells us that we should feel and hear two beats in each measure rather than four, and also the *ma non troppo* (not too much) with which Beethoven qualifies *Adagio*. No

8. It should be mentioned that one can often find startlingly *libre* elements in Bach's fugues as well. The E-minor Organ Fugue, BWV 548, the "Wedge," is a spectacular example.

EXAMPLE 22.   Op. 131, first movement, mm. 21–22

EXAMPLE 23.   Op. 131, first movement, mm. 66–72

less important is the further injunction, *e molto espressivo.* Beethoven's directions for *crescendos, diminuendos,* and accents are highly detailed, and this constant ebb and flow of the dynamics encourages an *espressivo* playing style.[9]

Example 21 shows the whole fugue subject. The four voices enter in descending order. As soon as they are in, Beethoven finds a way of making the first four notes still more *espressivo* by adding an appoggiatura to the last note (Ex. 22). As the lines progress, the harmonic horizons expand, to the point where Beethoven changes the key signature—something that never happens in a Bach fugue. He goes briefly into E-flat minor, then into B major, and, as he moves about, the rhythm also becomes more complex. Syncopations complicate the flow, and the motion is broken down into eighth notes.

Picking up an idea from the second half of the fugue subject (mm. 3 and 4 of Ex. 21), the music moves into a gentle episode in A major. The two violins begin it (Ex. 23), and the two lower instruments carry it forward. The full four-voice texture returns and, against a speeded-up version of Example 22 in eighth notes, the viola brings back the fugue

9. Carl Czerny based his 1838 edition of *The Well-Tempered Clavier* in part on his recollection of hearing many of these preludes and fugues played "by the great Beethoven." Beethoven's presence in this edition is reflected particularly in the prescriptions concerning tempos and dynamics, both of which Czerny adds liberally. The way the Op. 131 fugue looks on the page seems to confirm the accuracy of Czerny's representation of the highly inflected manner in which Beethoven played Bach.

EXAMPLE 24.   Op. 131, first movement, mm. 100–107

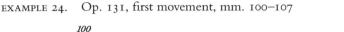

subject, not heard in its original form since the initial series of entrances. This long abandonment of the principal subject is as much an exceedingly *libre* element as was the range of the modulations earlier on.

The two violins follow the viola's example in returning to the fugue subject. When the cello does so as well, it brings it in augmentation— that is, in notes twice as long as the original (Ex. 24). This augmentation is the first in a series of powerful dynamic, harmonic, and rhythmic impulses (especially the syncopations in the inner voices) that propel the fugue toward a great cresting. From this it subsides onto a series of C-sharp major chords that softly throb almost into silence. Beethoven uses an idiosyncratic notation here, chords that are both separate and tied together. He wants a special effect—not a steady *decrescendo* across four beats but a quieting down by distinct stages, yet with no actual break in the sound.[10]

This is the first time that the music touches on the tonic major, and we shall have to wait a long time for this key to come back. Everything disappears from those final chords except the C sharps themselves. The cello rises an octave from C sharp to C sharp; viola and first violin imitate this. Then all three instruments echo this leap, but a half step higher, D to D (Ex. 25).

The second movement has begun. It is a scherzo, quick in tempo, gentle in mood (here is the first *pianissimo* in the quartet), and designed ever to keep in the listener's ear the connection with the first movement from which it emerged so organically. The theme itself introduces another way of ordering pairs of semitones—D/C sharp and A sharp/B. Insofar as the two pairs move in opposite directions, this resembles the opening of Op. 132 (see page 265), but the passages differ strikingly. Here the downward pair comes first; the vertical closeness of these two pairs, whose outer notes are only four semitones apart, makes for an

10. Bowed string instruments can manage this effect handily, but in his Sonata, Op. 110, Beethoven also expects it from the pianist. What string players accomplish with their bowstrokes the pianist must suggest with clever use of the pedal.

EXAMPLE 25.   Op. 131, first movement, mm. 119, to second movement, m. 1

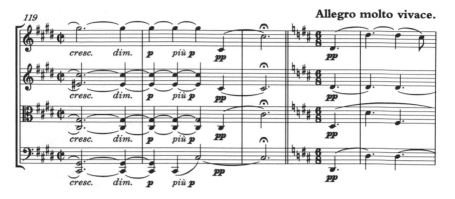

effect that is very different from that produced by the wide spaces between the two pairs in Op. 132; not least, the distinction between the
flowing rhythm here and the solemn half notes in Op. 132 makes a
whole world of difference.

Another connection with the first movement is more general, and
that is the way the smoothness of the lines reminds us of the gentle A-
major episode (Ex. 23). The music makes its way to the doorstep of F-
sharp minor, but after an expectant pause it resumes instead in E major.
The rhetoric is modest, all this being in *pianissimo,* but the effect is of a
delightful freshness. The return to D major is accomplished swiftly.
From time to time Beethoven breaks up the smooth flow with abrupt
accents, but he achieves his most dramatic surprise in a brief passage—
everything here is brief—in which the instruments play in austere, unharmonized octaves. No less startling is its sequel, a sudden spreading of
the voices in contrary motion, the first violin traveling from its bottom
G up two and a half octaves to high D, while the cello, starting from
the B flat just above the violin's G, descends to its lowest C sharp. This
outburst—I hear it as comic, tending a bit toward the petulant—is the
occasion for the first *fortissimo.*

The outburst is a bit much for everybody. Twice the music seeks to
resume with vigorous pairs of iambic chords, and twice it runs aground
with a sort of "Er, what was I saying?" And so the movement concludes
quickly with a few *mezza voce* and *pianissimo* chords. Their placement
amid the silences that separate them is provocatively and enchantingly

EXAMPLE 26.   Op. 131, fourth movement, mm. 1–4

vague. Throughout this quartet, Beethoven takes pains to distinguish degrees of finality in his closing cadences.

The last sound of the second movement is a D-major chord with F sharp on top. It is followed by a B-minor chord, also with F sharp on top, and this in turn is succeeded even more quickly by a first-inversion chord of F-sharp major. This is a formula from Italian operatic recitative, and its purpose here is to introduce a conversation. This third section is not so much a real movement as an eleven-measure bridge of recitative formulas. The tempo, *Allegro moderato* at first, slows to *Adagio* to allow the first violin space for a declaration that is at once ardent and, in its run of ornate thirty-second notes, proudly elegant. With the appropriate closing gestures the bridge is crossed and everything is ready for the next event.

This is the quartet's central movement, a theme with variations. The theme is utterly simple, and the beginning of its tune, in skeletal form, is A/G sharp, D/C sharp, another reshuffling of pairs of semitones (Ex. 26). What is far from simple, however, is the scoring. Regarding the third movement of Op. 130 I mentioned the miracle of the deaf Beethoven's fantasy and uncanny skill in the matter of scoring (see page 233). Here is another such marvel, though where that *Andante* in Op. 130 is delightfully "fancy," this page is of such simplicity that the music seems hardly to have been consciously scored at all. But how amazing it is— the subtle difference between the way the second violin quietly supports the first violin's phrases while the first violin stays silent when the second speaks, the contrast between the viola's long notes and the pizzicatos in

EXAMPLE 27.   Op. 131, fourth movement, mm. 32–37

the cello, the deemphasis throughout of the downbeats. And what comes later is no less wonderful—the double stops in the viola and cello, the increasing elaboration of the texture, the lovely detail of the just three notes that the cello plays arco rather than pizzicato.

The theme is of the simplest design, consisting of two sections of eight measures apiece, each section being repeated. With the sole exception of the second half of variation 5, the repeats are fully written out or, rather, recomposed, the movement always being from simplicity to complexity.

Example 27 shows how variation 1 begins. The texture at the beginning is 3 + 1: the three lower voices play together, carrying the theme, and the first violin spins out decorative filigree above. You discover almost immediately that while you can clearly hear the first phrase of the theme in the second violin, it is the middle voice, the viola, that supplies the continuation. For the phrase after that, the first violin is drawn in and thus no longer stands separate, and by the time the first eight-measure period comes to its end, all four instruments are engaged in equal play.

In the repeat of those eight measures, the viola carries the first fragment of the melody and the cello provides the decorative filigree, heightening the intensity of those lines. As the variation proceeds, the texture becomes ever more elaborated, subtilized, unpredictable. The tempo is that of the theme—*Andante ma non troppo e molto cantabile* (moving along, but not too much, and very songful)—but the effect is one of constant speeding up as the motion breaks down more and more consistently into sixteenth and thirty-second notes.

The suggestion of increased speed becomes truly increased speed when we reach variation 2. Here Beethoven prescribes a faster beat (*più mosso*), also changing the meter from 2/4 to 4/4 and preceding the real beginning with a vamp-till-ready measure. *Più mosso* also describes the sense of acceleration and increasing density that runs through this variation: there is more and more action as the music moves from a demure beginning to a wild ending. In this respect it resembles variation 1, but to still more heightened effect. Where in variation 1 the heightening was limited to the growing prominence of smaller note values, here every aspect of expression, dynamics, texture, and rhythmic eccentricity is intensified.

Variation 2 begins as a simple and casual exchange between violin and cello, for which the middle instruments provide a simple tick-tick accompaniment. The melody is present on a "now you hear it, now you don't" basis, and it is chiefly the very plain and graspable harmonic outline that connects us to the theme. The repeats of each half are thoroughly redesigned.

As the variation unfolds, the second violin and viola aspire to join the conversation of the first violin and cello. The second violin twice anticipates the cello's entrances as though too impatient to wait or not convinced that the cello will know what to do, and the viola actually joins the cello on some of its cadences. The second violin eventually succeeds in elbowing the first aside altogether. Finally all four instruments play in unharmonized octaves with big *sforzandi* on the offbeats, as if remembering—and recalling for us—the corresponding octave passage in the second movement. The contrary motion excursions return as well.

As though by now very cross with one another, the four instruments cannot agree to play the final cadence of the second part together either time it occurs. When, for example, they outline the final A-major chord one note at a time, each with its own choleric *sforzando* (Ex. 28), it reminds us of the way the orchestra begins the scherzo of the Ninth Symphony with a similarly split chord of D minor (Ex. 29).

That irascible gesture done, variation 3 can begin. It does so in a very different temper: the pace is slower, and the key word in the marking for the players is *lusinghiero,* for which "seductive" is not too strong a

EXAMPLE 28.   Op. 131, fourth movement, m. 97

EXAMPLE 29.   Symphony No. 9, second movement, mm. 1–8, piano
reduction

translation. In addition, Beethoven writes *dolce* over the cello's and viola's
first phrases. Much of this variation is cast as a series of two-part inven-
tions, though here too we shall find that the section as a whole describes
a general crescendo of intensity.

Cello and viola begin. The A/G sharp–D/C sharp pattern is made
part of a succession of soft melodic curves that once again hark back to
the gentle A-major episode in the first movement (Ex. 30). A couple of
trills appear at the close of the first eight-measure period. We shall hear
more about that. When this section is repeated, the violins take up the
two-part conversation. Viola and cello add a bass line, but the two instruments never play simultaneously. Not until the first half of the variation arrives at its cadence do we hear the whole quartet together.

The second half also starts as a two-part invention, but the mood is
beginning to change. Trills charge the proceedings with sudden extra

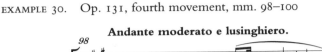

EXAMPLE 30.   Op. 131, fourth movement, mm. 98–100

spurts of energy, and Beethoven begins consistently to add sharp, offbeat accents. From genial and *dolce,* the atmosphere has turned ominous. The whole quartet plays the last eight measures, in effect doubling the previous two-part texture and of course also doubling the trills, *sforzandi,* and sudden *crescendos.*

The final cadential chord of variation 3 is also the first chord of variation 4. This *Adagio* is the first slow variation and, since the opening was an *Adagio ma non troppo* as well as in cut time, we can even say that this is the first truly slow music in the quartet. There are six eighth notes in each measure, but the beat we feel is that of a very slow two. Again, the melody is not obviously present, but we easily infer its shape from now very familiar harmonies. The chief element here is a gracefully limned melody in sixteenth notes; a subsidiary but striking element is the punctuation in pizzicato with which Beethoven marks the ends of phrases in the first part.

Once again Beethoven builds a constant increase of activity into this variation. The lines overlap more and more, and one result of that is that there are simply no more airspaces for the punctuating pizzicatos. Only in the very last measure, as the violins rise in an ecstatic scale, do viola and cello surprise us with an emphatic pair of final plunks. It is a lovable coming together of the serious and the humorous.[11]

Without pause, variation 5—*Allegretto* in 2/4—emerges from this final cadence. Here is one of Beethoven's strangest and most haunting pages. It begins with what sounds like tuning. Everything at first is off the beat, rhythmically "soft," virtually devoid of melody, and once again

---

11. I do not suppose that many quartet players since 1828 have been surprised by this—certainly none since recordings became available—but I do sometimes like to think of the raised eyebrows of the startled Joseph Böhm and his second violinist when they were so irreverently interrupted by the pizzicato plunks in the viola and cello while trying so hard to get their heavenbound A-major scale in octaves in tune.

EXAMPLE 31.   Op. 131, fourth movement, mm. 187–88

only the harmonies serve to maintain a clear connection with the theme. But even here Beethoven sticks to his pattern of getting more intense during the course of each variation: the meter is clarified and at least brief patches of clear melody emerge. This extremely "reduced" variation is the only one where Beethoven simply repeats the second part rather than varying or recomposing it.

Variation 5 is both a sudden speeding up after the spacious *Adagio* measures of the preceding variation and also a switch from the grounded to the wispy. When it disappears—and it does just disappear in mid-thought and mid-cadence rather than really finish—Beethoven takes us back to slow music. Here, too, *Adagio* is qualified by *ma non troppo,* but the meter is 9/4 (unique in Beethoven). The measures are very long, and the beat we feel is an extremely slow three.

The slowly pulsating chords of variation 6 outline the now familiar harmonies and shapes, but no longer at all literally (Ex. 31). There are a few *crescendos* and a few beats of *forte,* but for the most part the music moves in the world of *piano, pianissimo,* and *sotto voce.* Brief lines of melody emerge and the harmonies become more piquant as sharps and naturals collide. Beethoven also enlivens the textures with a few interventions, almost all of them in the cello, of the figure in Example 32. All in all, though, this is music of spellbinding stillness.

What seems to be a seventh variation is entered by way of a deceptive cadence, a particular kind that Haydn was fond of and also the one that Wagner, who treasured Op. 131 most among Beethoven's works, liked so well and used so much in *Die Meistersinger.* The new music that

EXAMPLE 32.   Op. 131, fourth movement, m. 195

EXAMPLE 33.   Op. 131, fourth movement, mm. 231–32

emerges is florid and very much like human speech (Ex. 33), but at what should be the end of the first paragraph it dissolves into a chain of trills. At this point we realize that this is not a new variation but the beginning of what turns out to be a long and fantastical coda. The violin trills, which at first seem about to settle the music in A major, instead divert it to C major, an area virtually untouched hitherto. There the violin seeks to pick up the theme in the most innocent manner imaginable, but fever intervenes. The music speeds up, then slows again, finally arriving in A major after all. There we hear the theme in a richly scored version decorated by trills from the first violin. It is a revisiting of variation 5, also in A major, of Op. 18 no. 5, and a page that Schubert found worth imitating in his "Trout" Quintet.

But this too gets lost in its trilling. Suddenly we find ourselves in the midst of another attempt to bring the theme back in its most naive form, this time in F major. This in turn is derailed. A songful and brilliant violin flourish takes us back to A major, and, in a witty confusion of hesitations, pauses, and rhythmic displacements, this immensely rich and elaborate variation movement comes to its close. Its coda is the wryly comic counterpart to the gropings Beethoven had earlier worked out in

EXAMPLE 34.   Op. 131, fifth movement, mm. 3–10

tragic-dramatic style at the beginning of the *Hammerklavier* Sonata's finale.

Here we have the closest event to a full stop so far. The cello rumbles noisily, and after a moment's shocked silence all four players begin a wild and very fast scherzo that makes the voyage to trio and da capo twice before winding up in a mad coda. Example 34 shows how the scherzo begins. The first violin's first measure is a repeat of the cello rumble. The sudden *forte* landing on the repeated G-sharp major chords is characteristic of the prevailing temper. A feature that we hear a great deal is a series of repetitions of a rising two-note figure derived from the second measure of the theme. Beethoven's attempt to indicate the degree of deceleration that he wants leads this master of complicated verbal directions into one of his stranger efforts, *molto poco adagio.* I think what he means by "very much a little bit slow" is that he wants the music to slow down, but only to *poco adagio;* the extra emphasis of *molto* refers to the *poco* and is intended to make sure that the *Adagio* is very *poco* indeed.

Later, Beethoven introduces a contrasting idea, which he marks *piacevole,* pleasing, agreeable, or amiable (Ex. 35). This in effect is the trio. The character is new, but the musical shape is related to that of Example 34; note the contrast of quarter and half notes and the specific reappearance of the B–E interval. The accompaniment is a rapid Ping-Pong of quarter notes for viola and cello. A moment later this Ping-Pong is heard by itself and then taken up by the two violins. To stay unflustered and steady there is one of the supreme tests of quartetsmanship. Soon Beethoven offers a further variant of this idea (Ex. 36). A bridge with more

EXAMPLE 35.   Op. 131, fifth movement, mm. 69–72

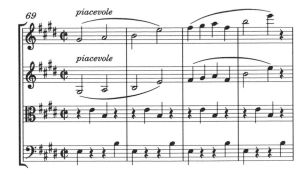

EXAMPLE 36.   Op. 131, fifth movement, mm. 113–18

Ping-Ponging and ending in a set of raucous pizzicatos leads back to the first reprise of the scherzo itself. It is typical of the humor and the pace of this music that the cello rumble, which is, as it were, the official initiation of the da capo, cuts impatiently across the last pizzicato twangs of the trio.

Scherzo and trio are recapitulated, though at the end of the trio Beethoven makes an amusing change by doubling the pizzicato notes so that there are two in each measure instead of one. He also varies this second repeat of the scherzo by asking for a large patch of it to be played *pianissimo,* an effect familiar from the corresponding movement in the Seventh Symphony.

For a moment it seems as though Beethoven will take us around the scherzo/trio cycle for a third time. This too is an old joke, familiar from the Fourth and Seventh symphonies. The *piacevole* phrase (Ex. 35) comes back but breaks off after four measures. Silence. First violin and cello resume with the third measure of the *piacevole* but take a wrong turn and find themselves in Example 36 instead. The second violin and the viola try the same thing, but a measure too late. Hideous dissonance, confusion, silence. This is the sound of a quartet getting lost: Beethoven, in a moment of mad Ivesian humor, has composed the breakdown of a performance!

Now we hear unconfident attempts to get back on track—efforts to find the main theme, another go at the pizzicatos, and again the baffled silences. Then the main theme does return, though Beethoven makes it still more strange by asking the musicians to play with the bow virtually at the bridge, which produces a ghostly "rats' feet on broken glass" effect.

The sonority returns to the ordinary, and the movement goes forward quickly to a close in *fortissimo*. The link between this movement and the next is parallel to the one between the first two movements, the final cadence simply being repeated at another pitch. G sharp is the note so dramatically introduced. This progression from E to G sharp echoes the one in the scherzo's first phrase, Example 34. G sharp is also the dominant of C sharp, the home key of the quartet, and this emphatic arrival on G sharp thus suggests that its purpose is to prepare the return to C sharp, from which we have been gone since the end of the first movement. So indeed it turns out; only the G sharp–C sharp cadence is much larger than we expect inasmuch as Beethoven takes time to turn G-sharp (minor) into a key in which we hear a brief songlike movement.

Opus 131 has no real lyric slow movement in the sense comparable to the variations in Op. 127, the cavatina in Op. 130, and the Song of Thanksgiving in Op. 132. Here, however, is another one of the passages of slow or fairly slow music—*Adagio quasi un poco andante* this time—that function as major structural and expressive markers in this work. The viola begins the singing of this poignant song whose harmonic life is so wondrously enriched by touches of Neapolitan harmony. This whole movement is a bridge from scherzo to finale, but a singularly beautiful deceptive cadence introduces the bridge within the bridge, the final phrase that turns the music toward its proper destination, C-sharp minor.

A violin phrase of wide range takes us into this new/old world. C sharp itself erupts as a single unharmonized note, brusque, staccato, and

EXAMPLE 37. Op. 131, seventh movement, mm. 2–5

EXAMPLE 38. Op. 131, seventh movement, mm. 6–9

fortissimo. And now for the first time since the opening fugue we are
back in C-sharp minor, in a stormy movement whose first idea—in
outline C sharp, G sharp, A, B sharp—presents yet another reshuffling
of the quartet's first notes (Ex. 37).

This is immediately expanded into a theme in which we can hear
another variant of the same idea (Ex. 38). Its contour also recalls the
curve of Example 23, smooth there but played here in excited dotted
rhythm. Another extension, shown in Example 39, recalls the rhythmic
pattern of the first movement's fugue subject, and its notes are the same
as well, though again rearranged. Altogether, as the music progresses,
Beethoven forges more and more links to establish the sense that a great
circle is closing.

EXAMPLE 39.   Op. 131, seventh movement, mm. 22–23

EXAMPLE 40.   Op. 131, seventh movement, mm. 56–59

His greatest marvel is a lyric theme, first heard in E major, richly scored, and whose phrases end in leaps that most extraordinarily convey both serenity and ecstasy (Ex. 40). Beethoven modulates to F-sharp minor. There he introduces a new and drastically simple rhythmic idea, a series of whole notes whose steadiness provides a counterpoise, highly charged emotionally, to the nervous energy of the surrounding material (Ex. 41).

Next (Ex. 42), Beethoven explores another harmonic area long unvisited, the Neapolitan, D major, the key of the second movement, and there the second violin plays a scurrying theme—*non ligato,* Beethoven

EXAMPLE 41. Op. 131, seventh movement, mm. 94–97

EXAMPLE 42. Op. 131, seventh movement, mm. 124–29

writes—that is clearly cousin to Example 40. This is explored further. The bass settles on G sharp, the dominant, and preparations begin to take place for the thrust into the recapitulation. This transition is accomplished by way of a Sibelius-like buzzing, suppressed and excited, the tension being resolved with a firm landing on C sharp. The recapitulation itself brings interesting rearrangements and reorderings.

Then epiphany. The serene-ecstatic theme (Ex. 40) reappears astoundingly in D major, the resonance of that chord on the string instruments yielding an even richer sound than before. In an even more astonishing sequel, Beethoven shifts this inspired theme into the tonic major, C sharp, a key not heard since the end of the opening fugue but, even if unconsciously, long awaited.

The music can now move resolutely toward its close, but even at this late stage Beethoven is not done with invention. Whole notes ring out in octaves—the only passage of sustained octaves anywhere in the Beethoven quartets. The D-major *non ligato* scurrying returns in different form, and after that flurry of energy everything begins to subside. The rate of harmonic change slows, and the tempo itself is reduced to *poco adagio*. In those few slow measures, the Es become E sharps. We are in C-sharp major. The final measures of quick music are also in that key, but they are far from a conventionally triumphant major-mode close to this, the last of Beethoven's great tragedies in music. For that they come too late and too quickly.

Yes, and it was about this, the greatest of his quartets, that Beethoven wrote to a friend that he would find "a new manner of part-writing and, thank God, less lack of imagination than before."[12]

STRING QUARTET IN A MINOR, OP. 132

Assai sostenuto—Allegro
Allegro ma non tanto

A Convalescent's Holy Song of Thanksgiving
    to the Deity, in the Lydian Mode:
Molto adagio—Andante
Alla marcia, assai vivace
Allegro appassionato—Presto

Opus 132 is the second in order of composition of the three quartets that Beethoven composed for Prince Nicholas Galitzin. (For more information about this commission, see the note on Op. 127, page 217.) Beethoven began to make sketches toward the end of 1824, just before the final push to finish Op. 127; as soon as that was accomplished, in February 1825, he began to concentrate on the present quartet. In the early spring, work was interrupted by a serious illness, some sort of intestinal inflammation, Beethoven eventually celebrating his recovery in the Song of Thanksgiving that is the quartet's third movement. By May, Beethoven was again well enough to compose, and he completed the score at the end of July. The Schuppanzigh Quartet gave two private performances in September 1825, followed by two public ones on 6 and 20 November. Schlesinger—of Berlin and Paris—contracted for the publication as early as September 1825 but took two years, which was six months after the composer's death, before managing to get the music into print.

12. Thayer-Forbes 1964, 982.

EXAMPLE 43.   Op. 132, first movement

a. mm. 9–11

b. mm. 9–11 in skeletal form

In the cello's first two notes—G sharp and A—we meet the musical idea that dominates this quartet as well as the two succeeding ones, Op. 130 and Op. 131. (In Beethoven's notebooks, the ideas for the introduction of Op. 132 are intermingled with those for the *Grosse Fuge,* the original finale of Op. 130.) The cello's phrase actually consists of two pairs of semitones, and in each of these three quartets Beethoven finds a different way of connecting two such pairs. Opus 130 has the simplest arrangements, the two pairs proceeding in straight sequence (see page 228), and Op. 131 the most complex, with one pair bracketing the other (see page 247). Here, in Op. 132, Beethoven begins with two pairs that move in opposite directions, the rising pair (G sharp/A) being followed by one that falls (F/E). When the cello has gotten no further than its third note, the viola joins in, followed one beat later by the second violin, and for eight measures, *pianissimo,* all the instruments discourse gravely on this idea.

Up to now the tempo has been fairly slow—*assai sostenuto.* Suddenly the first violin breaks free in a brief flight of quick notes, and the *Allegro* is under way. The violin swoops down through nearly two octaves, soars back to the note where it had begun its flight, then settles a semitone lower, on E (Ex. 43a). The whole flight is really an embellished upbeat (Ex. 43b). Under that E, in its high register, the cello suggests an idea (Ex. 44). The first violin immediately picks this up and continues it so that it becomes a real theme. A/G sharp and F/E are still very much with us. This gives way to an energetic passage in dotted rhythms for the

EXAMPLE 44.   Op. 132, first movement, mm. 11–12

EXAMPLE 45.   Op. 132, first movement, mm. 21–24

whole quartet. What sounds as though it were going to be a repetition of this in a higher octave turns instead into the double surprise of a single *Adagio* measure leading into a compressed return of the violin's down-and-up flight. All the components of the opening are there—the slow tempo leading to a quick tempo, the violin's fanciful flight, the F to E sequence in the violin, the beginning of the theme underneath—but everything is realigned, varied, fresh (Ex. 45). There is more to be said about Example 44, and what comes next is variation as well—an expansion both in actual length and in harmonic range—of the events that led up to that surprising *Adagio* intervention. The newest version of the violin flight introduces something new, division of the beat into triplets.

A vigorous *crescendo* leads to an expectant half cadence, and, almost without time to draw breath, the first violin launches a new and marchlike idea. This, however, turns out to be only the opening of the door to another preparatory *crescendo*. Then comes the real second

EXAMPLE 46.   Op. 132, first movement, mm. 103–6

theme. It is a smiling tune in F major, begun by the second violin and
continued by the first, which has already made a couple of moves to
chime in. Beethoven asks not only for *dolce* but adds *teneramente* (tenderly). Viola and cello accompany in a rapid Ping-Pong of triplets. The
music gathers energy. The dotted-rhythm passage reappears in more emphatic form, with an accent on each beat, and the exposition reaches its
final cadence in F major.

Beethoven, however, allows no moment for reflection. An expansive
ritard led into the cadence, but the continuation is immediate and in
tempo. After a brief series of chords that end in a curious hesitation, we
seem for a moment to be back at the beginning of the movement, to
long notes in *pianissimo* exploring sequences of semitones. After a silence
there is a strange passage in which the upper and lower halves of the
quartet team to oppose each other gruffly. This, by one of those vigorous
half cadences that are a hallmark of this movement, leads to a grand
statement of semitones in whole notes. One pair is in unison, the other
in contrary motion so that the earlier sequence of semitones in contrary
motion has been compressed into simultaneity (Ex. 46).

Further play with Example 44 leads to something familiar, the violin
flight, in yet another version. As before, it introduces Example 44, the
suggestion in the cello, the expansion, fancifully varied this time, in
the first violin. The strange thing, though, is that all this is happening in
the wrong key, E minor, instead of the tonic, A minor. But Beethoven
does mean to be doing exactly what he is doing. Thematically, the music
moves along the same path as before; only the harmonic design is askew.

EXAMPLE 47.   Op. 132, second movement, mm. 1–4

The marchlike beginning and the *dolce* second theme both return in C major.

This recapitulation ends as the exposition did, with a broad cadence and a hurried continuation. A few measures bring us to another presentation of the semitones in whole notes and in contrary motion, and this introduces what is in effect a second recapitulation, properly placed in A minor, and with the later *dolce* theme appearing in A major. (You could also say that the "wrong key" recapitulation is the humorously perverse final episode of the development and that only this is the real recapitulation.) In any event, the movement ends with a brisk coda. The brilliant writing for the first violin, reminiscent of the equivalently virtuosic but more expansive close to the first movement of Op. 74, gives it a rough trumpetlike energy.

The second movement is in a lilting triple meter—*Allegro ma non tanto* (*Allegro,* but not too much so). Once again we hear pairs of semitones (Ex. 47), and the figure defined by the first three notes is constantly kept in view as part of the fabric. An effect with which Beethoven made us very familiar in the first movement and that reappears here constantly is that of voices moving in contrary motion. This movement is an always surprising mixture of the gentle and the acid. The pace is easy-going, the gestures are soft, the dynamics rarely rise even as far as *forte;* on the other hand, the contrary motion often makes the harmonies a bit tart, and the rhythms are inclined to move with impish disregard of the barlines and with a constant and delightful inclination to surprise.

Beethoven can turn the most ordinary things into miracles. Nowhere does he do it more touchingly than in the trio, where a country dance tune, with bagpipe drone and all, becomes transfigured at a great height into something distant, mysterious, free of the pull of gravity. Here, too, is one of the moments at which Beethoven's imagination for sonority and texture—the imagination, one is once again startled to remember, of a deaf man—is unsurpassed in freedom and freshness. The middle section of this trio is something to make violists sweat.

Suddenly the world of firm basses must have its way. Cello and viola, eventually joined by the second violin, play an assertive passage in stark octaves, from which the first violin flees in a wide-ranging arpeggio. So disconcerting is this interruption of the mood that the meter goes to pieces and we have the jolt of four measures in duple meter before Beethoven resumes the dance with its intimations of heaven.

Heaven is, in a less elusive way, the subject of the next movement, one of Beethoven's most famous. He calls it "A Convalescent's Holy Song of Thanksgiving to the Deity, in the Lydian Mode." As I mentioned earlier, here Beethoven is drawing directly on his own life experience, himself having been extremely ill and in pain to the point where he had to interrupt his work on this quartet for many weeks.

Sometimes, in the most solemn moments of his later music, Beethoven leaves our familiar major and minor keys to explore the mystic realms of the old church modes. It was part of the renewal of his language at this time, a renewal that corresponded to a renewal of spirit. He might have said with Verdi: "Torniamo all'antico: sarà un progresso" (Let us turn to antiquity: it will be a step forward).[13] In 1817–18 he composed his B-flat major Piano Sonata, Op. 106, the so-called *Hammerklavier,* and the gravest cadences in the slow movement of that great work are modal. In 1818, probably in belated response to an invitation from the Philharmonic Society of London to visit England in the winter of 1817–18 and to bring two new symphonies, Beethoven made some jottings concerning such works: one was to be in D minor, the other to include a choral *"Adagio* Cantique . . . in ancient modes."[14] In these notations we can see the seeds, some of them at any rate of the Ninth Symphony, that would occupy him from 1822 until February 1824 and

13. Giuseppe Verdi to Francesco Florimo, 5 January 1871, in *Autobiografia dalle lettere,* ed. Carlo Graziani (Verona, 1941), 408.

14. In *Beethoven: Letters, Journals, and Conversations,* ed. and trans. Michael Hamburger (Garden City, N.Y., 1960), 161.

EXAMPLE 48.   Op. 132, third movement, chorale melody

EXAMPLE 49.   Op. 132, third movement, mm. 1–2

some of whose most significant moments are made so by touches of modal harmony. In February or March of 1819, Beethoven began to sketch a Kyrie, a skimpy notation of a few rising notes with the words "Elee" (eleison?) and "dor" (Dorian?). This was one of his first moves in the long gestation of the *Missa solemnis,* whose Dorian mode Et Incarnatus Est is of unearthly exaltation.

In the Song of Thanksgiving of Op. 132, Beethoven, as he points out in his long title, uses the Lydian mode. (The Lydian scale is like an F-major scale, only with B natural instead of B flat.) In the manner of a baroque chorale prelude, Beethoven frames the phrases of his hymn between more rapid figurations. In contrast to the solid chords of the hymn (Ex. 48)—the texture has, so to speak, been previewed in the first measures of the whole quartet—the introductory and connecting phrases are imitative in texture (Ex. 49).

EXAMPLE 50. Op. 132, third movement, mm. 85–86

The hymn is restated twice, with variations. Between its appearances comes the piercing contrast of brilliant D major, a quicker tempo (*andante*), and a dancelike triple meter; Beethoven in fact breaks off the hymn in mid-course for this interruption, which he marks "feeling new strength." The staccatos, the wide leaps, the exuberant upbeats in scurrying thirty-second notes, the jubilant violin trill that rides across the top of the music, the breathless excitement in the accompaniment, all contribute to the joyful atmosphere.

When the hymn returns, the polyphonic texture of the introductory measures persists throughout. The music is also elaborated rhythmically (Ex. 50), and the first violin alone carries the hymn tune. The "new strength" episode returns, though this time without that heading. It is fascinatingly revoiced, elaborated in detail, still more "physical."

Then the hymn returns. The connecting tissue is still more complex and intense in rhythm (Ex. 51), and the hymn itself is no longer the simple thing it was. Beethoven now concentrates on its first phrase, presenting this in a series of imitations. The harmonies become surprisingly dissonant. The range grows wider, the cello descending to its sonorous open C string, reinforced by the C an octave above, while the first violin ascends to ever greater heights. For a time, every beat is reinforced by a *sforzando*. There is also an extraordinary moment when the elaborate play with eighth and sixteenth notes ceases and the accompanying voices move only in half notes. The effect is heart-stopping—yet another wonderful example of Beethoven's powerfully imaginative use of rhythm to heighten expressive effect. From this radiant climax, this *Adagio*, the last

EXAMPLE 51.   Op. 132, third movement, mm. 169–70

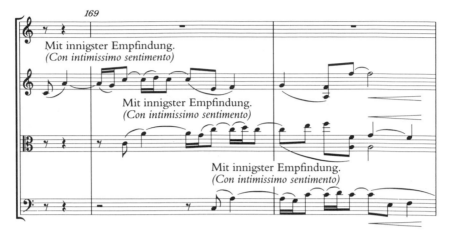

of Beethoven's long slow movements, descends slowly, to end in utmost serenity on a chord so airy that even the cello is in the treble register.[15]

The story is told that Beethoven not only could move listeners to tears with his improvisations at the piano but also on occasion enjoyed jarring them out of their emotional transport by laughing diabolically and scolding them for being fools. Nothing quite so drastic here; nonetheless, what happens next is far indeed from what any of us would predict. There is a special kind of Beethoven march, terse, full of unexpected twists and witticisms, and apt to be quite fierce. There is a fine theatrical example in the first act of *Fidelio,* another in the Three Marches for Piano Duet, Op. 45, and quite a mad and wonderful one in the A-major Piano Sonata, Op. 101. Here, in Op. 132, is its shortest and in some ways saddest incarnation. Beethoven delights in the rhythmic ambiguity he has built into his theme. The first two notes are a typical upbeat figure and sound as though they ought to be an upbeat, the impression being reinforced by the fact that the instruments other than the first violin, which carries the melody, enter only on the next beat. Just the same, what sounds like "four" is in fact "one" (Ex. 52).

15. A character in Aldous Huxley's *Point Counter Point* commits suicide while his gramophone endlessly repeats the last side of the Léner Quartet's recording of this movement.

EXAMPLE 52.   Op. 132, fourth movement, mm. 1–2

Without break, Beethoven moves into an impassioned recitative by the first violin. The urgent chords that introduce it may remind us of the chords that begin the development in the first movement as well as of the gruff octaves in the second movement; the wild declamation of the violin will bring back to our memories the fanciful flight of the same instrument in the first movement. Indeed, the recitative—which begins fast, *più* (more) *allegro* than the *assai vivace* of the march, and accelerates into *presto*—ends with yet another version of the flight, down and up. Even the pitches are the right ones. The flight begins and ends on F. Here, too, the F is a preparation for the real destination, which is E, the dominant of A minor, the key of the quartet as a whole and specifically of the finale that is about to begin. One striking difference here is that F/E is presented as an operatic recitative formula (Ex. 53).

The dying F/E cadence of that recitative is picked up by the second violin, in tempo, and that is the start of the urgent and febrile finale. The principal melody is one that Beethoven had sketched some years before—for the finale of the Ninth Symphony! There are contrasting elements—a more lyric melody given added grace by recurring trills, and a strangely creeping music in even quarter notes and gray *pianissimo*—but it never takes long before the sense of pressing forward returns. Near the end, Beethoven increases the speed from *allegro appassionato* to *presto*. The cello takes on the main theme in an extremely high register (always an exciting moment to see as well as to hear), and almost immediately the music is propelled from minor into a breathlessly

EXAMPLE 53.   Op. 132, fourth movement, mm. 44–46

ecstatic A major. As almost always in late Beethoven, formal closing gestures are kept to a minimum, everything remaining involved and "composed" right up to the epigrammatic final cadence.

GROSSE FUGE FOR STRING QUARTET, OP. 133

See the String Quartet in B-Flat Major, Op. 130, page 238.

STRING QUARTET IN F MAJOR, OP. 135

Allegretto
Vivace
Lento assai, cantante e tranquillo—Più lento—Tempo I
Grave ma non troppo tratto—Allegro

Almost as soon as Beethoven had finished Op. 131 in the summer of 1826, he started on another quartet, which he finished that October. The Galitzin commission for three quartets (see page 217) got Beethoven back to writing quartets after a twelve-year interval, but once started, he kept going on his own momentum. This F-major work was his last complete quartet, though it is followed by the new finale he composed for Op. 130 (see page 244). There is also a fragmentary sketch, also from 1826, for what seems to have been intended as a quartet in C major.

Published posthumously in September 1827 by Schlesinger, Op. 135

is dedicated to Beethoven's friend Johann Nepomuk Wolfmayer, a wealthy textile merchant and keen musical amateur. Originally, Wolfmayer was to have received the dedication of Op. 131: for that story see the essay on that work (p. 245). It was the suggestion of the violinist Karl Holz that Wolfmayer be compensated by the dedication of Op. 135.

By virtue both of its brevity and its "normality" of design, Op. 135 stands apart from the other late quartets. What if Beethoven could have recovered from the dropsy and cirrhosis that laid him low at the end of 1826? What if he had lived? Such speculations are in an obvious sense useless, but they need not be uninteresting. In the case of Beethoven, one question that immediately presents itself is whether the Tenth Symphony and whatever quartets and other works that followed would have continued on the path of new simplicity suggested by Op. 135 and the final *Allegro* of Op. 130.

Of course the latter had to be simple inasmuch as the sole reason for its existence was to provide an alternative to what was perceived as the impossibly knotty *Grosse Fuge*. Opus 135 did not have to be. That work, even though he grumbled to Schlesinger about really having had something bigger in mind, was, so to speak, a voluntary turning away from the crescendo of complexity that we can trace from Op. 127 to Op. 131. Opus 135 no more embodies nostalgia for the good old days of Op. 18 than the Eighth Symphony expresses longing to return to the manner of the First Symphony. It seems more like a quest for the ideal of *multum in parvo*. How would it be to provide an aesthetically and emotionally rich experience divorced from the staggering complexities and the expansive scale of the preceding quartets, particularly Opp. 130 and 131? A reminder: what came just before the last quartets was the *Diabelli* Variations, the *Missa solemnis,* the Ninth Symphony—gargantuan conceptions all.

Do we, in the works of the second part of 1826, have the beginning of a fourth period, vastly different from the awesome third, or would Op. 135 have come to seem like an intermezzo? We cannot know, but in spite of Beethoven's grumpiness to Schlesinger, this quartet sounds like the utterance of a heart and mind miraculously refreshed. Here, too, Beethoven might have said, as he did about Op. 131, "and thank God, not less imagination than before." [16]

16. Reported by Karl Holz, second violin in the Schuppanzigh Quartet, as something that Beethoven said to him. Holz is quoted in Wilhelm von Lenz's *Eine Kunststudie,* which in turn is quoted in Thayer-Forbes 1964, 982.

EXAMPLE 54.   Op. 135, first movement, mm. 1–2

EXAMPLE 55.   Op. 135, first movement, mm. 25–27

The gently conversational first movement—*Allegretto*—is an enchanting mixture of the plain and the curious. The viola, quietly supported by the cello, begins as though *in medias res,* and the first violin adds its *pianissimo* comment, a not quite suppressed snicker (Ex. 54). The hairpins contribute to the sense of caprice. The phrase is repeated, and this time both violins comment—with rather less restraint. The viola tries a slightly different tack, and this takes: with the cello still playing a supporting role, the two violins and the viola happily continue their exchange.

What astounds is not only the extreme simplicity of tone but how soon it is over. The first sentence complete, all the instruments switch to a solemn, even austere passage in unharmonized octaves. This too lasts only four measures before the first violin takes off on a brief flight that initiates yet another passage of conversation somewhat in the manner of the previous one. This leads to a new idea in sixteenth notes (Ex. 55), after which the exposition moves toward its breezy conclusion. On the way we hear one of those vigorous passages in contrary motion of which Beethoven is so fond in the late quartets.

EXAMPLE 56.   Op. 135, first movement, mm. 85–87

Actually the exposition never reaches a formal close. The expected cadence to C major, the dominant, is not completed; instead, Beethoven diverts the harmony so as to put us on the edge of D minor. There he begins the development. Within very few measures, the conversational passages from the beginning of the movement, the solemn octaves, and the vigorous sixteenth-note triplets that helped drive the exposition to its conclusion all come up for discussion. Then, surprisingly, Beethoven, after only two dozen measures, arrives at what sounds like the recapitulation. It is a witty reentry, cunningly spliced into the development.

It is also in the wrong key, B flat instead of F. All four players in unison enter a firm objection and swing the music around to F major. Everything now appears to be on track. The one remaining anomaly is that the development was too short, even for so brief an exposition. But Beethoven can take care of this, too. After two measures of what he has now convinced us is the proper recapitulation, he makes one change: he converts B flat to B natural. With that he sweetly and firmly undoes our sense of F major, of recapitulation, of being home (Ex. 56).

We are in A minor. A short excursion to G major distracts us further, but suddenly Beethoven propels us into the real recapitulation. This true reentry is as witty and surprising as the false one earlier on. Haydn would—at least should—have been proud of his difficult pupil.

The most striking change in the recapitulation itself is the way the serious octaves are expanded, in harmonic range as well as in sheer extension. Just like the exposition, the recapitulation ends in a deceptive cadence, Beethoven this time taking us to the doorstep of G minor. In

EXAMPLE 57.   Op. 135, second movement, mm. 1–9

the delightful coda, Beethoven shows us that the opening phrase, the flippant comment, the octaves, and the triplets can all be played at the same time. The end is whimsical and of perfect punctuality.

Next comes a fiery scherzo, very fast. The melody in the first violin is simplicity itself, just a shuttling back and forth along the first three notes of the F-major scale—F, G, and A. The bass line expands the repertory of notes. The middle parts are minimal with respect to pitch, but the second violin's syncopations add breathless excitement (Ex. 57).

These nine measures are repeated with the parts redistributed, but, practically before there is time to register that we have safely completed the paragraph, an accented E flat, thoroughly alien to the harmonic context, interrupts rudely. It insists for several measures. Then it is time for Beethoven to turn to one of his favorite tricks, the one where he simply picks up an idea bodily and puts it down again on another pitch the way you might pick up your cat and move it from your favorite chair to another. Here he just goes from E flat to E natural, and that, with C slipped under it, provides the most natural possible reentry into F major. There is something wonderful about watching Beethoven create such extreme disruption by such simple means and then restoring order with equal address.

The trio is wild. Its materials are an initial turn and a rising scale. At the end of the first sentence, Beethoven again turns his picking-up and putting-down trick, using the turn as the mechanism. He puts us down in G major, quite far from F, and there he repeats the trio's long first sentence. Then he does it again, this time dropping us into A major. It is an extremely unusual key sequence, this climbing by whole steps, and Beethoven presents it as jarringly as he can. At the same time it represents an extraordinary integration of elements inasmuch as the sequence of F, G, A is also the beginning of the scherzo's main theme (Ex. 57). In other words, the trio, with its big patches of F major, G major, and A major, is the movement's main theme writ large.

It may be that after the switch from F major to G major we could smell the further move to A major coming. At any rate, it is not and cannot be as much of a shock as the first modulation from F to G. Nonetheless, Beethoven has a major surprise in store for us. The F-major and G-major sections were brief. The A-major section grows huge. After a normal traversal, one comparable to those of the F-major and G-major sections, the first violin leads a frenzied dance with huge leaps; meanwhile the other three instruments get stuck on the turn, which they play over and over with mad obsessiveness.[17]

The transition out of this dizzy dance into the reprise of the scherzo is brilliantly done. Beethoven squashes the sound all the way down to triple *piano;* he also shows us how the figure of the turn, which he has thrown at us for fifty-four measures in a row, is related to the F/G/A cell of the scherzo. The end of the movement brings back the rhythmic disruptions of the E-flat interference earlier on, but of course in F major.

In the slow movement Beethoven returns for the last time to his beloved variation form. This is a piece almost too simple to be misunderstood and too deep ever to be exhausted. Beethoven meant it as "a sweet song of rest, a song of peace."[18] The tempo—*Lento assai, cantante e tranquillo*—is very slow, its character singing and calm.

Beethoven begins by building the tonic chord of the new movement upon the last notes of the old. The scherzo has just ended with a succession of F-major chords, the last five of them very high, so that the lowest note is the F above middle C. Now the viola enters alone, softly playing the F an octave lower. To this the second violin adds A flat. Then the first violin comes in on D flat, and when the cello adds its two D flats in octaves, the chord of D-flat major is complete. The first violin also adds an F, not only for richness but because putting the third of the

17. The first violin's dance is like a crazed parody of the mysterious country dance the same instrument plays in the corresponding section, also in A major, of Op. 132 (see p. 269).

18. Radcliffe, *Beethoven's String Quartets* (London, 1965), 170.

chord on top affects its character, making it more like a cushion or a screen on which a melody can be projected.

D-flat major in the context of F sounds rich, soft, and mellow, and with this new harmonic world established, the music can begin. The first violin plays, *sotto voce,* a melody in Beethoven's most hymnal voice. To begin with, the melody is held low and moves stepwise; only later does it begin to rise from the lowest string, and the last phrase rises and sinks again in quiet bliss. The harmonies are ordinary in the sense that tonic and dominant and other chords occur when you expect them to; decisively not ordinary are Beethoven's choices of voicings and inversions. The scoring, with the cello's double stops and the low-register musings of second violin and viola, is glorious.[19]

Four variations follow. The first continues the gait and texture of the theme, but in a higher register and in emotionally heightened form as well. In variation 2, Beethoven slows the tempo, and both the hesitations and the incorporeal *pianissimo* make for a sense of diminution of physical energy. For the player and score reader, the feeling of distance is further enhanced by the change of key signature from the five flats of D-flat major to the four sharps of C-sharp minor. To the pianist, D flat and C sharp are the same note, at least mechanically; players of nonfretted stringed instruments can distinguish between them. I can't say whether Beethoven intended the subtlety of going into C-sharp rather than D-flat minor or whether he was simply thinking of the players' convenience for reading: four sharps is a very much easier key signature than the six flats and one double-flat that D-flat minor would require. In any case, if the dramatic change of key signature inspires the players with some sense of mystery and awe, that is all to the good.

Variation 3 starts where variation 1 left off, in major and in flowing eighth notes. The cello carries the melody with the first violin imitating at a distance of one measure. The other instruments add an accompaniment that is made of the same substance and that constantly grows in intensity. In the fourth and final variation, Beethoven harks back to the strange *beklemmt* middle section of the cavatina in Op. 130 (see page 237). He again gives the theme to the first violin, but the declamation is fragmented. The music is full of pathos, yet Beethoven cautions that

---

19. It is easy to understand why Toscanini was tempted to play this movement with full string orchestra, and much of the movement is effective in that form. The scherzo, which he also conducted, works much less well.

EXAMPLE 58.   Op. 135, fourth movement, epigraph

the playing must be *semplice*. It is with this wondrous "speaking" that Beethoven's last slow movement ends.[20]

The finale begins with a slow introduction whose first idea later appears upside down as the opening motif of the *Allegro*. But before we even get to that, Beethoven, in an epigraph, lays these two ideas out separately and marks them, respectively, "Muss es sein?" (Must it be?) and "Es muss sein! Es muss sein!" (It must be! It must be!). The whole is headed *Der schwer gefasste Entschluss* (The Difficult Decision) (Ex. 58).

To his publisher Moritz Schlesinger, Beethoven wrote in a letter from which I quoted earlier: "You see what an unhappy man I am, not only that [this quartet] was difficult to write because I was thinking of something else much bigger, but because I had promised it to you and needed money, and that it came hard you can gather from the 'it must be.' Now add to that . . . my being unable to find a copyist anywhere . . . and so I had to copy it myself, and was that ever a nice piece of work! Oof, it's done. Amen."[21]

The introduction—*Grave ma non troppo tratto* (Seriously and slow, but not too drawn out)—begins by presenting "Muss es sein?" in the cello and viola, to which the violins add impassioned commentary. They feel exceedingly sorry for themselves. "Muss es sein?" continues, punctuated by ever more urgent chords. Finally this slows to *adagio* and sinks to *pianissimo,* and without pause the cheerful *Allegro* begins. "Es muss sein!" It is a taut movement in sonata form. The second group appears in A major, unexpectedly and to delightfully fresh effect. The recapitulation includes the "Muss es sein?" introduction, with everyone in still more desperate straits than before. The recapitulation goes about its business swiftly, and Beethoven particularly asks for "the second part"—that is, the development and recapitulation—to be repeated as well as the expo-

20. The combination of pathos and simplicity is exceedingly difficult to find. Adolfo Betti of the Flonzaley Quartet was one who achieved it to perfection.
21. Thayer-Forbes 1964, 1010.

sition. There is a little hesitation—two measures of *poco adagio*—before the coda. That section itself begins in playful pizzicato, and it stays in *pianissimo* right up until a four-measure *fortissimo*—thematic, not formulaic—that brings this miracle of a quartet to its witty end.

And so Beethoven's string quartets end where humor and the deepest seriousness meet. He, whose most accustomed face to the world is one of defiance, ends his musical life with the laughter of Op. 135 and the new finale for Op. 130. Perhaps Nietzsche can help us understand. He once wrote: "Whosoever has built a new Heaven has found the strength for it only in his own Hell."[22]

22. *On the Genealogy of Morals,* trans. Walter Kaufmann (New York, 1969), third essay, section 10, p. 115.

Glossary

While some readers may be familiar with such terms as "sonata form," "tonic," "dominant," and other items of technical talk that occur in the text, especially in the section "Notes on the Quartets," it is also possible that others are not entirely sure what some of these mean or how they are used. Hoping to be helpful, we have provided a glossary. Some of the explanations are drastically and no doubt dangerously simplified. There is no topic here that is not hung about with exceptions and complications. More comprehensive and leak-proof definitions and explanations are readily available in reference books such as *The New Harvard Dictionary of Music*, edited by Don Randel (Cambridge, Mass., 1986); *Harvard Concise Dictionary of Music*, edited by Don Randel (Cambridge, Mass., 1978); *Oxford Dictionary of Music*, edited by Michael Kennedy (Oxford, 1985); and *Harper Dictionary of Music*, 2d ed., edited by Christine Ammer (New York, 1991).

Adagio. Literally "at ease"; in practice, slow.

Affettuoso. Tender, affectionate.

Alla breve. A tempo mark, also expressed by the symbol ¢, indicating that even though there are four quarter notes in each measure, the rhythmic unit is the half note. In other words, the motion should be felt as two beats per measure, not four. Or in still other words, don't drag!

Alla marcia. In the manner of a march.

Allegretto. Somewhat fast, one step down from *allegro*. *Allegretto* often connotes something a bit on the light side in spirit and weight.

Allegro. Literally "cheerful," "good-humored"; in practice, quick. *Allegro* is often modified by such words as *molto, moderato, vivace,* etc. See under individual entries.

Andante.   Literally "moving"; in practice, on the slow side, but still with a real sense of forward motion. During the nineteenth century, *andante* came more and more to mean "slow," thus giving rise to some confusion whether, for example, *più andante* (more andante) means faster or slower.

Appassionato.   Impassioned.

Assai.   Very.

Attacca.   Go on immediately, without a break.

Ben.   Well.

Cadence.   A cadence is a harmonic formula that functions like a punctuation mark at the end of a musical thought, whether large (a movement or entire composition) or small (a phrase). The progression from dominant to tonic is called a perfect cadence (see *Dominant* and *Tonic*). This is the most final form of cadence and is like the period at the end of a sentence. The reverse of a final cadence—tonic to dominant—is called a half cadence. It is a place to take a breath, but you don't want to stop there. The progression from the subdominant to the tonic is called a plagal cadence or, less formally, an "amen" cadence. Sometimes a composer will make all the preparations for a final cadence but at the last moment put some other chord in place of the expected tonic: that is called a deceptive cadence.

Cantabile.   In a singing style.

Cantante.   Singing.

Chord.   A chord is a stack of two or more notes, most often three or four. (A more exact theorist might use the term "pitch class" instead of "note.") Beethoven's Quartet in E-Flat Major, Op. 127, begins with a chord that consists of three E flats, two Gs, and two B flats, seven notes in all (Ex. G1). Nonetheless, in common, informal parlance, the crucial and characteristic feature of this chord is that it is made up of three kinds of notes—E flats, Gs, and B flats.

   "Chord" is also commonly used for triad, a three-note chord that is the most common coin in the harmonic currency of Beethoven's time. We talk, for example, about a C-major chord and we mean specifically the triad or three-note chord C/E/G. Similarly, a C-minor chord means C/E flat/G.

   How you stack triads makes a difference. The C in a C-major chord is called the root, and when we distribute the notes of a C-major chord so that the lowest note is C, we say that the chord is in root position. The other distributions (i.e., with either E or G as the bass note) are called inversions. A root-position chord sounds stable: we are content to end a piece on such a chord. In this, the two inversions differ from the root position. The first inversion, the one with E in the bass, is delicately and alertly poised for further adventures: this is the chord you hear a lot as the introduction to a new thought or new sentence in recitatives in opera and oratorio. The second inversion, the so-

EXAMPLE G1.   Op. 127, first movement, m. 1

EXAMPLE G2.   Figured-bass notation of a six-four chord

6
4

called six-four chord, is almost defiantly unstable: for a familiar example of its use and sound, this is the chord that immediately precedes the cadenza in classical concertos. The term "six-four chord" comes from the useful shorthand, called figured bass or basso continuo, that was used to tell seventeenth- and eighteenth-century keyboard players how to derive full chords from just a bass line. Numbers of figures indicated the distance from the bass of the needed notes. Example G2 shows a second-inversion or six-four chord. C and E are four and six steps above G, respectively, and so, to a keyboard player skilled in reading figured bass, this notation means, "play the G in the bass, and build upon it a chord including at least one C and one E, and perhaps another G or two as well."

A chord presented one note at a time instead of simultaneously is called an arpeggio (from *arpa,* the Italian for harp) or broken chord.

Circle of fifths.   In tonal music, the most important note is the tonic or keynote. The next most important is the dominant, the fifth note of the scale, and the chord built on that note is the one with the strongest magnetic pull toward the tonic (see *Tonic* and *Dominant*). If you keep going up a fifth at a time—e.g., from C to G to D to A and so forth—you will touch all twelve notes in the chromatic scale and eventually come back to your starting point, a voyage you can represent graphically by means of a circle (Ex. G3).

EXAMPLE G3. Circle of fifths

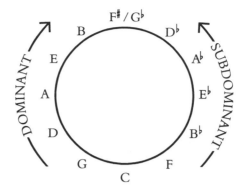

If you go around the circle clockwise, the next note is always the dominant of the one you have just left—for example, C to G. To go one step clockwise is also to go from subdominant to tonic. Conversely, to move counterclockwise is to go both from dominant to tonic and from tonic to subdominant—for example, G to C.

The circle of fifths also illustrates something else important. What we call closely related keys are those that have the greatest number of notes in common. For example, C major and G major are closely related because their scales differ by only a single note: C major has F natural, G major has F sharp. On the other hand, C major and F-sharp major are distant from one another because their scales have only one note, B, in common. (While F in the C-major scale and E sharp in the F-sharp major scale are indistinguishable on the piano, they are theoretically not the same note, and a fine string player or sensitive singer would differentiate between them.) The most closely related keys are the ones closest to each other on the circumference of the circle; the most remote relationships are those between keys directly opposite one another on the circumference.

Coda.   This word is Italian for "tail." The coda is that part of a piece that comes after the basic design is complete—e.g., what happens after the recapitulation in a sonata-form movement or after the last variation in a variation movement. A coda can be anything from a few measures of lightweight afterthought to an extended passage including elaborate development and of great rhetorical and formal weight.

Codetta.   A close that functions like a coda but for a section of a movement rather than for a whole movement or piece.

Con brio.   Fiery.

Con moto.   Moving along.

Deceptive cadence.   See *Cadence*

Development.   See *Sonata form*

Dolce.   Sweet, gentle.

Dominant.   The fifth note of the scale—e.g., G in the key of C. The dominant chord is the one that most powerfully pulls toward the tonic. Dominant to tonic is the most common form of final cadence.

E, ed.   And.

Exposition.   See *Sonata form*

First ending.   Sometimes, when a passage like a sonata-form exposition is to be repeated, the composer will throw the switch some measures before the actual return to the opening so that the performer takes one path to go back and another to go on. These two different paths are indicated by a horizontal bracket with either a "1." or a "2." These are called respectively first ending and second ending.

Grave.   Slow, serious.

Grazioso.   Graceful.

Half-cadence.   See *Cadence*

Key.   The harmonic—and thus, in a wider sense, the structural—center of gravity of a substantial section, of a movement, or of an entire composition. If, for example, the note C is given prime place in the hierarchy of notes—and a composer always has plenty of ways of making this primacy obvious to the listener's ear—we say that the piece or section is in C. The note and the chord erected upon it assume the structural and psychological function of "home." The chord built upon this keynote can be either major (C/E/G) or minor (C/E flat/G), and we say accordingly that the music is in C major or C minor. In general we perceive major as bright and affirmative, minor as dark and melancholy or tragic. (See also *Chord.*)

Many composers, for reasons either practical (e.g., the particular effectiveness for mechanical reasons of certain instruments in certain keys) or purely personal, associate particular keys with particular moods. The result may be that, for example, Beethoven's C-minor compositions all have some kinship and that they differ from his F-minor pieces, which also have a family resemblance of their own.

Key is a vast, immensely complex subject, and these sentences barely touch, let alone scratch, the surface.

Key relationships.   See *Circle of fifths*

Larghetto.   Fairly broad.

Largo.   Broad.

Leggiero, leggieramente.   Light, lightly.

Lento.   Very slow.

L'istesso.   The same.

Lusinghiero.   Literally "flattering," "coaxing"; carries implication of "seductive."

Ma.   But.

Maestoso.   Majestic, grand.

Mancando.   Fading away. Characters in opera often exclaim "io manco" when they are about to swoon.

Marcato.   Marked, articulated.

Mediant.   The third degree of the scale—e.g., E in the key of C major. The note a third below the tonic and its associated chord—e.g., A in the key of C—is called the submediant. In the key of C major, E flat and A flat are called the flat mediant and flat submediant respectively.

Meno.   Less.

Mesto.   Sad.

Mezza voce.   Half voice. Much like *sotto voce.*

Moderato.   Moderate.

Modulation.   The maneuver that moves the music from one key to another.

Molto.   Very.

Morendo.   Dying.

Motif.   See *Theme*

Neapolitan.   The chord based on the note one half step up from the tonic—e.g., D flat in the key of C—is, for no very convincing reason, called Neapolitan. By extension we also speak of Neapolitan relationships.

Non tanto.   Not very much.

Non troppo.   Not too much.

Open strings.   The four strings of the violin are tuned G, D, A, E (Ex. G4a); those of the viola are tuned C, G, D, A (Ex. G4b); and those of the cello are also tuned C, G, D, A, but an octave lower than the viola (Ex. G4c). The more these strings are allowed to sound unstopped by the player's finger, either be-

EXAMPLE G4.   Tunings of instruments in the string quartet

a. violin tuning

b. viola tuning

c. cello tuning

cause they are actually played or because they resonate in sympathy with other notes being played, the more sonorous the effect. This, for example, makes D a particularly gratifying violin key because the four notes to which the violin strings are tuned are all part of the D-major scale and therefore appear prominently in music in that key.

Pedal (also *Pedal point*).   A long note, most often but not necessarily in the bass, that is stubbornly held even though the harmonies around it change.

Perdendosi.   Disappearing.

Piacevole.   Pleasing, agreeable.

Più.   More.

Più mosso.   With more movement, faster.

Poco.   A little.

Poco a poco.   Gradually.

Prestissimo.   Extremely fast, as fast as possible.

Presto.   Really fast.

Quasi.   Almost.

Recapitulation.   See *Sonata form*

Relative major/minor.   Keys that contain the same basic set of notes but that use different tonics are called "relative keys." Each major key has a relative minor, and each minor key has a relative major key. C major is the relative major of A minor, and A minor is the relative minor of C major. The keynotes of "relatives" are always a minor third (or three semitones) apart. We also speak of tonic major and tonic minor to denote the major and minor keys based on the same keynote or tonic—e.g., C major and C minor.

But notice that while major scales are stable (e.g., a C-major scale always consists of C, D, E, F, G, A, and B), minor scales are variable. In a C-minor scale, C, D, E flat, and G are certain, but A is sometimes A flat and sometimes A natural, and B can also appear in both its flat and natural forms. In all there are three forms of the minor scale for each keynote, so while relative keys share the same basic set of notes, they may vary by a semitone in one or two spots.

Ritmo di quattro battute.   In four-measure units.

Ritmo di tre battute.   In three-measure units.

Scherzando.   Jesting, playful.

Scherzoso.   See *Scherzando*

Second ending.   See *First ending*

Semplice.   Simple, unaffected.

Sempre.   Always, constantly.

Smorzando.   Dying away, literally "becoming extinguished."

Sonata form.   Sonata form, also called sonata *allegro* form, is a flexible and powerful way of organizing musical material that has served composers from the middle of the eighteenth century to the present. It was described by various eighteenth-century theorists and first named in a treatise, *Die Lehre von der musikalischen Komposition,* published in 1837 by Adolf Bernhard Marx. You find sonata form most often in the first movements of multimovement sonatas, trios, quartets, symphonies, etc.; however, slow movements and finales are often in sonata form as well; so, occasionally, are scherzos.

Sonata form unfolds essentially in three stages. In the first of these, the material is presented, and two important things happen with respect to the harmony. To begin with, the composer establishes a firm sense of key (see *Key*), firm enough so that we really notice when the music goes to a different key. And that, in fact, is the second important thing: modulating (see *Modulation*) to and settling in a new key. When the piece is in a major key, the new key is most likely to be the dominant (see *Dominant*); if it is in a minor key, the most probable destination is the relative major (see *Relative major/minor*). Often, the arrival in the new key coincides with the appearance of a striking new theme (see *Theme*). Some composers, for example Mozart and Dvořák, are notably lavish with the number of themes they will offer during the first stage of the sonata form. Others incline toward economy; Haydn, for instance, will sometimes make do with a single theme. This portion of the movement is called the exposition, and, up to the end of the nineteenth century, composers often ask that it be repeated.

Next, the material that was presented in the exposition is put through its paces. This section is called the development. Themes are taken apart, and their components are recombined, invested with new character, perhaps scrutinized in detail and at length. Here, too, the composer deals with two major phases in the harmony. Most of the development is likely to be active and to range across wide areas of harmonic territory. The rate of harmonic change is much faster than in the exposition, and in most ways this is going to be the most restless section of the movement. Development is essential to the sonata style. For Claude Debussy, who rebelled against the sonata tradition, the development section of a sonata movement was "the laboratory of the void."

One further point should be made. It is a mistake to infer from the standard exposition/development/recapitulation terminology that development happens only in the development section. Some of the kind of treatment of material we call development almost always occurs in the exposition, and certain composers—Haydn, Beethoven, and Brahms are notable examples—continue to develop, often quite adventurously, in the recapitulation.

Eventually the composer must prepare a return to the home key and, probably, the first theme. This leadback can be simply efficient, or it can be made into a dramatic, suspenseful process. The return might also be managed unexpectedly, through the back door, as it were, or through a door that we hadn't spotted in the wall and whose existence the composer was careful to draw our attention away from, much as a skillful magician knows how to distract our eye from what he or she does not wish us to see. Beethoven occasionally likes to have us home before we realize that we have even found the door.

Now, at any rate, we are back. The word "recapitulation" refers both to the moment of return and to the part of the movement that begins with this moment. Most often the return to the home key and the return to the first theme coincide; it is possible, however, for the composer, for purposes of humor, dramatic surprise, or balance, to misalign these two returns so that they do not occur simultaneously, or even to omit the return of the first theme entirely (for example, if that theme has received an extraordinary amount of attention in the development). Some clear signal of homecoming will, at any rate, be given, and there will be an unmistakable release of tension.

The basic task of the recapitulation is to reproduce the events of the exposition, but with one crucial difference: while the exposition has to modulate away from the home key, the whole point of the recapitulation is not to modulate but to affirm the stability of the home key after the turbulence and harmonic instability of the development. This can be done smoothly or the difference can be dramatized. The hinge, the place that led out of the home key in the exposition but that now must dig into that key even more firmly, may well provide the most strikingly beautiful detail in the entire movement. To balance the push toward the dominant in the exposition, the composer may make a point of creating a strong bias in the opposite direction in the recapitulation (see *Circle of fifths*). In a larger sense, the recapitulation, with its paradoxical double assignment of being the same as the exposition yet not the same, of bringing both confirmation and freshness, is the section that gives the composer the most interesting challenge in the composition of a sonata-form movement. In many movements by Haydn and Mozart, and in a few by Beethoven, the development and recapitulation are also meant to be repeated. These repeats are observed far less devoutly than those of the exposition, though there are movements in which this second repeat is very much worthwhile.

The three principal sections of sonata form—exposition, development, recapitulation—may be preceded by an introduction and followed by a coda. The introduction is usually slower than the main part of the movement. Often its purpose is to provide suspense and contrast; sometimes it adumbrates some of the material that is to be presented more fully later on. (See also *Coda*.)

Sostenuto.   Sustained.

Stringendo.   Literally "tightening"; in practice, speeding up.

Subdominant.   The fourth note of the scale—e.g., F in the key of C major or minor. Subdominant to tonic is also a relatively familiar form of final cadence. It is the one to which the word "amen" is sung at the end of a hymn, whence it is also known as the "amen cadence."

Subito.   Immediately, suddenly.

Tempo I.   Revert to the original tempo.

Teneramente.   Tenderly.

Theme.   A substantial musical idea from which a composition is made. Within a theme, we can usually identify one or more motifs, a motif being the smallest distinctive and identifiable musical unit. Example G5 is the first theme of the first movement of Beethoven's F-major Quartet, Op. 18 no. 1; the passage marked with a bracket is its principal motif. (See also *Variations*.)

Tonic.   The keynote—e.g., C in the key of C major or minor; also the chord built on the keynote.

Tratto.   This means both "treated" and "dragged." Thus, when Beethoven writes at the head of the slow movement of Op. 59 no. 2, "Si tratta questo pezzo con molto di sentimento," he means that "this piece must be treated with much feeling." On the other hand, his "Grave ma non troppo tratto" at the beginning of the finale of Op. 135 means "Very slow and serious, but not too drawn out."

EXAMPLE G5. Op. 18 no. 1, first movement, mm. 1–20

Variations.   The systematic presentation of a theme in different guises. "Theme" is used here rather differently from its ordinary use as in, for example, "the first theme of this movement begins. . . ." The theme of a set of variations might be anything from a neutral four-measure formula to an elaborate paragraph that takes two or three minutes to play.

Vivace.   Lively, vivacious.

Index

Compositor:	Graphic Composition, Inc.
Music setter:	George W. Thomson
Text:	11/13 Bembo
Display:	Bembo
Printer:	Maple-Vail Book Mfg. Group
Binder:	Maple-Vail Book Mfg. Group